Probation

Fergus McNeill • Ioan Durnescu • René Butter
Editors

Probation

12 Essential Questions

Editors
Fergus McNeill
School of Social and Political Sciences
University of Glasgow
Glasgow, United Kingdom

René Butter
HU University of Applied Sciences
Utrecht, The Netherlands

Ioan Durnescu
Faculty of Sociology
University of Bucharest
Bucharest, Romania

ISBN 978-1-137-51980-1 (hardback)   ISBN 978-1-137-51981-8 (paperback)
ISBN 978-1-137-51982-5   (eBook)
DOI 10.1057/978-1-137-51982-5

Library of Congress Control Number: 2016942453

Cover illustration: © Hip Hip! / Alamy Stock Photo

Printed on acid-free paper

This Palgrave Macmillan imprint is published by Springer Nature
The registered company is Macmillan Publishers Ltd. London

Contents

Introduction: Questions, Questions, Questions   1
Ioan Durnescu, Fergus McNeill, and René Butter

Why Do People Commit Crimes?   9
Rob Canton

What Are the Most Important Studies of Desistance and
What Are the Future Research Needs?   35
Lila Kazemian

What Is the Impact of Probation in Advising Sentencing
and Promoting Community Sanctions and Measures?   61
George Mair

Has Probation Any Impact in Terms of Reparation to
Victims and Communities? Complicating a Simple Question   85
Leo van Garsse

What Is the Impact of Community Service?   107
Gill McIvor

What Is Probation's Role in Successful Social Integration
(Resettlement) of People Leaving Prison? A Piece in
the Jigsaw   129
Maurice Vanstone

What Is the Impact of Probation on Satisfying the Public's
Desire for Justice or Punishment?   153
Rob Allen

What Are the Costs and Benefits of Probation?   179
Faye S. Taxman and Stephanie Maass

Experiencing Supervision: From 'Sparing the First
Offenders' to 'Punishment in the Community' and
Repairing the Harm Done   197
Ioan Durnescu

Electronic Monitoring and Probation Practice   217
Mike Nellis

Explaining Probation   245
Fergus McNeill and Gwen Robinson

Conclusion: The 12th Question   263
Fergus McNeill, René Butter, and Ioan Durnescu

Index   275

Notes on Contributors

Rob Allen is an independent researcher and consultant and co-founder of Justice and Prisons (www.justiceandprisons.org). A former director of the International Centre for Prison Studies, Rob is currently an associate of Penal Reform International (www.penalreform.org).

René Butter is Associate Professor with the Research Group on Applied Research Methodology at HU University of Applied Sciences Utrecht in the Netherlands of which he is a co-founder. Being a research methodologist and assessment psychologist, he is responsible for the theme Assessment of Research and Innovation Competencies. He also works with the Research Group on Working with Mandated Clients where he publishes on public attitudes towards probation and professionalism in probation. In his company RBPA he develops contextualized assessment tools, such as the PhD Personality Questionnaire that is used at several Dutch Universities to support the selection and coaching of PhD candidates.

Rob Canton is Professor in Community and Criminal Justice at De Montfort University, Leicester, UK. He worked in the Probation Service in England for many years before joining De Montfort. He has been extensively involved in recent years in work to help other countries to develop their practices in supervising offenders. He was appointed by the Council of Europe to contribute to framing the Recommendation that was subsequently adopted (2010) by the Council of Europe as the European Probation Rules.

Ioan Durnescu is Professor in the Faculty of Sociology and Social Work at the University of Bucharest, Hungary, where he teaches and conducts research in areas including prisons, probation and resettlement. He is the co-editor of *European Probation Journal*. He is a member of several professional organizations, such as the European Society of Criminology and Confederation of European Probation. He acts as consultant in the field of criminal justice in countries such as Armenia, Croatia and Kosovo.

Lila Kazemian earned her PhD at the Institute of Criminology of Cambridge University in the UK in 2005. She was awarded a one-year post-doctoral fellowship by the Economic and Social Research Council (ESRC, UK). She joined the faculty as an Assistant Professor at John Jay College of Criminal Justice in the fall of 2006, and was promoted to Associate Professor in 2011. Her research interests include life-course and criminal career research, desistance from crime, prisoner reentry and comparative criminology.

Stephanie Maass is Research Associate at the Center for Advancing Correctional Excellence (ACE!) in the Criminology, Law and Society department at George Mason University, USA. Using a range of methodologies, Stephanie's research focuses on the adoption of evidence-based practices (EBPs) within community corrections agencies, the influence of individual- and agency-level factors in organizational change, and interventions for individuals with substance abuse and/or co-occurring disorders.

George Mair is Professor of Criminal Justice and Head of the Department of Social Science at Liverpool Hope University in the UK. He has researched and written extensively on community penalties. He was a member of Merseyside Probation Board from 2001 to 2007. His most recent book is *Redemption, Rehabilitation and Risk Management: A History of Probation* (Routledge).

Gill McIvor is Professor of Criminology at the University of Stirling in Scotland, UK, Co-Director of the Scottish Centre for Crime and Justice Research and she was previously Professor of Criminology at Lancaster University in the UK and Professor of Social Work and Director of the Social Work Research Centre at the University of Stirling. Her research interests include alternatives to imprisonment (including specialist courts), young offenders and women who offend.

Fergus McNeill is Professor of Criminology and Social Work at the University of Glasgow, Scotland, UK. Prior to becoming an academic in 1998, Fergus worked for a number of years in residential drug rehabilitation and as a criminal justice social worker. His many research projects and publications have examined institutions, cultures and practices of punishment and rehabilitation—and questions about their reform. Currently, he is Chair of an EU funded research network on 'Offender Supervision in Europe', which involves about 100 researchers from across 23 jurisdictions.

Mike Nellis is Emeritus Professor of Criminal and Community Justice at the University of Strathclyde, Glasgow, Scotland, UK. He has a PhD from Cambridge University, worked as a youth justice social worker and trained probation officers. He has written widely on electronic monitoring and worked with the CEP and the Council of Europe on issues relating to it.

Gwen Robinson is Reader in Criminal Justice at the University of Sheffield, UK. After qualifying as a probation practitioner in 1996, she has pursued a career in academic research, and has published widely in the areas of community sanctions, offender rehabilitation and restorative justice. Her recent publications include *Community Punishment: European Perspectives*, co-edited with Fergus McNeill (Routledge). She is co-leader of the COST Action on Offender Supervision in Europe's Working Group on Practicing Supervision.

Faye S. Taxman is University Professor in the Criminology, Law and Society Department and Director of the Center for Advancing Correctional Excellence at George Mason University, USA. She is recognized for her work in the development of systems-of-care models that link the criminal justice system with other service delivery systems, as well as her work in reengineering probation and parole supervision services and in organizational change models. She has active 'laboratories' with the Maryland Department of Public Safety and Correctional Services. She is Co-editor of *Health & Justice*. The American Society of Criminology's Division of Sentencing and Corrections has recognized her as Distinguished Scholar twice as well as conferring on her the Rita Warren and Ted Palmer Differential Intervention Treatment award. She has a PhD from Rutgers University's School of Criminal Justice.

Leo Van Garsse is working at the Department of Social Agogics at Ghent University in Belgium. He is also attached to the Leuven Institute of Criminology as a voluntary researcher.

Maurice Vanstone is Professor Emeritus, Criminology and Criminal Justice at Swansea University, Wales, UK. He has published extensively on, among other things, community penalties, probation history, and the effectiveness of rehabilitation. His books include *Offenders or Citizens: Readings in Rehabilitation* (Willan 2010, co-edited with Philip Priestly) and *Supervising Offenders in the Community: A History of Probation Theory and Practice* (Ashgate 2004).

Introduction: Questions, Questions, Questions

Ioan Durnescu, Fergus McNeill, and René Butter

This book addresses some key questions about probation. In order to avoid long and difficult discussions (see McNeill and Beyens 2013), we agreed at the outset to define probation somewhat loosely as referring both to the set of practices and to the organisations that are associated with the implementation of community-based sanctions and measures in the criminal justice system. Whatever the limits of its imprecision, this broad definition allowed us to explore a wide range of sanctions and measures that are applied in many jurisdictions (including probation, parole, supervised suspended or conditional sentences, and so on) and the diverse organisations that deliver these sanctions and measures.

I. Durnescu (✉)
Faculty of Sociology, University of Bucharest, Bucharest, Romania

F. McNeill
University of Glasgow, Glasgow, UK

R. Butter
HU University of Applied Sciences, Utrecht, The Netherlands

© The Editor(s) (if applicable) and The Author(s) 2016   **1**
F. McNeill et al. (eds.), *Probation*,
DOI 10.1057/978-1-137-51982-5_1

The book's origins lie at a conference that took place in December 2009, in Agen, France. Leo Tigges, then the Secretary General of the Confederation of European Probation (CEP) asked a simple question of the academic delegates: what do we know about probation so far? Obviously, the question was meant to be challenging, Participants offered a range of different answers to different interpretations of the initial question. Some stressed the effectiveness issues. Some others emphasised questions of public perception and legitimacy. A few raised issues about victim involvement and impact. Quickly, it became obvious that the question needed clarification: there are lots of different forms of knowledge about probation and a great deal of research has been undertaken. So how might Leo's question be refined?

Leo continued to think about how to reframe his question; or rather, as someone working tirelessly to promote the appropriate use of probation at the European level, he wanted and needed to articulate what were the most important questions for the probation field, particularly from the perspectives of policy and practice. His ambition became to identify and seek answers to a range of key questions; short, authoritative, evidence-based answers that might reach and influence a broad audience: the general public, the judiciary, the probation practitioners, policymakers, managers and so on.

As researchers interested in probation and in regular contact with CEP, the co-editors of this volume had the chance to see how Leo's questions evolved—and to some extent we played a part in helping to shape them. Although it was and remains almost impossible to develop a comprehensive list of questions addressing all the relevant probation subjects, we could agree at least that, by the beginning of 2014, a list of 10 important questions was ready. The 10 questions were these:

1. Why do people offend?
2. How and why do people stop offending?
3. What is the impact of the role of probation staff in advising sentencing and in promoting community sanctions and measures?
4. What is the impact of probation on reducing re-offending and supporting desistance?
5. What is the impact of probation on satisfying the public's desire for justice or punishment?

6. What is the impact of probation on the offender's social integration (resettlement)?
7. What is the impact of probation in terms of reparation to victims and communities?
8. How do people subject to supervision experience it (as punishment, as assistance, as constraint)?
9. What is the impact of community service?
10. What are the costs and benefits of probation?

The editors of this volume were then invited to act as the curators of a collection of short papers answering (or at least addressing) these questions. The Research Group on Working with Mandated Clients at the Hogeschool Utrecht (HU) University for Applied Sciences coordinated the project.

Our next challenge was to identify authors who could summarise (in just 500 words!) the kernel of an answer to each question, and to do so in easily accessible language. Scholars in many disciplines and for many centuries have recognised this as one of the most difficult tasks for any scientist: as Pascal once remarked pithily in his *Lettres Provinciales*: 'I have made this longer than usual because I have not had time to make it shorter.'

Several meetings were organised and different strategies were employed to generate a list of potential authors. The authors were chosen primarily for their well-established reputations for doing good work on the topics about which they were invited to write. After a few months, they submitted their answers and these were uploaded on the CEP website under the very optimistic but somewhat questionable title, 'Probation Works!' (http://cep-probation.org/probation-worksfacts-about-probation/). We say 'questionable' since, as a matter of fact, the answers are much more nuanced and equivocal in their judgments than the website's exclamatory confidence suggests.

Partly with those nuances and subtleties in mind, the idea of publishing more extensive versions of these syntheses was an obvious and attractive one. An edited collection would provide more space to express ideas and present evidence for different points of view. Experts who had proven their ability to be brief, we reasoned, could also be relied upon to provide more extensive analyses. And indeed, all of the authors welcomed this opportunity and duly embarked upon their tasks.

Reviewing this list of the 10 original questions now—and with the benefit of the greater critical distance that comes with hindsight—it poses two main problems. First and most fundamentally, it reflects the understandable concern of their original author (Leo) with advocating for greater use of probation at the European level, in particular as a way of addressing the excessive, expensive and unnecessary use of imprisonment in many states. As academic editors and as citizens, we share the commitment to penal reductionism. However, we also realise that, as has been noted by many authors and confirmed in many studies, probation growth is *not* an unqualified good; indeed it often accompanies rather than displacing prison growth (see for example, McNeill 2014a; Phelps 2013). And, given that the available forms of supervision seem to be intensifying as well as expanding, if probation displaces not more but less serious and intrusive sanctions, then this raises complex questions of parsimony, proportionality and justice (see McNeill and Beyens 2013; van Zyl Smit et al. 2015).

A related second problem—doubtless partly a result of the origins of this project in probation advocacy—is that all but two of the questions concern probation's impact or effectiveness (although question 8 gives primacy to how supervision is experienced rather than what it achieves). Important though these questions may be, we would argue that there are other, perhaps more fundamental ones that tend to be ignored where the focus is on impact, outcomes or effects. Indeed, at the same time as our ideas about this collection were evolving, debates within the European Society of Criminology's Working Group on Community Sanctions and Measures and in the COST Action on Offender Supervision in Europe (www.offendersupervision.eu) had begun to expose the lack of explicit theories to explain probation's social and penal purposes and its complex evolutions in different states (see Robinson and McNeill 2015). It seemed to us and to our colleagues in these groups that most anglophone probation studies focused directly or indirectly on *rehabilitation* as a penal ideal and as a practice (see McNeill 2014b). In other words, they tended to be more interested in how to make probation more effective in reducing reoffending or promoting desistance, and less concerned with understanding, explaining, justifying or critiquing probation itself.

As we debated this, increasingly we came to recognise that, in fact, probation organisations are sophisticated institutions that serve many different formal and informal purposes and that probation scholarship needs a more developed sociological account of probation's emergence and development, forms and functions. Hence the inclusion in this collection of a chapter dedicated to providing some theoretical resources for explaining probation itself as a social institution.

We also realised that the development of new technologies—in particular technologies of electronic monitoring—have already profoundly influenced the development of probation in many states, and that a critical appreciation of the impact of such technologies and of associated practices is essential to considering probation's possible futures. We are delighted that Mike Nellis agreed to contribute a chapter on this topic.

With these revisions in place, and having permitted our authors to reinterpret their brief and to rephrase their allotted questions, the chapters of this book now address the following questions in this order:

1. Why do people commit crimes?
2. What are the most important studies on desistance and what are future research needs?
3. What is the impact of the role of probation staff in advising sentencing and in promoting community sanctions and measures?
4. Does probation have any impact in terms of reparation to victims and communities?
5. What is the impact of community service?
6. What is probation's role in successful social integration (resettlement) of people leaving prison? A piece in the jigsaw
7. What is the impact of probation on satisfying the public's desire for justice or punishment?
8. What are the costs and benefits of probation?
9. How is probation supervision experienced by offenders?
10. What is the nature of the debate that has taken place about electronic monitoring, what is the available evidence, how should we appraise this and what is its prospect for the future?
11. How we can best account for probation's emergence and development as a penal institution and as a set of connected penal discourses and practices?

Observant readers will have noted that we did not commission Fergus McNeill to further develop his short answer to the question: What is the impact of probation on reducing re-offending and supporting desistance? While we accept that this is a critically important question (or rather a conflation of two related questions), Fergus's short answer argues, in effect, that the question cannot be answered (at least not yet). The reasons are both conceptual and methodological. There are problems with the outcome measure (rearrest, reconviction, reimprisonment), but more fundamentally, many desistance scholars would argue (1) that desistance implies more than not offending and (2) that probation (even where it is constructive and helpful) does not 'produce' desistance, since desistance is a personal and social process of development that is properly seen as belonging to the human subjects involved in it. Furthermore, any assessment of the apparent effect of probation on reoffending would also need to examine the influence of the social and structural contexts of desistance. And if 'effects' were to be attributed to practices or systems, that would require a sufficiently rich understanding of those specific practices or systems. So, in this case, Leo's original question begs several others that we are not yet able to answer.

The conclusion summarises what we have learned from answering the 11 questions explored in the individual contributions to the collection. But it also itself addresses an important 12th question: What next? The last question is crucial since, as with any account of the state of art in any given field, this account is a product of its origins, of a specific moment in time and of the preferences of its authors. It reflects our limitations but perhaps it can also help to shape the agenda for the future of probation research.

In sum, we are proud of this collection and grateful to our contributors. We think this book represents a useful resource—and one that has emerged from intensive and constructive research–practice dialogue. This time, the challenge came from the practice and the answer come from the research. We hope this book will contribute to reducing the traditional gap between these two interdependent fields, both so that probation practice and institutions can develop in progressive ways that contribute to penal reductionism and, ultimately, to the delivery of justice—and so that probation scholarship can develop in ways that support those vital aspirations.

References

McNeill, F. (2014a, June 18). *Probation: Myths, realities and challenges.* Retrieved October 19, 2015, from http://www.offendersupervision.eu/blog-post/probation-myths-realities-and-challenges

McNeill, F. (2014b). Punishment as rehabilitation. In G. Bruinsma & D. Weisburd (Eds.), *Encyclopedia of criminology and criminal justice* (pp. 4195–4206). New York: Springer. A final draft version of this paper is available open access online at: http://blogs.iriss.org.uk/discoveringdesistance/files/2012/06/McNeill-When-PisR.pdf

McNeill, F., & Beyens, K. (Eds.). (2013). *Offender supervision in Europe.* Basingstoke: Palgrave Macmillan.

Phelps, M. (2013). The paradox of probation: Community supervision in the age of mass incarceration. *Law and Policy, 35*(1–2), 55–80.

Robinson, G., & McNeill, F. (Eds.). (2015). *Community punishment: European perspectives.* London: Routledge.

van Zyl Smit, D., Snacken, S., & Hayes, D. (2015). One cannot legislate kindness: Ambiguities in European legal instruments on non-custodial sanctions. *Punishment and Society, 17*(1), 3–26.

Why Do People Commit Crimes?

Rob Canton

In this chapter, some of the main theories of criminology will be introduced. This is a brief and introductory overview and those who wish to
look at these theories in any depth are referred to the further reading recommended at the end of the chapter and to the references in the text itself.
The account will, however, attempt to draw out some of the implications
of these ways of understanding offences and offenders for the policies and
practices of criminal justice social work and probation. The aspiration of
the chapter is to show that these various theoretical accounts offer more
than academic insights and can be *applied* to enhance probation's work.

What Is Criminology?

Criminology is an academic discipline that draws upon the insights and
methods of other subjects—including sociology, psychology, law, philosophy,

R. Canton (✉)
De Montfort University, Leicester, UK

© The Editor(s) (if applicable) and The Author(s) 2016   **9**
F. McNeill et al. (eds.), *Probation*,
DOI 10.1057/978-1-137-51982-5_2

pedagogy and social work—in its attempt to understand aspects of crime and punishment. Among the questions that criminology sets for itself, this chapter looks like the central, even the defining, concern of the discipline. The question has a political and moral import: this is not (not only) a theoretical matter, but one that bears on people's safety and well-being. This is by no means the only aspect of criminological study, of course, which is also properly concerned with crime prevention (or more realistically its reduction), with criminalisation (the processes by which some kinds of act come to be crimes while others do not), with the institutions of criminal justice and the practices of its agencies (including the police, the court and prison and probation agencies), and with the experiences, rights and needs of victims. Even so, for many people, the causes of offending ought to be a central topic of study, and attempts to understand this better have been at the heart of the criminological enterprise from its beginnings.

Garland (2002) finds the origins of modern criminology in the coming together of two projects. One of these he names the *Lombrosian project* (after Cesare Lombroso (1835–1909), the Italian criminologist), which drew on the developing methods of the natural sciences in order to identify the causes of crime. Human conduct is just a particular kind of event in the world and therefore just as amenable as any other kind of event to scientific explanation. The rigorous application of scientific method—systematic observation, the recording of human behaviour and characteristics, the research for connections, correlations and causes—could be employed to develop a 'science of the natural born criminal'. Hypotheses about causation could be put to test to find out why some individuals come to commit crimes. This method of inquiry is sometimes referred to as *positivism*.

The other parent of modern criminology Garland calls the *governmental project*. Governments always and everywhere are concerned with the social order and offences against it. Crimes had traditionally been understood to be the actions of people exercising their free will. Effective crime control therefore called for an examination of the institutions of criminal justice (especially policing), to ensure the efficient detection and punishment of criminals, and a setting of penalties at a level that would deter people from offending. But from the 19th century radical changes in society and social organisation, linked with changing modes of production, were raising urgent questions about how to respond to new kinds of crime and criminal and especially to perceptions of increases in levels of offending.

The insights of the Lombrosian project held the promise of serving the governmental project by identifying the causes of criminality. This should afford opportunities to intervene to treat these causes and thus prevent offending. The convergence of these two projects gave birth and nurture to modern criminology, demonstrating the link between social science knowledge production and the historical contexts in which such knowledge is applied.

What Are Crimes and Who Are Criminals?

Years of research and scholarship, however, have brought us little closer to being able to give satisfactory answers to questions about 'the causes of crime'—in ways that are either intellectually persuasive or else useful in supporting efforts at crime reduction. Whenever a question is found to be so intractable, it is often worth pausing and pondering whether it is the right question in the first place. So before reviewing some of the answers that have been proposed, a few preliminary observations may be useful.

First, definitions of crime are contested. Some scholars are keen to include actions that are not normally studied by mainstream criminology—for example, the crimes of states and their leaders, the crimes of companies against their customers or their workers (like health and safety violations) or other crimes of the powerful. Yet even if we set aside this debate and accept the conservative position that criminology should confine itself to *the study of those actions that are forbidden by the criminal law and liable to attract a punishment*, 'crime' includes an indefinitely wide and diverse range of conduct. How likely is it that there is such a thing as 'the cause' of actions as varied as theft, rape, drunk driving, murder, tax evasion, taking drugs, polluting the environment or fraud—or (to take some examples from the law of my own country) selling grey squirrels, impersonating a traffic warden, offering air traffic control services without a licence, swimming in the wreck of the *Titanic*, defacing an ancient monument, creating a nuclear explosion or allowing a chimney to be on fire? Within the UK (and no doubt many other countries), there are thousands of 'crimes' and it is not clear that there is anything that such a varied range of actions have in common (apart from being forbidden by law and a consequently liable for punishment).

A second (and related) point is well expressed by Christie's observation that 'Crime does not exist. Only acts exist, acts often given different meanings within various social frameworks' (Christie 2004, p. 3). He makes an instructive distinction between crimes and 'deplorable acts'. Some deplorable acts (and of course there will be disagreements among people about which acts are deplorable) are made into crimes while others are not. This way of putting it immediately raises several rather better questions, for example: Are all crimes deplorable acts? (Probably not.) Are all deplorable acts crimes? (Definitely not.) Is making a deplorable act into a crime the best way of reducing its incidence? (Not always, for sure.) Does making an act a crime have undesirable consequences? (Sometimes, for example, drug enforcement strategies may have the effect of steering users into the company of pushers who will exploit them and involve them in more crimes. And later in this chapter other undesirable consequences will be discussed.) The implications of this critical distinction have been insufficiently appreciated in criminal justice policy. In many countries, the recognition that some type of behaviour is giving rise to concern can lead to demands for its criminalisation or, if it is a crime already, for greater punishment, without sufficient regard to the questions we have just raised.

A third preliminary point is that the Lombrosian project could not study 'offenders' or 'criminals', but only those who had been detected—or indeed were available for 'study'. Lombroso studied prisoners, not offenders. As Foucault (1977) influentially explained, criminology and the prison are interdependent: without the prison there could be no study of prisoners, while studies of prisoners have been used to guide the regime of the prison. Most obviously, very many crimes are not cleared up and studies of convicted offenders could only illuminate the behaviour of 'criminals' on the assumption that they are *typical* and somehow representative of all the others. There are no grounds for such an assumption and many reasons to doubt it. It is still the case that almost all generalisations about 'criminals' refer to prisoners or people under probation supervision—that is, almost exclusively those who commit crimes 'on the streets' rather than state, corporate or otherwise powerful criminals.

Finally, as well as differences among the many acts that are crimes, there are other differences among offenders that criminology has sometimes disregarded. Notably, many early studies of offenders were, in effect, about men. The experiences of women were often invisible or considered irrelevant to these investigations. Feminist criminology has been influential in redressing this, by identifying *gender* as a critical criminological variable, shedding light not only on *women offenders*, but also on the significance of *masculinity* in an understanding of (some kinds of) crime committed by men. Similarly, it may not be assumed that criminological theories can apply in quite the same way to all groups—for instance, age, differences in social class, culture and ethnicity may be important variables in understanding crimes and in how to respond to them, but have received uneven (and often insufficient) attention.

Implications for Probation Policy and Practice

There are several possible responses to misbehaviour and incivility ('deplorable acts') and, if the political choice is made to make many of them into crimes, then there will be more crimes and more criminals. In a significant sense, then, societies can have as much crime as they choose. Crime cannot be studied in isolation from the processes of criminalisation and the practices of enforcement, and a preoccupation with the characteristics of 'criminals' is likely to be self-defeating. In working with 'offenders', their diversity is always an important consideration and there can be no assumption that the pathways into and out of offending (or the services they require) are the same for all.

The Search for a Difference

The Lombrosian project supposed that criminals, behaving in ways others do not, must have some kind of constitutional difference—*something that makes them different* from these others. Different events, after all, must have different causes. Lombroso himself dedicated much of his career to searching out this difference by examining criminals, measuring the size and shapes of skulls and faces. Other researchers studied body shapes. Perhaps such physiological factors might be 'the difference' between criminals and others. Again, while some such differences may be genetic, there may be other factors like diet—for example, food additives—that are (or are a part of) the explanation. It is well known that neurological disorders and substances like alcohol and other drugs can affect brain functioning and consequently behaviour. A connection has been posited between offending behaviour and the amount of lead in petrol (and therefore levels of lead in the air from vehicle emissions) or in paint (Nevin 2012).

Others have looked instead for differences in offenders' upbringing, seeking psychological rather than biological causes. Most of the major psychological schools (notably the psychodynamic tradition, associated especially with Freud, and behaviourism) have supposed that early life experiences are profoundly influential in determining the behaviour of the adult. Perhaps childhood experiences lead to ways of thinking that make offending more likely—for example, cognitive limitations may make some people less able to think through the consequences of their behaviour; or deficiencies in empathy or in moral sensibilities may be such that offenders are not checked by constraints of conscience, or by feelings of shame or guilt.

Certainly it is psychology that dominates the criminologies that modern probation staff draw upon in their work. The findings of 'what works' research suggested that the difference between those who offend and those who do not might lie in the ways in which they *think*. The insights of cognitive behavioural psychology, which emphasises the dynamic influences among thinking, feeling and behaving, have inspired a great deal of contemporary probation policy and practice (McGuire 2004). Offending behaviour programmes that were founded on this psychological theory were discovered to be relatively successful in reducing reconvictions.

Research (McGuire and Priestley 1995) attempted to summarise the characteristics of effective programmes and concluded that guiding principles were as follows:

• Risk   The higher the risk of reoffending, the more intensive and extended the supervision programme should be. The risk principle can accordingly be used to determine who should be worked with and to what level.

• Need   The need principle insists that the focus of intervention must be on those needs or factors associated with their offending. These are often called 'criminogenic' needs. (The word criminogenic, however, means *crime-causing* and it would be more accurate to say that these factors are known to be associated with offending: the causal relationships are often complex.) They are also often referred to as dynamic risks—dynamic because they are current and in principle susceptible to change as 'static' risks (often historical factors) are not.

• Responsivity   This principle has been well defined as 'Ensuring that all interventions, programmes and activities with offenders are run in a way which is engaging, encourages full participation and takes account of issues of identity and diversity' (Dominey 2007, p. 270). This recognises that not every approach is likely to be effective for everybody and that the best way of working with people needs to be assessed person-by-person.

These principles, which give the name to the RNR model, were supplemented by others, including the following:

• Community base   Programmes in the community are, other things being equal (which they rarely are), more likely to be effective than those delivered in prison.

• Multi-modality   Offenders' problems are diverse, calling for a correspondingly diverse repertoire of interventions.

• Programme integrity   If the programme is to have its effect, it must be delivered in the manner intended (and this is not always easy to achieve).

More recent research has added further ideas about effectiveness (see, for example, Raynor 2004; Robinson and Crow 2009; Raynor and Robinson 2009; McGuire 2007; Lösel 2012).

Others again have looked for *social* factors that might be associated with offending. Perhaps the differences to be found are neither biologically constitutional nor specifically psychological, but are rather associated with social structure. One extremely influential attempt to understand this was advanced by Robert Merton, whose 'strain' theory posited that much offending in USA was a response to the tension between the cultural aspiration for material affluence and, on the other hand, the reality that this was achievable only by a few people. This is a very crude summary of a sophisticated thesis, but for the present purpose the point is that some have argued that the origins of much crime are to be found to be in the socio-economic and cultural order rather than in any inherent differences in individual offenders.

The 'Chicago School' famously studied *place*, introducing ideas of understanding the geography of offending, so to speak, mapping the residences of offenders and the locations where crimes occur—a type of analysis that modern technologies are making ever more refined and (at least potentially) illuminating. In an associated tradition, scholars and advocates of community justice like Todd Clear and David Karp have focused on 'the local' and have offered an invaluable counterweight to the 'placeless' and decontextualized accounts of offenders that seem to characterise much forensic psychology (see for example Clear et al. 2010). Flynn (2012) has also convincingly demonstrated the importance of an awareness of place in understanding the origins of offending—and its significance in the process of desistance (see below).

Culture is another critical and complex consideration. By this is meant not only the cultural aspiration to affluence that Merton had in mind, reflecting and reproducing the values of capitalism, but the specific influences, within and beyond the family, that may more directly shape attitudes and behaviour. This includes schools, mass media and religious institutions. Peer groups in particular may exercise a strong influence on conduct, not only by moulding the beliefs and values of their members, but by creating opportunities to acquire skills in the arts and crafts of crime: for example, people learn to steal cars by watching others, while knowledge about where to obtain drugs, paraphernalia and how to use substances is commonly learnt in groups. It seems that fraudsters in the financial sector too learn from and collude with one another in their malpractices. Techniques of neutralisation (see below) are also developed and rehearsed within groups.

Implications for Probation Policy and Practice

Almost all of the approaches in this search for the 'causes of crime' have continuing relevance to policy and to the work of probation staff and other criminal justice personnel. Physiology may well make a difference, even if it is unfashionable to think in these ways in a discipline dominated by social (rather than biological) sciences. The connections between substance use and offending is the most obvious example: even if detoxification is just the start of the process, it is often an essential element of intervention, if only because it is exceptionally hard to work with someone who is under the influence of drugs or alcohol. In my own career as a probation officer, I worked with the following people:

• A middle-aged, middle-class woman of excellent character who had hit her mother on the head with a hammer (with near fatal consequences)—inexplicably, until a hitherto undiagnosed and immediately treatable glandular disorder was discovered;
• A defendant who had cut someone's face with a broken glass as he went into an epileptic seizure;
• A persistently violent man whose behaviour improved rapidly and dramatically after he had been diagnosed with diabetes and his behaviour linked with hypoglycaemia.

Psychology has informed a great deal of contemporary practice, as we have seen. The Risks-Needs-Responsivity model (RNR) is widely held to have demonstrated its effectiveness in reducing reoffending (Andrews and Bonta 2010). The model has been enriched and developed by more recent attention to the potential of pro-social modelling, the significance of relationships, the importance of motivational work and associated ideas about what is involved in offender engagement (see for example Raynor and Robinson 2009).

A sociological perspective is a necessary reminder of the considerable social disadvantage with which so many probation service users have to struggle. It is not necessary to adopt a radical political perspective to recognise the wisdom in the words of Steven Box:

[A]lthough people choose to act, sometimes criminally, they do not do so under conditions of their own choosing. Their choice makes them responsible, but the conditions make their choice comprehensible. These conditions, social and economic, contribute to crime because they constrain, limit or narrow the choices available. Many of us, in similar circumstances, might choose the same course of action. Furthermore, if we understand the intimate relationship between economic and social circumstances and criminal behaviour, then we might be in a better position to intervene effectively and humanely to reduce the incidence of crime. (Box 1977, p. 29)

Criminal justice interventions cannot do much to influence the conditions to which Box draws attention, although some interventions make the problems very much worse—for example, by stigmatising people who have offended to further reduce life opportunities that were already limited, by blocking desistance through excessive use of imprisonment and by undermining the stability and well-being of some deprived communities through mass incarceration of their younger members (especially those who are poor, male and black). The erroneous belief that criminal justice holds the solution to the problem of crime has also diverted large sums of money away from social initiatives that would improve people's chances, channelling funds instead into prisons (Reiman and Leighton 2013). Since the types and amounts of crime so much depend on socioeconomic factors, criminal justice policy is best regarded as one aspect of social policy, rather than a distinct and decontextualized strategy to respond to individual wrongdoers. Again, probation staff might often do well to look more closely at the neighbourhoods and areas in which offenders live and try to understand the problems that their clients share, as well as the opportunities they may have, rather than focusing simply on individual characteristics.

It rarely makes sense for probation workers to think of a 'cause' of a crime and even less to think of *the* cause. If we think in terms of causes at all (see below) there are many interacting factors associated with offending, which is among the reasons why one of the principles of 'what works' is a multi-disciplinary approach, with a range of interventions required to respond to a diverse and complex set of criminogenic needs. It is not that people are a product of their biology or their psychology or their society: all these factors are influential all of the time and some kind of *bio-psycho-social theory* is needed to explain criminality.

One aspect of this debate is of particular interest to probation workers. Some critics of RNR have argued that psychological approaches distract attention from social disadvantage. As Smith says, 'an exclusive stress on offending behaviour entails the expectation that offenders, and not their social circumstances, must change, and encourages the abstraction of the offending act itself from the personal and relational context which could make it intelligible.' (Smith 1998, p. 108). This criticism has particular weight when considering the position of groups—the poor and socially excluded, women and offenders from minority ethnic groups—whose offending behaviour and experiences of criminal justice can only be properly understood within that broader socio-political context. On the other hand, those who are working to try to help offenders may object that their responsibility is to support and guide them in finding ways of living that do not add the further burdens of punishment—and the pains that their crimes bring to other people, many no less disadvantaged than they are—to their many other troubles. Offenders must find ways of negotiating through the world as they encounter it, without causing harm to others and to themselves, and criminal justice social workers should support them in these endeavours, at the same time as doing as much as possible to redress (or at least not aggravate) the injustices that oppress their clients.

While a social critique should be part of probation's self-awareness, it is unnecessary to insist on a working distinction between *agency* (how individuals think, decide and act) and *social structure*, since both of these are influential all of the time. The question then becomes one about the best way of bringing about change, the point of intervention. Finally, these positivist theories should not be taken to *determine* offending in any fatalistic sense. Probation believes in the possibility of change, and its work would be pointless if there was no place for *choice* in understanding human behaviour.

Perhaps There Is No Difference: (i) Labelling

The search for difference assumes that offenders must somehow be different because 'most people' do not offend. But this assumption should be inspected. Even the most prolific offenders spend most of their lives without committing crimes, while most people are willing to admit that they have committed crimes at some time or another in their lives. Research has found that crime committed by 'ordinary people' is perfectly common (Karstedt and Farrall 2007). Some of this crime is trivial—but then so is some of the crime that comes before the courts in most countries. Yet the (self-proclaimed) 'law-abiding majority' does not regard its members as criminals and would be indignant at being described in this way.

These reflections have led some people to conclude that the search for an intrinsic difference is misplaced. Just as crimes are those acts that have been designated as crimes, *criminals are those who have been criminalised*. There are differences in patterns of enforcement—in arrest, prosecution and punishment—that lead some people to be regarded as offenders while others, whose behaviour may have been quite as bad or worse, are not. In what may be the most quoted paragraph in criminological literature, Howard Becker wrote:

> [S]*ocial groups create deviance by making the rules whose infraction constitutes deviance*, and by applying those rules to particular people and labeling them as outsiders. From this point of view, deviance is *not* a quality of the act the person commits, but rather a consequence of the application by others of rules and sanctions to an 'offender'. The deviant is one to whom that label has successfully been applied; deviant behavior is behavior that people so label. (Becker 1973, p. 9)

Note that this does not attempt to explain the initial offence (the 'primary deviance'). In this regard, labelling theory could argue that there is nothing in need of explanation—in the sense that the breaking of rules is common and familiar. If there is a difference between offenders and others, it lies in the reactions to their behaviour. Nor are these differential responses random or arbitrary: on the contrary, criminal justice practices systematically target and criminalise the poor, the disadvantaged and the vulnerable (Reiman and Leighton 2013).

Once the label of 'offender' or 'criminal' has been applied, it can be very hard to remove and can make a difference to how people so labelled are viewed by others and indeed sometimes how they view themselves. People respond differently to (those labelled) offenders; for example, an employer may well be less willing to offer a job to someone with a criminal conviction. These responses make desistance (see below) much harder to achieve. Moreover, in a process known as secondary deviance (Lemert 1967), individuals themselves can come to 'internalise' the label: someone who has stolen may come to regard herself *as a thief* and therefore as a person who might steal again in future.

Implications for Probation Policy and Practice

Among the most important implications of this way of understanding offending is that policymakers and practitioners should always be aware that their interventions can sometimes—perhaps even often—make things worse. Schur (1973) famously argued for 'radical non-intervention'—'leave the kids alone': almost all of them will grow out of it and most criminal justice interventions will slow this process down and can do little to hasten it. Many policymakers are tempted by the idea of early intervention: to identify those who (according to some positivist understanding) are likely to become offenders and to intervene with them as early as possible—maybe even before offending has taken place. But this approach has struggled to prove its worth and has often resulted in disappointment (Goldson 2007). Similarly, the 'risk principle' suggests that too much involvement with low-risk offenders can increase their risks of reconviction. Again, there is evidence to show that offenders who begin offending behaviour programmes *but do not complete them* are more likely to be reconvicted than those who never began them in the first place (Raynor 2004).

Most obviously of all, imprisonment frequently makes people more rather than less likely to re-offend, sometimes by associations with others (Kropotkin called prisons 'universities of crime' and has been frequently echoed), but also by damaging positive influences in people's lives (like family relationships, accommodation and employment) that could, if supported and nurtured, contribute to their desistance. Formal criminal justice interventions, then, can aggravate or even cause crime problems.

Perhaps There Is No Difference: (ii) Rational Choice

Reporter: 'Why do you keep robbing banks, Willie?'
Sutton: 'Because that's where the money is.'
(Attributed to Willie Sutton, Jr. (1901–80), American bank robber—although, sad to say, it is doubtful if he ever said exactly this.)

Rational choice theory claims that too much has been made of differences or 'pathologies' that are supposed to afflict offenders: in fact, they take opportunities and decide what to do by working out the costs and benefits—just like everyone else (Cornish and Clarke 1986). One principal justification of punishment rests precisely on this assumption. Deterrence—the idea that the prospect of punishment frightens people off from offending—depends upon their making some calculation of gains and losses (although also about their chances of being caught). While positivist criminology had been looking for 'causes', this perspective encourages us to try to understand purposes—and, as Willie Sutton reminds us, sometimes there is nothing very mysterious about these purposes.

This account is not without its limitations. It is at its most persuasive in the case of acquisitive crime, but perhaps less convincing in understanding other types of crime (for example crimes of violence). Rational choice gains much of its persuasiveness from its claim that in the ways in which offenders decide to act they are *just like everybody else*, but is this really how people take their decisions? This 'economic' model of decision making is increasingly thought to be an incomplete and often misleading account of the way in which people behave in most other circumstances. Even where they are able to calculate and plan, people are prone to systematic errors and biases in their reasoning. The influence of *emotion* also seems altogether absent from the 'rational choice' account, despite compelling evidence of its influence in decisions of all kinds (Kahneman 2011). The rationality that people bring to their actions in many circumstances is bounded and limited and this is all the more likely to be true in the kinds of circumstances in which crimes often occur, where reasoned calculation may be distorted by anger, fear, excitement or intoxication.

As Willie Sutton suggests, sometimes (perhaps often) the answer to the question 'why?' is perfectly obvious, the motives apparent. At other times, perhaps especially in the case of grave crimes, 'why?' is unanswerable: the offender's own account of their own motivations seems inadequate and the speculations of psychologists and commentators unconvincing. (What would even count as an answer to the question why someone (for example) committed a series of murders? Any answer seems to raise more questions than it settles.)

Willie Sutton is not the only one who knows that the money is kept in banks, but most people do not do as he did. So perhaps the better question here is not so much *why do they?* as *how could they?* Sykes and Matza (1957) challenged the then common assumption that the values of offenders were different, 'an inversion of the values held by respectable, law-abiding society' (1957, p. 664). On the contrary, they argued, offenders in many respects share mainstream values. The question then becomes: how is it that delinquents can behave in ways that violate values to which they do after all subscribe? Sykes and Matza found the answer in what they referred to as *techniques of neutralisation*. These are stories that offenders tell themselves and others to resolve the dissonance that arises from their awareness that they have done things that they are willing to recognise would normally be morally reprehensible. By the use of these techniques, 'Social controls that serve to check or inhibit deviant motivational patterns are rendered inoperative, and the individual is freed to engage in delinquency without serious damage to his self-image' (1957, p. 667).

Implications for Probation Policy and Practice

Rational choice theory, with its insistence that offenders reason and calculate just as others do, is a valuable corrective to any straightforward assumption of difference or of pathology. In exploring offending behaviour, probation staff must try to make sense of offenders' accounts—to appreciate purposes and reasons, not merely focusing on supposed deficiencies. At the same time, this theory pays insufficient attention to the complex mix of feelings and motivations associated with offending. It is ironic that while the concept of 'the reasoning criminal' has been used to show that offenders are not pathologically irrational but no different from everyone else, psychology is increasingly discovering that decision taking is much less a matter of rational calculation than had been supposed. In truth, offenders act on decisions taken on intuitive and emotional grounds, variably influenced by 'reason'—*just like everybody else.*

The psychological preconditions for a crime to take place are, first, motivation (the offender must in some sense want to do this) and, second, a neutralising of what have been called internal inhibitors (conscience, for example, shame or fear—all those considerations that are in people's minds that may check them from doing what they are motivated to do) (Finkelhor 1986). Arguably our motivations are quite often obscure, ambivalent and hard to change: our motives are unclear even to ourselves (Nisbett and Wilson 1977). Attempts to change behaviour could instead focus on strengthening internal inhibitors, working to challenge neutralisations, encouraging offenders to be aware of the effects of their conduct on other people, drawing attention to the effects on their families and on raising victim awareness. This is often part of the work of probation officers and criminal justice social workers.

Better Questions: Control Theory and Desistance

Since the original question *why do people commit crimes?* has, for so many reasons, proved impossible to answer simply or satisfactorily, this may be a sign that there is a need for better questions. One instructive reframing involves asking instead *why doesn't* everyone *commit crime(s)?* As Willie Sutton pointed out, the advantages of some crimes are obvious, yet *al*most all of us do not offend for almost all of the time. An influential approach to this reframed question is known as *control theory*. One version of this posits that there are four factors that explain conformity:

- Attachment—caring about what others think about us, especially those who are important to us (like our families) and about the effects of our behaviour upon them.
- Commitment—the investment we have made into our personal ambitions, projects and activities making us keen not to spoil them or place them in jeopardy.
- Involvement—many people (perhaps most) are too involved in living their lawful lives even to think about offending.
- Belief—this includes the moral constraints which Sykes and Matza believe offenders attempt to neutralise, as we have just seen.

Where these influences towards conformity are weakened or absent, offending is more likely to take place.

Another and better question than that of *why people commit crimes* is *how do people come to stop offending?* Attempts to answer that question are known as desistance studies (for an excellent review, see McNeill and Weaver 2010). Most people manage to stop offending, especially as they get older. The process is uneven and commonly marked by lapses, so that Burnett (1992), referring to 'the switching, vacillating nature of desisting from offending', aptly describes it as a zigzag path. One way of understanding this process and its successful outcome is known as the *Good Lives Model* (GLM): people typically come to stop offending in the context of living good and meaningful lives, with new purposes and significance and often marked by a sense of personal achievement and fulfilment (Ward and Maruna 2007). It is not so much, as RNR implies, that desistance is accomplished by the direct overcoming of criminogenic needs or dynamic risks: rather, these are *transcended* in a life in which offending has less and less of a place. While there is (of course) no single way of achieving this, it is not perhaps too much of an over-simplification to say that desistance is often associated with the attachments, commitments, investments and beliefs that constitute the framework of control theory.

There is dispute about the extent to which desistance studies add to the insights and practice implications of RNR (see Andrews et al. 2011; Ward et al. 2012). It may be more a matter of emphasis than substance, but desistance studies have stressed some aspects that are less salient in RNR accounts, specifically the following:

- The importance of social capital—psychological interventions are and could not be enough without social inclusion and fair opportunities to access resources that are a precondition of most people's conception of a 'good life'.
- Attention to offenders' own accounts—what they have found to be incentives and obstacles to desistance, what they experience as more and less valuable in their dealings with probation. Since self-identity and 'narrative' are central to the process of sustaining desistance, offenders' perceptions become the start and focus of working to support change.

- Emphasis on strengths. RNR attends to shortcomings—cognitive deficiencies, risks and needs. Desistance encourages attention to strengths and potentials, taking seriously people's personal goals and ambitions (Ward and Maruna 2007). Positive goals—things to strive for—constitute a much more powerful motivation than aversive goals—things to avoid. This perspective also develops the sense of agency or 'self-efficacy' which is commonly associated with successful desistance.
- The central place of relationships. Offenders often speak of the value of a probation officer's practical help in identifying and resolving obstacles to desistance, but especially emphasise the sense of personal interest and concern, of partnership and cooperation (Farrall 2002).

Desistance research further suggests that while life events, for instance forming intimate relationships and finding employment, often support desistance, it is the *meaning* that people find and invest in these events that makes the difference. It is not only 'the perceived strength, quality and interdependence of these ties', but also 'the individual's reaction to and interaction with those circumstances' (Weaver and McNeill 2007, p. 90; see also Maruna 2000). It is in and through these interactions that people come to find new ways of understanding themselves—for example, as workers, as artists, as sports men and women, and, very commonly, as partners and as parents. The narratives that they construct to make sense of their lives are changed, reversing the effects of secondary labelling to achieve a 'secondary desistance'. It is not surprising, then, that desistance research has encouraged an inquiry into the reasons and meanings that people find in their behaviour and in their aspirations to change.

And it is in terms of reasons that people normally seek to understand one another. Usually if we want to know why someone has behaved as they have, we ask them and they will give *reasons* and *meanings* in their account—not *causes*. If you want to know why I took the train to Strasbourg, you are inquiring about my reason for going there (or maybe why I didn't go by air), but you are unlikely to be interested in an answer that refers to my neurological state, my genetic inheritance or my upbringing. Human behaviour is in this respect precisely *not* like other events in the world, as the positivists supposed: we take our decisions for reasons and invest our actions with meanings. Yet criminology, with its positivist preoccupation with causes, has not usually approached offenders in this way, losing a rich and indeed indispensable source of understanding. One of the hallmarks of desistance research is an attempt to access these opportunities of understanding by attending carefully to individuals' own accounts.

Some people are reluctant to 'understand' types of conduct that it is psychologically and politically more comfortable to denounce and suppress. (A former British Prime Minister once said that 'Society needs to condemn a little more and understand a little less' (Independent 1993, although those who think that crime reduction is more important than righteous indignation may feel that we can ill-afford *not* to understand.) Criminal justice professionals, typically charged with a responsibility to reduce (re)offending, are especially likely to begin with what Matza called a 'correctional perspective'. But this priority to denounce and repudiate increases the possibility of 'losing the phenomenon, reducing it to that which it is not' (Matza 1969, p. 17). In other words, the urge to suppress crime may interfere with a proper understanding. Yet much of the criminological tradition treats offenders as objects rather than subjects, inquiring into causes rather than reasons. Both the Lombrosian project (with its positivist preoccupations) and the governmental project (with its ambitions to reduce crime) reflect a correctional aspiration that leads to the neglect of the sense that offenders make of their behaviour and their circumstances and can result in a failure to understand.

Implications for Probation Policy and Practice

There is a synergy between control theory and desistance studies. In their different ways, they reframe the intractable question, *why do people commit crimes?* The bonds that control theory identifies to explain why most people do not offend (or offend much) are very close to the ties that research has found to be supportive of desistance. At the least, the implications of this way of understanding should include a strong presumption against any intervention that blocks desistance and weakens the bonds of conformity—imprisonment above all.

Matza contrasted the correctional perspective with what he called an 'appreciative' inquiry which takes seriously offenders' accounts of their own behaviour, but without romanticisation or collusion. As we have seen, this would involve exploring reasons rather than causes, entailing dialogue and a relationship—a level of engagement which positivism does not require. It is not surprising, then, that the influence of desistance research on practice has been paralleled by the rediscovery of the importance of the professional relationship in supporting change; for a short review of *relationship* in contemporary probation practice see Canton (2011, Chap. 9).

Indeed the professional relationship can contribute to the 'attachment' that control theory takes to be conducive to abiding by the law. It can be a sense of obligation and loyalty to a probation officer, who demonstrates concern for and personal interest in the offender, that bring a reason to cooperate and indeed to 'go straight' (Rex 1999). Smith (2006, p. 371) speaks of the potential of 'the quality of the relationship with the supervising officer, if he or she becomes someone whom the offender would rather not let down, and whose good opinion the offender values and wishes to keep.' This is not to exaggerate probation's influence: other life events and opportunities are what are most needed to accomplish desistance. But the contribution of a concerned individual—offering encouragement, willing to discuss and explore opportunities, enabling access to services to develop personal skills and/or gain resources, and, perhaps above all, believing in the possibility of change—is always likely to make a difference and may even be decisive.

Criminology, Criminal Justice and Probation

This chapter has been concerned with *applied criminology*: how the insights of research and scholarship in the discipline can enhance the work of probation and criminal justice social work. Most of these theoretical perspectives have advice (proposals or cautions) to contribute to probation's policies and practices, as we have seen. We have also seen that some of criminology's questions—including the one that gives this chapter its title—are not well framed, and the subject needs different and better questions.

What are the main findings from this outline of a range of criminological theories? Within the positivist traditions, authoritative reviews of the personal and social characteristics of offenders (see, for example, Farrington 2007) and of the influences that appear to be associated with offending across the life course (Smith 2007) draw attention to the influence of parents and carers, of other associates, of school, as well as socioeconomic factors, notably poverty and limited access to resources and opportunities (social exclusion). Some scholars would also want to consider genetic influences on offending, as well as biochemical factors, diet and other examples of biological positivism.

Yet most of these factors are entirely beyond the reach of criminal justice. The implications of criminological research point policy towards a range of social and educational measures, but very few of these are *criminal justice* interventions. This does not mean that criminal justice is unimportant: on the contrary, trustworthy and effective criminal justice institutions have an intrinsic worth and can make a decisive difference for many people. But it is not reasonable to suppose that the agencies of criminal justice can solve the problems of crime.

One way of summarising this chapter would be to suggest that people's behaviour in general, and their capacity to change in particular, depends upon the following:

Motivation　Within the limits of the possibilities open to them, people will do what they choose to do. There is a crucial role for probation in offering encouragement and sustaining motivation to change, especially at difficult times. RNR literature and theories of motivation have given many valuable insights here to guide practice. Few things are more disheartening and demotivating than the belief that change is impossible and this is among the reasons why many accounts of probation values affirm this belief in the possibility of change. This involves a rejection of any deterministic or fatalistic interpretation of a positivist theory, even though workers will be mindful of the influence of structure, culture and biography on their clients' behaviour, on their circumstances and on their prospects of desistance (Hebdige 1976).

Abilities　People will only do what they are personally capable of doing. This is another aspect of 'human capital' and draws attention to the need to develop skills that may conduce to a 'good life'. People have their own conceptions of what may count for them as a good life, but it commonly involves activities like gainful employment that provide the means of living and building 'commitments' and 'investments', as well as personal relationships. To achieve this can require skills—some specifically related to particular occupations, but also broader educational development (notably literacy and numeracy), as well as general social skills, communication, thinking and problem-solving. Criminal justice social workers can try to help people to develop these skills or, in some societies, liaise with specialised organisations to ensure that their clients have access to the necessary services.

Opportunities   People can only do what they have an opportunity to do. Although RNR nowhere denies its significance, desistance research has foregrounded the importance of social capital. Very many probation clients experience enormous social disadvantage and it is not fatalistic to say that the persistence of these disadvantages will make desistance very much harder to accomplish. Part of probation's responsibility, then, is to encourage society to support social inclusion and to enable its clients to access the services and opportunities that they need by advocating on their behalf. Rehabilitation, and associated ideas like reintegration and resettlement, imply not only a person who has changed, but a society willing to accept that they have changed and to give them a fair chance to lead the better life to which they aspire.

Motivation, abilities and opportunities should be the focus of probation's work to bring about change. Both agency (human capital, motivation and abilities) and structure (social capital, fair opportunities and resources) are central to an understanding of the origins of offending and of the processes of desistance. Criminology can offer some valuable insights to refine policy and enhance practice. Criminal justice social workers are likely to employ these theories eclectically, taking guidance from the different ways of approaching crime and desistance and making pragmatic choices to help them in their work. Many theories capture a truth and then present it as the complete truth, reducing the significance of other ways of understanding. But this chapter has tried to show that attempts to confine the complex and many-sided questions of criminology to a single discipline are likely to lead to over-simplification and distortion.

Further Reading

For a very short but authoritative introduction to many of the topics discussed in this chapter, see Gelsthorpe (2003). There are a large number of general criminology textbooks available and different commentators will have their own favourites. Mine are Newburn (2012); Maguire et al. (2012); and (older, but certainly useful still) Smith (1995). Carrabine et al. (2014) and Hale et al. (2013) are also recommended. Christie (2004) is wise and thought-provoking, as Christie always is.

References

Andrews, D., & Bonta, J. (2010). Rehabilitating criminal justice policy and practice. *Psychology, Public Policy, and Law, 16*(1), 39–55.

Andrews, D., Bonta, J., & Wormith, J. (2011). The Risk-Need-Responsivity (RNR) model: Does adding the good lives model contribute to effective crime prevention? *Criminal Justice and Behavior, 38*(7), 735–755.

Becker, H. (1973). *Outsiders*. New York: Free Press.

Box, S. (1977). *Recession, crime and punishment*. Basingstoke: Macmillan.

Burnett, R. (1992). *The dynamics of recidivism*. Oxford: University of Oxford Centre for Criminological Research.

Canton, R. (2011). *Probation: Working with offenders*. Abingdon: Routledge.

Carrabine, E., Cox, P., Fussey, P., Hobbs, D., South, N., Thiel, D., et al. (2014). *Criminology: A sociological introduction* (3rd ed.). London: Routledge.

Christie, N. (2004). *A suitable amount of crime*. London: Routledge.

Clear, T., Hamilton, J., & Cadora, E. (2010). *Community justice* (2nd ed.). London: Routledge.

Cornish, D., & Clarke, R. (Eds.). (1986). *The reasoning criminal: Rational choice perspectives on offending*. New York: Springer.

Dominey, J. (2007). Responsivity. In R. Canton & D. Hancock (Eds.), *Dictionary of probation and offender management*. Cullompton: Willan.

Farrall, S. (2002). *Rethinking what works with offenders: Probation, social context and desistance from crime*. Cullompton: Willan.

Farrington, D. (2007). Childhood risk factors and risk focused prevention. In M. Maguire, R. Morgan, & R. Reiner (Eds.), *The Oxford handbook of criminology* (4th ed.). Oxford: Oxford University Press.

Finkelhor, D. (1986). *A sourcebook on child sexual abuse.* New York: Sage.

Flynn, N. (2012). *Criminal behaviour in context: Space, place and desistance from crime.* London: Routledge.

Foucault, M. (1977). *Discipline and punish: The birth of the prison.* Harmondsworth: Penguin.

Garland, D. (2002). Of crimes and criminals: The development of criminology in Britain. In M. Maguire, R. Morgan, & R. Reiner (Eds.), *The Oxford handbook of criminology* (3rd ed.). Oxford: Oxford University Press.

Gelsthorpe, L. (2003). Theories of crime. In W. H. Chui & M. Nellis (Eds.), *Moving probation forward: Evidence, arguments and practice.* Harlow: Pearson.

Goldson, B. (2007). Child criminalisation and the mistake of early intervention. *Criminal Justice Matters, 69*(1), 8–9.

Hale, C., Hayward, K., Wahidin, A., & Wincup, E. (Eds.). (2013). *Criminology.* Oxford: Oxford University Press.

Hebdige, D. (1976). The meaning of mod. In S. Hall & T. Jefferson (Eds.), *Resistance through rituals: Youth subcultures in post-war Britain.* London: HarperCollins.

Independent. (1993, February 21). Major on crime: 'Condemn more, understand less'. *The Independent.* Retrieved May 2015, from http://www.independent.co.uk/news/major-on-crime-condemn-more-understand-less-1474470.html

Kahneman, D. (2011). *Thinking, fast and slow.* Harmondsworth: Penguin.

Karstedt, S., & Farrall, S. (2007). *Law-abiding majority? The everyday crimes of the middle classes.* Retrieved May 2015, from http://www.crimeandjustice.org.uk/publications/law-abiding-majority-everyday-crimes-middle-classes

Lemert, E. (1967). *Human deviance, social problems and social control.* Englewood Cliffs, NJ: Prentice Hall.

Lösel, F. (2012). Offender treatment and rehabilitation: What works? In M. Maguire, R. Morgan, & R. Reiner (Eds.), *The Oxford handbook of criminology* (5th ed.). Oxford: Oxford University Press.

Maguire, M., Morgan, R., & Reiner, R. (Eds.). (2012). *The Oxford handbook of criminology.* Oxford: Oxford University Press.

Maruna, S. (2000). *Making good: How ex-convicts reform and rebuild their lives.* Washington, DC: American Psychological Association.

Matza, D. (1969). *Becoming deviant.* Englewood Cliffs, NJ: Prentice Hall.

McGuire, J. (2004). *Understanding psychology and crime: Perspectives on theory and action.* Maidenhead: Open University Press.

McGuire, J. (2007). Programmes for probationers. In G. McIvor & P. Raynor (Eds.), *Research highlights in social work: Vol. 48. Developments in social work with offenders.* London: Jessica Kingsley.

McGuire, J., & Priestley, P. (1995). Reviewing 'What Works': Past, present and future. In J. McGuire (Ed.), *What works: Reducing reoffending—Guidelines from research and practice.* Chichester: Wiley.

McNeill, F., & Weaver, B. (2010). *Changing lives? Desistance research and offender management.* Retrieved May 2015, from http://www.sccjr.ac.uk/pubs/Changing-Lives-Desistance-Research-and-Offender-Management/255

Nevin, R. (2012). The answer is lead poisoning. Retrieved May 2015, from http://www.ricknevin.com/uploads/The_Answer_is_Lead_Poisoning.pdf

Newburn, T. (2012). *Criminology* (2nd ed.). London: Routledge.

Nisbett, R., & Wilson, T. (1977). Telling more than we can know: Verbal reports on mental processes. *Psychological Review, 84*(3), 231–259.

Raynor, P. (2004). Rehabilitative and reintegrative approaches. In A. Bottoms, S. Rex, & G. Robinson (Eds.), *Alternatives to prison: Options for an insecure society.* Cullompton: Willan.

Raynor, P., & Robinson, G. (2009). *Rehabilitation, crime and justice.* Basingstoke: Palgrave Macmillan.

Reiman, J., & Leighton, P. (2013). *The rich get richer and the poor get prison: Ideology, class and criminal justice* (10th ed.). New York: Pearson.

Rex, S. (1999). Desistance from offending: Experiences of probation. *Howard Journal, 38*(4), 366–383.

Robinson, G., & Crow, I. (2009). *Offender rehabilitation: Theory, research and practice.* London: Sage.

Schur, E. (1973). *Radical non-intervention.* Englewood Cliffs, NJ: Prentice Hall.

Smith, D. (1995). *Criminology for social work.* Basingstoke: Palgrave Macmillan.

Smith, D. (1998) 'Social work with offenders: the practice of exclusion and the potential for inclusion' in Monica Barry and Christine Hallett (eds.) *Social Exclusion and Social Work: Issues of theory, policy and practice,* Lyme Regis: Russell House

Smith, D. (2006). Making sense of psychoanalysis in criminological theory and probation practice. *Probation Journal, 53*(4), 361–376.

Smith, D. J. (2007). Crime and the life course. In M. Maguire, R. Morgan, & R. Reiner (Eds.), *The Oxford handbook of criminology* (4th ed.). Oxford: Oxford University Press.

Sykes, G., & Matza, D. (1957). Techniques of neutralization: A theory of delinquency. *American Sociological Review, 22*(6), 664–670.

Ward, T., & Maruna, S. (2007). *Rehabilitation.* London: Routledge.

Ward, T., Yates, P., & Willis, G. (2012). The good lives model and the risk need responsivity model: A critical response to Andrews, Bonta, and Wormith (2011). *Criminal Justice and Behavior, 39*(1), 94–110.

Weaver, B., & McNeill, F. (2007). Desistance. In R. Canton & D. Hancock (Eds.), *Dictionary of probation and offender management.* Cullompton: Willan.

What Are the Most Important Studies of Desistance and What Are the Future Research Needs?

The Relevance of Desistance Research

The association between age and crime is one of the best- established facts in the field of criminology. It is generally agreed that aggregate crime rates peak in late adolescence/early adulthood and gradually drop thereafter, but there remains some debate about the cause of this decline. Information about protective factors that foster or accelerate desistance also informs interventions after the onset of criminal careers. Once onset has occurred, efforts should be invested in limiting the length, intensity and seriousness of criminal careers. Identifying life-course transitions and cognitive factors that contribute to desistance from crime can provide useful information for post-onset interventions. This chapter provides

---

This chapter draws from various sections of the following publication:
Kazemian, L. (2015). Desistance from crime and antisocial behavior. In Morizot, J. & Kazemian, L. (eds), *The Development of Criminal and Antisocial Behavior: Theory, Research and Practical Applications* (pp. 295–312). New York: Springer.

L. Kazemian (✉)
Department of Sociology, John Jay College of Criminal Justice,
University of New York

© The Editor(s) (if applicable) and The Author(s) 2016
F. McNeill et al. (eds.), *Probation*,
DOI 10.1057/978-1-137-51982-5_3

an overview of the most important studies on desistance and underlines future research needs.

Explanations of Desistance

This section aims to provide a brief summary of some of the key findings derived from influential studies on desistance from crime. Major findings on the social, cognitive, and genetic predictors of desistance are presented. While the focus is on desistance from crime, findings are likely to be generalizable to other forms of problem behaviors. Laub and Sampson's (2001, p. 38) extensive review suggested that "the processes of desistance from problem behaviors such as alcohol dependency are quite similar to the processes of desistance from predatory crime."

It should be noted that results may vary from one study to another as a result of divergent definitions of desistance (Kazemian 2007). Although several researchers have acknowledged the relevance of perceiving desistance as a process rather than an event that occurs abruptly (Bottoms et al. 2004; Bushway et al. 2001, 2003; Laub et al. 1998; Laub and Sampson 2001, 2003; Le Blanc 1993; Loeber and Le Blanc 1990; Maruna 2001; Shover 1983), the dichotomous definition of desistance as the opposite of recidivism remains common.[1] Reviews of the literature have suggested that when prospective longitudinal data are not available, observation periods are short, and dichotomous measures of desistance are employed, desistance is likely to indicate a temporary lull in offending as opposed to the permanent cessation of crime (see Kazemian 2007).

Over 25 years ago, Le Blanc and Fréchette (1989, followed by Loeber and Le Blanc 1990 and Le Blanc and Loeber 1998) developed a definition of desistance that extended beyond the dichotomous measure. This definition integrated four dimensions. The authors argued that before criminal activity ceases completely, the frequency of offending declines (deceleration), offenders engage in less-diverse offense types (specialization),

---

[1] The process view of desistance has been more prevalent in recent research. Adopting this approach in their analysis of desistance among parolees, Bahr et al. (2010, p. 674) did not focus solely on specific events (i.e., recidivism) but rather "... on how well parolees were able to perform across a period of 3 years".

transition to committing less serious offenses (de-escalation), and a culmination point is reached. This definition is consistent with the operationalization of desistance as a process, but it remains underutilized in desistance research. Most (quantitative) desistance research continues to adopt a dichotomous definition of desistance, most likely owing to the convenience and availability of recidivism data as opposed to data on other criminal career parameters.

Social Predictors of Desistance

A large body of research on desistance has drawn attention to the importance of social bonds in the process of desistance. Desistance from crime is said to be gradual, resulting from an accumulation of social bonds (see Horney et al. 1995). Irwin (1970) identified three key factors in the explanation of desistance from crime: a good job, a good relationship with a woman, and involvement in extracurricular activities. Giordano et al. (2002) made reference to the "respectability package", and argued that marriage and job stability exert a more substantial impact on desistance if they occur jointly. In this respect, turning points (marriage, employment, etc.) are likely to be interdependent. Life events can either be positive or negative, depending on the "quality, strength, and interdependence of social ties" (Sampson and Laub 1993, p. 21). In this respect, adult crime would largely result from weak bonds to social institutions, and desistance from crime would entail some "social investment" in conventional institutions.

Employment

The general consensus in the literature is that job stability promotes desistance from crime (Giordano et al. 2002). Using data from the National Supported Work Demonstration Project, Uggen (2000) explored the effect of employment on recidivism. This project recruited participants from underprivileged neighborhoods and randomly assigned them to control or experimental groups. Offenders, drug users and dropouts were targeted. Individuals in the treatment group were given minimum-wage employment opportunities. Results showed that the program had a more substantial impact on older individuals (over 26 years of age). This finding is consistent with Morizot and Le Blanc's (2007) analyses of a sample of adjudicated French-Canadian males, which showed that employment exerted a positive effect on desistance only at specific developmental periods. Furthermore, "offenders who are provided even marginal employment opportunities are less likely to reoffend than those not provided such opportunities" (Uggen 2000, p. 542). Although the general consensus in the literature is that employment (and employment stability) exerts an impact on desistance, some studies have found that employment did not have an impact on the likelihood of desistance from crime (Giordano et al. 2002).

The life narratives explored in Laub and Sampson's (2003, p. 129) study suggested that "stable work may not trigger a change in an antisocial trajectory in the way that marriage or serving in the military does, even though employment may play an important role in sustaining the process of desistance". Analyzing data from a random sample of Texas male parolees, Tripodi et al. (2010) found somewhat similar results. Their findings showed that employment was not significantly associated with a reduced likelihood of reincarceration, but was linked to longer time lags to reincarceration (i.e., more time "crime-free in the community"). As highlighted by the authors, this interesting finding underlines the importance of studying desistance as a process:

> The explanation for this insignificant finding, however, requires a shift in perspective from a "black and white" view of ex-prisoners as either recidivists or nonrecidivists. This traditional view of parolees leaves little middle ground for ex-prisoners who are in the process of changing. Instead, a more complex view of offenders is needed to recognize that they may fall on a spectrum of behavior change that consists of various stages. (p. 714)

Interestingly, a study drawing on a sample of recidivist Norwegian males found that employment is a consequence, and not a cause, of desistance (Skardhamar and Savolainen 2014). Modeling changes in offending behavior before and after exposure to employment, the authors found that most individuals had desisted from crime prior to obtaining employment, and that being employed did not result in additional decreases in criminal behavior. Skardhamar and Savolainen (2014) did detect a small group of individuals who exhibited reductions in offending behavior after obtaining employment, but they were a very small minority of the sample. This study is important because it demonstrates the crucial influence of selection effects in explaining the association between turning points and desistance.

Laub and Sampson (2003) argued that the processes underlying the relationship between work and desistance are similar to those underlying the relationship between marriage and desistance.

Employment promotes desistance through four main processes: (1) a reciprocal exchange of social capital between employer and employee; (2) more limited exposure to criminal opportunities and a reduced "probability that criminal propensities will be translated into action"; (3) direct informal social control; and (4) the development of a "sense of identity and meaning to one's life" (Laub and Sampson 2003, p. 47). Finally, the impact of employment as a turning point appears to also act conjointly with other social transitions. Sampson and Laub's (1993) results reveal interaction effects between various social institutions and desistance from crime. For example, they find that the impact of job stability on desistance is not as significant among married men.

Marriage

The strong link between marriage and desistance has been highlighted in various studies for the past few decades, and continues to hold in contemporary research (Bersani et al. 2009; Craig and Foster 2013; Doherty and Ensminger 2013; Farrington and West 1995; Horney et al. 1995; McGloin et al. 2011; Sampson and Laub 1993, 2003). The most influential findings have emerged from the Glueck data, the Cambridge Study in Delinquent Development, and Horney et al.'s (1995) classic analysis of criminal careers in the short term.

Drawing on a sample of Nebraska inmates, Horney et al. (1995, p. 658) explored the association between crime and local life circumstances, which they defined as "conditions in an individual's life that can fluctuate relatively frequently." According to the authors, variables explaining short-term variations in criminal behavior are similar to variables explaining long-term variations (i.e. the strength of the bonds to conventional social institutions). Horney et al. (1995, p. 669) found that individuals were "less likely to commit crimes when living with a wife" (see also Farrington and West 1995; Laub and Sampson 2003; Sampson and Laub 1993). The authors argued that time invested in conventional social institutions was time away from sources of temptation (bars, delinquent peers, etc.). Horney et al. (1995, p. 670) added that these events may not have been randomly distributed, and that "local life circumstances can change criminal careers by modifying the likelihood of offending *at particular times.*" Since their analyses were limited to a short period of the life course, it is difficult to assess whether these changes were permanent, and whether they reflected stable changes in life-course trajectories.

Farrington and West (1995, p. 265) found that "individuals who had married and never separated were the least antisocial at age 32 while those who had married and separated and were now living alone were the most antisocial." They studied rates of offending before and after marriage, and concluded that getting married led to a decrease in offending compared with staying single. However, their results did not allow determining "how far marriage and separation may be causes, consequences, or symptoms" (p. 265). The effect of marriage on desistance may have been dependent on "the reasons for getting married (e.g. pregnancy), on the happiness of the marriage, and on the extent to which the wife is conventional and prosocial" (Farrington and West 1995, p. 278). In a follow-up of the Cambridge Study in Delinquent Development of males up to age 48, Theobald and Farrington (2009) found significant declines in the number of convictions after marriage, though this effect was less pronounced for late marriages as opposed to early or mid-range marriages. The authors argued that "there may be an interaction effect between marriage and some variable that is correlated with age such as malleability—a willingness to change or be more flexible in behaviour" (p. 512).

Laub et al. (1998) also found that high-rate offenders had weaker marital bonds compared to other offenders. In agreement with Farrington and West's results, Laub et al. (1998) argued that the timing and quality of marriage were important (see also Rutter 1996), with stable marriages exerting a greater preventive effect (see also Sampson and Laub 1993). In agreement with Farrington and West's study, Laub et al. (1998)

argued that the inhibiting effect of marriage on crime is gradual rather than abrupt. Laub and Sampson (2003) defined the effect of marriage on crime as an "investment process"; the more that individuals invest in social bonds (e.g. marriage), the less likely they are to engage in criminal activities because they have more to lose. Laub and Sampson (2003, p. 33) rejected the idea that the effect of marriage on crime is merely a result of self-selection (i.e., the idea that people who decide to reform are more likely to get married), and claimed that marital effects remained strong despite selection effects. In contrast to these claims, many studies have suggested strong assortative mating effects (i.e., the idea that the selection of a partner is a nonrandom process that involves various similarities between the mates; see Boutwell et al. 2012; Krueger et al. 1998). Boutwell et al.'s (2012, p. 1250) findings suggested that "the similarity in mates existed prior to the commencement of their relationship," providing support for "the role of assortative mating, not behavioral contagion, in structuring mate similarity for antisocial behaviors." The contrasting results between Laub and Sampson's work and the assortative mating literature show that there is still much to learn about the link between marriage/romantic partnerships and desistance.

Laub and Sampson (2003) summarized the key processes involved in the effect of marriage on desistance from crime, many of which revolve around shifts in routine activities. Marriage leads to reduced deviant peer associations, new friends and extended family, as well as overall changes in routine activities. Spouses also constitute an extra source of social control, and an effective means of monitoring routine activities. Marriage also often results in residential changes and children, which may also promote changes in routine activities. Laub and Sampson (2003, p. 43) also argued that "marriage can change one's sense of self."

Findings from recent research provide support for Laub and Sampson's (2003) hypotheses and further specify the marriage–desistance link. In addition to the quality of relationship, the characteristics of the partner also appear to be important. Van Schellen et al. (2012) argued that the crime-reduction benefits of marriage may be reduced among convicted individuals, because they "have a tendency to marry criminal partners" (p. 567). Bersani and Doherty (2013) found that the dissolution of the marriage is associated with increased offending, which prompted the authors to hypothesize that marriage is likely to exert temporary or situational effects on desistance.

Not all studies found a significant effect of marriage on desistance (e.g., Kruttschnitt et al. 2000). Recent European studies found divergent results. Lyngstad and Skardhamar (2013) investigated the marriage–desistance link among a sample of Norwegian males. The study used a within-individual design and followed up individuals for a period of 5 years before and after marriage, and investigated the likelihood of engaging in crime during these periods. A reduction in crime is observed before marriage, and a slight increase in offending occurs after marriage. These findings suggest that the drop in offending among married individuals is initiated in the years preceding marriage, and is not a result of marriage (a similar drop was observed in an analysis of the effect of parenthood on offending, using the same data; see Monsbakken et al. 2013). Lyngstad and Skardhamar (2013) hypothesized that the reduced involvement in crime prior to marriage may be due to the social control influences of the courtship period, as well as the potential selection effect of individuals who show disinterest in offending (and who select partners who share the sentiment). Using a Dutch sample, van Schellen et al. (2012) found that although individuals who were highly active in offending were less likely to marry, they were more likely to marry a deviant partner than to remain (potentially reflecting assortative mating effects, see discussion above). These results prompted the authors to recommend that we revisit the marriage–desistance link, arguing that "offenders are less likely to experience the protective effects of marriage, because of their lower marital chances," and that the crime-reducing effects of marriage are lost on individuals who marry a deviant spouse (p. 567). These interesting findings highlight the need to better document changes before and after marriage, as well as information about partner selection.

While marriage is regarded as a major turning point in desistance research, much less attention is granted to the effects of cohabitation (for one of the first analyses of cohabitation with longitudinal data, see Farrington and West 1995) In an analysis based on a sample of Finnish recidivists, Savolainen (2009, p. 300) found that the "transition to cohabitation is associated with greater reductions in criminal activity than getting married," highlighting once again the relevance of taking into account the stability of the relationship as opposed to uniquely focusing on marital status. Savolainen (2009, p. 301) also noted a cumulative effect of parenthood and union formation on desistance from crime, concluding that "offenders who formed a union and became fathers enjoyed the greatest reductions in criminal activity." Drawing on a sample of 500 women living in underprivileged communities in Denver, Kreager et al. (2010) found that the transition to motherhood was significantly associated with reduced delinquency and substance use, and that this effect was more pronounced than that of marriage. Conjugal relationships often coincide with having children, and further research is needed to better understand the impact of parenthood on desistance, as well as its differential impact across gender groups (see Laub and Sampson 2001, for a discussion on the more pronounced impact of parenthood on women when compared with men; see also Lanctôt 2015).

Peers

The social learning perspective suggests that the effect of marriage on crime is mediated through peer associations. This perspective attributes desistance to associations with conventional peers, increased noncriminal routine activities, and reduced exposure to definitions favorable to crime (e.g., Farrington et al. 2002; Warr 1998; Wright and Cullen 2004). Using a sample from the National Youth Survey (NYS), Warr (1993) found that changes in offending behavior with age were related to changes in peer associations. The author concluded that, when controlling for peer affiliations, "the association between age and crime is substantially weakened and, for some offences, disappears entirely" (1993, p. 35). In a later study, Warr (1998) found that married people tend to spend less time with their friends than unmarried individuals, and that married individuals tend to have fewer delinquent friends than their unmarried counterparts.

Wright and Cullen (2004) replicated Warr's (1998) study and also used data from the National Youth Survey (NYS), but focused on work rather than marriage. The authors found that employment increased the interactions with prosocial co-workers, which "restructure friendship networks by diminishing contact with delinquent peers" (2004, p. 185). Work was said to promote desistance not through the development of increased social capital, but rather through increased associations with prosocial co-workers. In other words, relationships with prosocial co-workers minimized interactions with delinquent peers and promoted desistance from crime. Wright and Cullen (2004, p. 200) argued that the effects of unemployment on desistance were not dependent on the quality of the job (as argued by Sampson and Laub), but rather on the "*quality of peer associations* that occur within the context of work." In the Pittsburgh Youth Study, Farrington et al. (2002) found that, while affiliations with delinquent peers were strongly correlated with delinquency in between-individual analyses, this was not the case for within-individual analyses, suggesting that peer delinquency may not have had a causal effect on offending.

Peer networks may be associated with the environment or the neighborhood. Kirk's (2012) research suggests that residential change may be an important turning point in criminal careers, a question that has been largely ignored in life-course research.

Military

Sampson and Laub's (1993; see also 2003) analysis of the Glueck men sample suggested that the military was an important turning point in the life course. In contrast, Bouffard (2005) found that military service was not associated with offending outcomes (see also Craig and Foster 2013, for similar results). Craig and Foster (2013, p. 219) explained that the divergence in results with Sampson and Laub "may indicate a change in the military". However, the authors did find that involvement in the military was predictive of desistance among women. There is a need for research with contemporary samples of individuals having completed military service in order to assess the impact of the military on desistance from crime, as well as the differential gender effects.

Incarceration

Most empirical studies and meta-analyses that have investigated the impact of incarceration on recidivism have found that imprisonment has either no impact or undesirable effects on subsequent offending (Bales and Piquero 2012; Gendreau et al. 1999; Nagin et al. 2009; Villettaz et al. 2006; Weatherburn 2010). Gendreau et al. (1999) conducted a meta-analysis of studies that have investigated the link between prison and recidivism. Controlling for relevant risk factors, the authors found that both incarceration (in comparison with community sanctions) and length of time in prison led to increases in recidivism. Gendreau et al. (1999, p. 7) concluded that prison may promote offending behavior by damaging the "psychological and emotional well-being of inmates" (see also Maruna and Toch 2005). Clemmer (1958) discussed the concept of *prisonization*, which refers to the process by which inmates adopt the customs, values and norms of prison, some of which may be inappropriate for life on the outside and impede desistance efforts. In addition, the significant prevalence of traumatic experiences and mental health disorders among the prison population (e.g., Fazel and Danesh 2002; Wolff et al. 2009) highlights yet another impediment to desistance. In its current form, the prison environment may not be conducive to the development of a reformed, prosocial identity. Very little is known about the identity shifts that occur among inmates during periods of incarceration, and how these shifts impact their attitudes, behaviors, and relationships.

Substance Use

Substance use issues constitute an important barrier to successful desistance and reintegration (Belenko 2006; Mumola and Karberg 2006; Travis et al. 2001). Drug and alcohol use may promote impulsivity and violent behavior (Raskin White et al. 2002). Substance use is likely to impede the desistance process, since it impacts the offender's ability to think rationally; Longshore et al. (2004) unsurprisingly found that drug use was higher among individuals with low self-control.

Giordano et al. (2002) explained that drug and alcohol use limit accessibility to prosocial life events, cloud judgment and limit cognitive abilities. Substance use was so widespread in Maruna's (2001, p. 64) sample that the author concluded that "The study of desistance, therefore, is almost necessarily a study of abstaining from both types of behavior." Laub and Sampson (2003) also found that substance use, especially alcohol, played an important role in persistence in crime over the life course. Laub and Sampson (2003, p. 284) also highlighted the indirect effects of substance use on offending, arguing that "drug and alcohol abuse sustains crime in part because of the negative consequences and social difficulties caused by heavy drinking and drug use in the domains of work, family, and the military" (see also Belenko 2006).

Cognitive Predictors of Desistance

The study of subjective changes that promote desistance from crime has generally been addressed in ethnographic studies and qualitative analyses of crime. Maruna (2001, p. 8) argued that "subjective aspects of human life (emotions, thoughts, motivations, and goals) have largely been neglected in the study of crime, because the data are presumed to be either unscientific or too unwieldy for empirical analysis."

Anderson and McNeill (forthcoming) perhaps offer the most comprehensive review of cognitive factors associated with desistance from crime. The authors identify three main types of cognitive transformations: (1) shifts in *narrative identity*; (2) changes in the *content of cognitions* (i.e., shifts in pro-criminal attitudes, emotions pertaining to criminal behavior, and motivation and hope); and (3) transformation in *cognitive skills* (i.e., changes in self-control, executive functioning, and cognitive strategies that may to sustain desistance efforts).

The notion of *human agency* (i.e., the idea that offenders have free will and remain active participants in their life journey) is central to our understanding of desistance from crime. Sampson and Laub (2003) argued that human agency is not a stable trait, but rather an emergent property within situations; offenders are not mindless participants pushed or pulled to break the law. This argument is consistent with analyses that have investigated changes in personality traits over time (Morizot 2015).

According to Gove (1985), desistance from crime is a result of five key internal changes: a shift from self-centeredness to consideration for others, the development of prosocial values and behavior, increasing ease in social interactions, greater consideration for other members of the community, and a growing concern for the "meaning of life." Through life history narratives, Giordano et al. (2002) developed the theory of cognitive transformation and discussed the cognitive shifts that promote the process of desistance. The authors described four processes of cognitive transformations. First, the offender must be open to change (see also Abrams 2012). Second, through a process of self-selection, Giordano et al. (2002) argued that the individual exposes himself/herself to prosocial experiences that will further promote desistance (e.g., employment). Third, the individual adheres to a new prosocial and noncriminal identity. Finally, there is a shift in the perception of the criminal lifestyle, that is the negative consequences of offending become obvious. As such, desistance is regarded as a gradual process.

Shover and Thompson (1992) found that the relationship between age and desistance was mediated by *optimism for achieving success via legitimate pursuits* and *expectations of criminal success*. Burnett (2004) also found that pre-release self-assessments of optimism about desistance were positively associated with actual desistance outcomes after release (see Farrall 2002, for similar results). Maruna (2001, p. 9) concluded that desisting ex-offenders "displayed an exaggerated sense of control over the future and an inflated, almost missionary, sense of purpose in life." In addition, the ability to envision a future self has also been found to be associated with the process of desistance (Paternoster and Bushway 2009). Paternoster and Bushway (2009) argued that developing a negative image of one's future self may stimulate desistance by making clear to the individual what he/she does not want to become.

The individuals' motivation and determination to cease offending has also been found to be an important factor promoting in the desistance process (Burnett 2004; Shover 1983; Shover and Thompson 1992; Sommers et al. 1994). Through interviews with a sample of incarcerated burglars, Shover (1996) highlighted the importance of *resolve and determination* in the desistance process. He argued that "men who are most determined to avoid crime are more successful in doing so than their equivocating peers, even allowing for the possible influences of other factors" (1996, p. 130). Some of the interviewees expressed increasing concern with getting caught as they got older, fearing that they might spend the rest of their lives in prison and therefore miss out on the opportunity to make something of their lives. Furthermore, with age, some offenders gave less importance to material gain, which reduced the appeal of crime.

Overall, crime (and all caveats associated with it) has a cumulative effect on offenders and sooner or later, they get "worn down" by a life in crime.

These findings suggest that it may not be age in itself that causes a decline in offending, as argued by Gottfredson and Hirschi (1990), but rather the accumulation, over time, of failures, contacts with the criminal justice system, betrayals and other problems associated with crime. Shover (1996, p. 138) suggested that "aging makes offenders more interested in the rewards of conventional lifestyles and also more rational in decision making," Individuals will be more willing to cease offending if the perceived benefits of refraining from engaging in criminal behavior are greater than those of crime. These findings suggest that desistance requires both internal and external changes.

The Role of Identity Change in the Desistance Process

The importance of identity transformation in the process of desistance has been highlighted by many researchers (Anderson and McNeill forthcoming; Bottoms et al. 2004; Burnett 2004; Giordano et al. 2002; King 2013; Laub and Sampson 2003; Maruna 2001; Shover 1983). Maruna (2001, p. 7) argued that "to desist from crime, ex-offenders need to develop a coherent, prosocial identity for themselves" (see also Shover 1983). In his sample, Maruna identified a need for desisting offenders to separate their past self from their current self. *Making good* refers to a process of "self-reconstruction" (Maruna 2001). *Making good* entails an understanding of why past offenses were committed, and of the reasons supporting the decision to stop. Additionally, it also involves an ability to see the link between past mistakes and current accomplishments, to make the best of past experiences and to discover one's "true self." Maruna and Farrall (2004) made the distinction between primary desistance (the initial decision to abandon criminal behavior) and secondary desistance (a shift in self-identity and maintenance of desistance efforts), which underlines the reality that the initial decision to cease offending is often only the first step in the desistance process.

The narrative approach to studying desistance has become increasingly popular in recent years, and several studies have provided support for the idea of the "redemption script" and its role in sustaining desisting identities (e.g., Burnett 2004; Gadd and Farrall 2004; Halsey 2006; Maruna 2001). The construction, deconstruction and reconstruction of self-stories is at the core of many traditional correctional interventions. Laub and Sampson (2003) have been critical of this perspective, arguing that desistance does not necessarily require cognitive transformation. The authors maintained that "offenders can and do desist without a conscious decision to 'make good' … and offenders can and do desist without a 'cognitive transformation'" (p. 279). Although desistance does eventually occur for all offenders, it occurs earlier for some individuals than others. Evidence from the studies presented in this chapter seems to suggest that, rather than being a process that occurs "naturally", desistance tends to be prompted and supported by strong social networks and an individual resolve to change. What remains less understood, however, is how the cognitive and social processes interact to cause a shift towards desistance.

It is interesting to note that many of the cognitive factors investigated in criminological studies of desistance bear many similarities to personality traits identified by psychologists, and yet this literature has been largely overlooked in criminological research. Longitudinal studies have shown that there is a "normative maturation" in personality traits, and a growing number of studies have confirmed that these changes in personality traits are correlated with decreases in offending and substance use (Morizot 2015).

The Interaction Between Social and Cognitive Factors

One of the most interesting dimensions of the desistance process refers to the way in which individual predispositions and life events converge to promote this process. Giordano et al. (2002, p. 1026) argued that "given a relatively 'advantaged' set of circumstances, the cognitive transformations and agentic moves we describe are hardly necessary; under conditions of sufficiently extreme disadvantage, they are unlikely to be nearly enough". Giordano et al. (2002) supported the idea that permanent desistance from crime may be a result of both cognitive changes and turning points ("hooks for change"). Through a process of self-selection, life events promote shifts in identity and act as *catalysts* for permanent changes in offending. Some of the main hooks for change identified in the narratives included the links to formal institutions (prison and religion) and intimate or informal networks (spouse and/or children), which is consistent with Sampson and Laub's (1993) theory of formal and informal social control. Various other studies have emphasized the important roles of both internal and external factors in the explanation of desistance (Farrall and Bowling 1999; Laub and Sampson 2003; Sommers et al. 1994).

LeBel et al. (2008) highlighted the distinction between *social* (i.e. life events, situational factors, "objective" changes) and *subjective* (cognitive factors, internal changes) components in the explanation of desistance. The authors presented three models explaining the interaction between social and subjective factors. First, the *strong subjective model* stipulates that it is the individual's motivation and desire to change that increases the likelihood that bonds will be strengthened by conventional social sources (marriage, legitimate employment, etc.). In this respect, turning points that promote desistance would be the result of a process of self-selection and would not cause a change in behavior. Second, the *strong social model* asserts that life events occur randomly among individuals, and that these turning points are directly responsible for desistance from crime. From this viewpoint, subjective characteristics are not essential to desistance from crime. Finally, the third model, the *subjective-social model*, supports the idea that life events may contribute to the desistance process, but that the impact of these events will be dependent on the *mindset* of the individuals. As argued above, although motivation is a crucial component of change, it nonetheless requires support from conventional social networks to maintain desistance efforts. This last model thus integrates both objective and subjective factors (external and internal changes) in its explanation of desistance.

LeBel et al.'s (2008) findings suggested that the desistance process is a system in which various internal and external factors interact in different ways. On one hand, the authors suggested also that some social problems occur independently of the optimistic views of the offender. On the other, they also concluded that individuals displaying the greatest motivation to change were also the least likely to recidivate. Individuals who had the right mindset and social networks to support them were better equipped to face problems, resist temptations and avoid setbacks, provided that the problems faced were not tremendous. However, the authors also concluded that the desire to change may be insufficient when social problems are overwhelming and excessive (see also Bottoms et al. 2004; Giordano et al. 2002; Farrall and Bowling 1999; Maruna 2001). Maruna (2001) explained that the decision and desire to desist from crime is often put to the test by situational factors, such as temptations and frustrations, and in such scenarios the desire to desist from crime may not always be sufficient.

Genetic/Biological Factors and Desistance

The maturation framework, discussed by Glueck and Glueck (1940), stipulates that physical, intellectual, emotional and psychological development (i.e., maturation) is the main cause for decline or cessation of offending behavior. Gottfredson and Hirschi (1990) argued that aging is a major reason for the decline in crime observed over time, and that offending declines for all offenders with age. Few studies have explored the role of genetic and biological factors in the desistance process (for extensive research on the biosocial explanations of offending behaviors, see Beaver et al. 2015). In a recent study, Barnes and Beaver (2012) investigated the influence of genetic factors in the marriage–desistance link. The authors drew on prior research having examined the genetic foundations of adult social bonds and focused on active gene-environment correlations (rGEs), which "occur when a person selects into an environment on the basis of his or her genetic propensities" (p. 22). They found significant genetic influences on both marriage and desistance from crime. Marriage remained a significant predictor of desistance even after controlling for genetic influences, but its effect was greatly attenuated. Similarly, Beaver et al. (2008) also found a significant interaction between marital status and genetic polymorphisms in the prediction of desistance. This is a relatively new area of inquiry in desistance research, and more studies are needed to better understand the complex interplay between genes and the environment. Loeber et al.'s (2007) study suggested that the evidence base for physiological and biological factors linked to desistance is highly underdeveloped.

Summary

There is an increasing consensus regarding the relevance of perceiving desistance as a process rather than an event. The decision to abandon criminal behaviors is unlikely to occur abruptly, particularly for those individuals who display longer and more intense criminal careers. Intermittency in criminal careers is the norm. Decisions to desist from crime may involve several relapses and reversals of decisions before reaching the final point of termination from crime, which renders the prediction of desistance challenging. Desistance is likely to occur as a result of various turning points and cognitive shifts that occur throughout the life course, rather than being determined by early risk factors. Social bonds, particularly marriage and employment, are generally found to be significant predictors of desistance. However, the quality of the bond, the nature of the relationships with the spouse or the fellow employees/ employer, and the timing of life event are also important considerations. In addition, some research has suggested that these turning points are consequences, rather than causes, of desistance, suggesting strong selection effects. Various cognitive factors (or personality traits), such as the decision to change or the development of a prosocial identity, have been found to be predictive of successful desistance efforts. These measures are typically excluded from quantitative analyses. The process of desistance is likely to occur as a result of the combined influence of life events, cognitive/personality changes, and potentially genetic/biological factors.

Conclusion

Despite the substantial progress in desistance research, some important issues warrant more attention. First, the assessment of desistance should extend beyond traditional measures of offending. Additional outcome measures for successful desistance may include improvements in mental and physical health outcomes, social bonds and integration, personality traits, and behavioral variables other than offending (e.g., substance use, routine activities, etc.). Second, we need to better understand the interplay between individual traits and turning points in the explanation of desistance. For instance, while we generally regard life events as objective turning points, they may in fact be subjective owing to the fact that personality influences how these events are perceived. Third, desistance research has, for the most part, failed to integrate the concept of resilience (for exceptions, see Born et al. 1997; Lösel and Bender 2003). In the psychological literature, resilient individuals refer to those who are exposed to life stresses but who "defy expectation by developing into well-adapted individuals" (Luthar 1991, p. 600). In the context of desistance research, better knowledge about resilience would shed some light on the factors that contribute to the success of individuals who, theoretically and statistically, may be less likely to desist given their exposure to influential risk factors. Finally, efforts should be undertaken to better integrate knowledge generated in areas of desistance and prisoner reentry research. While desistance research has primarily emphasized theoretical advancements, research on prisoner reentry has focused on the practical implications of the desistance process of formerly incarcerated individuals as they return to the community. Findings drawn from desistance research have obvious implications for reentry practices, but these two areas of study often appear to be disjointed. Similarly, life-course and criminal career research has largely neglected to study how the desistance process unfolds during periods of incarceration (Kazemian and Travis 2015). Consequently, we know little about whether our knowledge base on desistance is applicable to prisoners.

References

Abrams, L. S. (2012). Envisioning life "on the outs": Exit narratives of incarcerated males youth. *International Journal of Offender Therapy and Comparative Criminology, 56*(6), 877–896.

Anderson, S., & McNeill, F. (forthcoming). Desistance and cognitive transformations. In D. P. Farrington, L. Kazemian, & A. Piquero (Eds.), *The Oxford handbook on developmental and life-course criminology*. New York: Springer.

Bahr, S. J., Harris, L., Fisher, J. K., & Armstrong, A. H. (2010). Successful reentry: What differentiates successful and unsuccessful parolees? *International Journal of Offender Therapy and Comparative Criminology, 54*(5), 667–692.

Bales, W. D., & Piquero, A. R. (2012). Assessing the impact of imprisonment on recidivism. *Journal of Experimental Criminology, 8*, 71–101.

Barnes, J. C., & Beaver, K. M. (2012). Marriage and desistance from crime: A consideration of gene—Environment correlation. *Journal of Marriage and Family, 74*, 19–33.

Beaver, K. M., Schwartz, J. A., & Gajos, J. M. (2015). A review of the genetic and gene-environment interplay contributors to antisocial phenotypes. In J. Morizot & L. Kazemian (Eds.), *The development of criminal and antisocial behavior: Theory, research and practical applications* (pp. 109–122). New York: Springer.

Beaver, K. M., Wright, J. P., DeLisi, M., & Vaughn, M. G. (2008). Desistance from delinquency: The marriage effect revisited and extended. *Social Science Research, 37*(September), 736–752.

Belenko, S. (2006). Assessing released inmates for substance-abuse-related service needs. *Crime & Delinquency, 52*(1), 94–113.

Bersani, B. E., & Doherty, E. E. (2013). When the ties that bind unwind: Examining the enduring and situational processes of change behind the marriage effect. *Criminology, 51*, 399–433.

Bersani, B. E., Laub, J. H., & Nieuwbeerta, P. (2009). Marriage and desistance from crime in the Netherlands: Do gender and socio-historical context matter? *Journal of Quantitative Criminology, 25*(3), 3–24.

Born, M., Chevalier, V., & Humblet, I. (1997). Resilience, desistance and delinquent careers of adolescent offenders. *Journal of Adolescence, 20*, 679–694.

Bottoms, A., Shapland, J., Costello, A., Holmes, D., & Muir, G. (2004). Towards desistance: Theoretical underpinnings for an empirical study. *Howard Journal of Criminal Justice, 43*(4), 368–389.

Bouffard, L. A. (2005). The military as a bridging environment in criminal careers: Differential outcomes of the military experience. *Armed Forces & Society, 31*(2), 273–295.

Boutwell, B. B., Beaver, K. M., & Barnes, J. C. (2012). More alike than different: Assortative mating and antisocial propensity in adulthood. *Criminal Justice and Behavior, 39*(9), 1240–1254.

Burnett, R. (2004). To reoffend or not to reoffend? The ambivalence of convicted property offenders. In S. Maruna & R. Immarigeon (Eds.), *After crime and punishment: Pathways to offender reintegration* (pp. 152–180). Cullompton: Willan.

Bushway, S. D., Piquero, A. R., Broidy, L. M., Cauffman, E., & Mazerolle, P. (2001). An empirical framework for studying desistance as a process. *Criminology, 39*(2), 491–515.

Bushway, S. D., Thornberry, T. P., & Krohn, M. D. (2003). Desistance as a developmental process: A comparison of static and dynamic approaches. *Journal of Quantitative Criminology, 19*(2), 129–153.

Clemmer, D. (1958). *The prison community*. New York: Holt, Rinehart and Winston.

Craig, J., & Foster, H. (2013). Desistance in the transition to adulthood: The roles of marriage, military, and gender. *Deviant Behavior, 34*, 208–233.

Doherty, E. E., & Ensminger, M. E. (2013). Marriage and offending among a cohort of disadvantaged African Americans. *Journal of Research in Crime and Delinquency, 50*(1), 104–131.

Farrall, S. (2002). *Rethinking what works with offenders: Probation, social context and desistance from crime*. Cullompton: Willan.

Farrall, S., & Bowling, B. (1999). Structuration, human development and desistance from crime. *British Journal of Criminology, 39*(2), 253–268.

Farrington, D. P., Loeber, R., Yin, Y., & Anderson, S. J. (2002). Are within-individual causes of delinquency the same as between-individual causes? *Criminal Behavior and Mental Health, 12*(1), 53–68.

Farrington, D. P., & West, D. J. (1995). Effects of marriage, separation, and children on offending by adult males. In Z. S. Blau & J. Hagan (Eds.), *Current perspectives on aging and the life cycle* (Vol. 4, pp. 249–281). Greenwich, CT: JAI Press.

Fazel, S., & Danesh, J. (2002). Serious mental disorder in 23 000 prisoners: A systematic review of 62 surveys. *Lancet, 359*, 545–550.

Gadd, D., & Farrall, S. (2004). Criminal careers, desistance and subjectivity: Interpreting men's narratives of change. *Theoretical Criminology, 8*(2), 123–156.

Gendreau, P., Goggin, C., & Cullen, F. T. (1999). *The effects of prison sentences on recidivism*. Ottawa: Corrections Research Branch, Solicitor General of Canada.

Giordano, P. L., Cernkovich, S. A., & Rudolph, J. L. (2002). Gender, crime, and desistance: Toward a theory of cognitive transformation. *American Journal of Sociology, 107*(4), 990–1064.

Glueck, S., & Glueck, E. (1940). *Juvenile delinquents grown up*. New York: Commonwealth Fund.

Gottfredson, M. R., & Hirschi, T. (1990). *A general theory of crime*. Stanford, CA: Stanford University Press.

Gove, W. (1985). The effect of age and gender on deviant behavior: A biopsychological perspective. In A. S. Rossi (Ed.), *Gender and the life course* (pp. 115–144). New York: Aldine.

Halsey, M. J. (2006). Negotiating conditional release: Juvenile narratives of repeat incarceration. *Punishment & Society, 8*, 147–181.

Horney, J., Osgood, D. W., & Marshall, I. H. (1995). Criminal careers in the short-term: Intra-individual variability in crime and its relation to local life circumstances. *American Sociological Review, 60,* 655–673.

Irwin, J. (1970). *The felon.* Englewood Cliffs, NJ: Prentice Hall.

Kazemian, L. (2007). Desistance from crime: Theoretical, empirical, methodological, and policy considerations. *Journal of Contemporary Criminal Justice, 23*(1), 5–27.

Kazemian, L. & Travis, J. (2015). Forgotten prisoners: Imperative for inclusion of long termers and lifers in research and policy. *Criminology & Public Policy, 14*(2), 355–395.

King, S. (2013). Early desistance narratives: A qualitative analysis of probationers' transitions towards desistance. *Punishment & Society, 15*(2), 147–165.

Kirk, D. (2012). Residential change as a turning point in the life course of crime: Desistance or temporary cessation? *Criminology, 50*(2), 329–358.

Kreager, D. A., Matsueda, R. L., & Erosheva, E. A. (2010). Motherhood and criminal desistance in disadvantaged neighborhoods. *Criminology, 48*(1), 221–258.

Krueger, R. F., Moffitt, T. E., Caspi, A., Bleske, A., & Silva, P. A. (1998). Assortative mating for antisocial behavior: Developmental and methodological implications. *Behavior Genetics, 28*(3), 173–186.

Kruttschnitt, C., Uggen, C., & Shelton, K. (2000). Predictors of desistance among sex offenders: The interaction of formal and informal social controls. *Justice Quarterly, 17*(1), 61–87.

Lanctôt, N. (2015). Development of antisocial behavior in adolescent girls. In J. Morizot & L. Kazemian (Eds.), *The development of criminal and antisocial behavior: Theory, research and practical applications* (pp. 399–411). New York: Springer.

Laub, J. H., Nagin, D. S., & Sampson, R. J. (1998). Trajectories of change in criminal offending: Good marriages and the desistance process. *American Sociological Review, 63,* 225–238.

Laub, J. H., & Sampson, R. J. (2001). Understanding desistance from crime. In M. Tonry (Ed.), *Crime and justice.* Chicago: University of Chicago Press.

Laub, J. H., & Sampson, R. J. (2003). *Shared beginnings, divergent lives: Delinquent boys to age 70.* Cambridge, MA: Harvard University Press.

LeBel, T. P., Burnett, R., Maruna, S., & Bushway, S. (2008). The 'chicken and egg' of subjective and social factors in desistance from crime. *European Journal of Criminology, 5*(2), 130–158.

Le Blanc, M. (1993). Late adolescence deceleration of criminal activity and development of self- and social control. *Studies on Crime and Crime Prevention, 2,* 51–68.

Le Blanc, M., & Fréchette, M. (1989). *Male criminal activity from childhood through youth: Multilevel and developmental perspectives.* New York: Springer.

Le Blanc, M., & Loeber, R. (1998). Developmental criminology updated. In M. Tonry (Ed.), *Crime and justice* (Vol. 23, pp. 115–198). Chicago: University of Chicago Press.

Loeber, R., & Le Blanc, M. (1990). Toward a developmental criminology. In M. Tonry & N. Morris (Eds.), *Crime and justice.* Chicago: University of Chicago Press.

Loeber, R., Pardini, D. A., Stouthamer-Loeber, M., & Raine, A. (2007). Do cognitive, physiological and psycho-social risk and promotive factors predict desistance from delinquency in males? *Development and Psychopathology, 19,* 867–887.

Longshore, D., Chang, E., Hsieh, S.-C., & Messina, N. (2004). Self-control and social bonds: A combined control perspective on deviance. *Crime and Delinquency, 50*(4), 542–564.

Lösel, F., & Bender, D. (2003). Protective factors and resilience. In D. P. Farrington & J. W. Coid (Eds.), *Early prevention of adult antisocial behaviour.* Cambridge: Cambridge University Press.

Luthar, S. S. (1991). Vulnerability and resilience: A study of high-risk adolescents. *Child Development, 62,* 600–616.

Lyngstad, T. H., & Skardhamar, T. (2013). Changes in criminal offending around the time of marriage. *Journal of Research in Crime and Delinquency, 50*(4), 608–615.

Maruna, S. (2001). *Making good: How ex-convicts reform and rebuild their lives.* Washington, DC: American Psychological Association.

Maruna, S., & Farrall, S. (2004). Desistance from crime: A theoretical reformulation. *Kölner Zeitschrift für Soziologie und Sozialpsychologie, 43,* 171–194.

Maruna, S., & Toch, H. (2005). The impact of imprisonment on the desistance process. In J. Travis & C. Visher (Eds.), *Prisoner reentry and crime in America* (pp. 139–178). New York: Cambridge University Press.

McGloin, J. M., Sullivan, C. J., Piquero, A. R., Blokland, A., & Nieuwbeerta, P. (2011). Marriage and offending specialization: Expanding the impact of turning points and the process of desistance. *European Journal of Criminology, 8*(5), 361–376.

Monsbakken, C. W., Lyngstad, T. H., & Skardhamar, T. (2013). Crime and the transition to parenthood. *British Journal of Criminology, 53*(1), 129–148.

Morizot, J. (2015). The contribution of temperament and personality traits to criminal and antisocial behavior development and desistance. In J. Morizot & L. Kazemian (Eds.), *The development of criminal and antisocial behavior: Theory, research and practical applications* (pp. 137–165). New York: Springer.

Morizot, J., & Le Blanc, M. (2007). Behavioral, self, and social control predictors of desistance from crime: A test of launch and contemporaneous effect models. *Journal of Contemporary Criminal Justice, 23*(1), 50–71.

Mumola, C. J., & Karberg, J. C. (2006). *Drug use and dependence, state and federal prisoners, 2004 (NCJ 213530).* Washington, DC: U.S. Department of Justice, Bureau of Justice Statistics.

Nagin, D. S., Cullen, F., & Jonson, C. L. (2009). Imprisonment and reoffending. In M. Tonry (Ed.), *Crime and justice* (Vol. 38). Chicago: University of Chicago Press.

Paternoster, R., & Bushway, S. (2009). Desistance and the feared self: Toward an identity theory of criminal desistance. *Journal of Criminal Law and Criminology, 99*(4), 1103–1156.

Raskin White, H., Tice, P. C., Loeber, R., & Stouthamer-Loeber, M. (2002). Illegal acts committed under the influence of alcohol and drugs. *Journal of Research in Crime and Delinquency, 39*(2), 131–152.

Rutter, M. (1996). Transitions and turning points in developmental psychopathology: As applied to the age span between childhood and mid-adulthood. *Journal of Behavioral Development, 19*, 603–626.

Sampson, R. J., & Laub, J. H. (1993). *Crime in the making: Pathways and turning points through life.* Cambridge, MA: Harvard University Press.

Sampson, R. J., & Laub, J. H. (2003). Life-course desisters: Trajectories of crime among delinquent boys followed to age 70. *Criminology, 41*(3), 555–592.

Savolainen, J. (2009). Work, family and criminal desistance: Adult social bonds in a Nordic welfare state. *British Journal of Criminology, 49*, 285–304.

Shover, N. (1983). The later stages of ordinary property offender careers. *Social Problems, 31*(2), 208–218.

Shover, N. (1996). *Great pretenders: Pursuits and careers of persistent thieves.* Boulder, CO: Westview.

Shover, N., & Thompson, C. Y. (1992). Age, differential expectations, and crime desistance. *Criminology, 30*(1), 89–104.

Skardhamar, T., & Savolainen, J. (2014). Changes in criminal offending around the time of job entry: A study of employment and desistance. *Criminology, 52*(2), 263–291.

Sommers, I., Baskin, D. R., & Fagan, J. (1994). Getting out of the life: Crime desistance by female street offenders. *Deviant Behavior, 15,* 125–149.

Theobald, D., & Farrington, D. P. (2009). Effects of getting married on offending: Results from a prospective longitudinal survey of males. *European Journal of Criminology, 6*(6), 496–516.

Travis, J., Solomon, A. L., & Waul, M. (2001). *From prison to home: The dimensions and consequences of prisoner reentry.* Washington, DC: Urban Institute Justice Policy Center.

Tripodi, S. J., Kim, J. S., & Bender, K. (2010). Is employment associated with reduced recidivism? The complex relationship between employment and crime. *International Journal of Offender Therapy and Comparative Criminology, 54*(5), 706–720.

Uggen, C. (2000). Work as a turning point in the life course of criminals: A duration model of age, employment, and recidivism. *American Sociological Review, 67,* 529–546.

van Schellen, M., Poortman, A.-R., & Nieuwbeerta, P. (2012). Partners in crime? Criminal offending, marriage formation, and partner selection. *Journal of Research in Crime and Delinquency, 49*(4), 545–571.

Villettaz, P., Killias, M., & Zoder, I. (2006). *The effects of custodial vs. noncustodial sentences on re-offending: A systematic review of the state of knowledge.* Philadelphia, PA: Campbell Collaboration Crime and Justice Group.

Warr, M. (1993). Age, peers, and delinquency. *Criminology, 31,* 17–40.

Warr, M. (1998). Life-course transitions and desistance from crime. *Criminology, 36*(2), 183–216.

Weatherburn, D. (2010). *The effect of prison on adult re-offending.* New South Wales, UK: Bureau of Crime, Statistics, and Research, Number 143.

Wolff, N., Shi, J., & Siegel, J. (2009). Understanding physical victimization inside prisons: Factors that predict risk. *Justice Quarterly, 26*(3), 445–475.

Wright, J. P., & Cullen, F. T. (2004). Employment, peers, and life-course transitions. *Justice Quarterly, 21*(1), 183–205.

What Is the Impact of Probation in Advising Sentencing and Promoting Community Sanctions and Measures?

George Mair

Introduction

Probation services provide a wide variety of tasks. In England and Wales, for example, besides the supervision of offenders who are sentenced to community penalties by the courts, they are involved in crime prevention initiatives, carry out bail information work, work with the police in Multi-Agency Public Protection Arrangements, have a presence in prisons, work with the victims of crime and with those released from custody, and prepare reports for the courts which are intended to provide sentencers with information which will assist in the sentencing process. While the bulk of probation research has focused on its work with offenders, it can be argued that the provision of reports for the courts is—in some ways—the most significant task. Pre-sentence reports (PSRs) are the primary point of contact with sentencers, who are the main customers for probation work; they are a key probation task in many countries, although they

G. Mair (✉)
Department of Social Science, Liverpool Hope University, Liverpool, UK

© The Editor(s) (if applicable) and The Author(s) 2016
F. McNeill et al. (eds.), *Probation*,
DOI 10.1057/978-1-137-51982-5_4

may have different names. This chapter will explore the role of probation staff in advising on sentencing and in promoting community sanctions and measures. It will, for the most part, focus on England and Wales but the implications of the discussion will be relevant to any countries where PSRs (or their equivalents) are prepared by the probation service.

The Historical Context

In the last quarter of the nineteenth century, when police court missionaries were responsible for delivering what became probation, their work comprised two tasks: (a) making a plea for mercy or leniency in the court for the offender, in order that, if successful (b) the missionary might then help redeem sinners from the evils that caused their crimes. The role of the missionary in court was to promote the work of the Church of England Temperance Society in dealing with offenders; essentially, to 'sell' their services to sentencers. They would only do this for those whom they judged to be capable of redemption, so they were advising sentencers of what they considered to be the most effective method of dealing with these individuals and thereby promoting their services. At this time, the missionaries had no statutory duties so their presence in (a few) courts was vital in ensuring that some offenders had the opportunity of being placed under their supervision. If a missionary was not present to make the case for supervising an offender, then this was not a sentencing option that would be considered. Clearly, in a situation such as this the impact of the missionary was considerable, as without his presence 'probation' simply did not exist in practice.

The Probation of Offenders Act 1907 did not include carrying out preliminary inquiries for the courts as one of the duties of a probation officer, but it is obvious from the Report of the Departmental Committee that was set up to examine the workings of the Act that such inquiries continued to be part of a probation officer's work:

> (22) That the probation officer should, if possible, be present in court at the hearing of the case, but that *the result of any preliminary inquiries which he has made* should not be communicated to the court till it has reached a conclusion on the truth of the charge. (Home Office 1910, p. 14; emphasis added)

Reports to the court continued to be used informally and became a routine part of the process of helping courts in deciding on a probation order. There can be little doubt that they played an important role in helping to establish the probation order as a sentencing option. By the mid-1930s they were acknowledged as invaluable by the National Association of Probation Officers: '[I]nvestigation is the foundation, without which no superstructure can safely be erected' (Le Mesurier 1935, p. 100). Their usefulness for magistrates was also noted:

> Speaking generally, however, it is often a help to a magistrate to be able to turn to the probation officer for an opinion regarding a person before the Court, or to refer to him a request that a general investigation should be made into the defendant's circumstances, or that parents or employers should be consulted. (Le Mesurier 1935, p. 81)

The Streatfeild Committee, which reported in 1961, proposed a major change to reports by emphasising their importance not just as providing background and contextual information for sentencers but by offering an informed opinion (*not* a recommendation) about the effect of a sentence (not just probation) on an offender:

> [A] probation report may properly supply the court with information about the offender and his background which is relevant to his culpability or to stopping him from offending again and with an opinion as to the likely effect on the offender of probation or some other form of sentence. (Home Office 1961, p. 123)

By the mid-1960s, what McWilliams calls 'the diagnostic ideal' (1986) had reached its height and alongside this the social enquiry report was an indispensable part of the probation process. If social casework lay at the heart of probation, then effective diagnosis by way of a report to the court was the key to successful treatment. It is easy to look back at what now seems to be a naïve and simplistic process: probation officers were officers of the court who were in a subordinate role to help sentencers make their decisions; they would almost certainly be known to magistrates and trusted; and sentencers would have confidence in 'their' probation officers and trust their judgement—although this would not necessarily mean that they would follow their opinions about sentence or suitability for a probation order. Davies (1974) notes the three fold rise in social enquiry reports between 1956 (77,175) and 1971 (224,977) and the clear confidence that existed in the usefulness of such reports:

> [P]rofessional commentators from within probation, magistrates, the press and many criminologists have all tended to argue that the availability of more comprehensive social information in cases will lead to more appropriate sentencing, not just by keeping the prison population down ... but by increasing the 'effectiveness' of the court's decision. (Davies 1974, p. 20)

Davies, however, takes a sceptical approach to such claims by asserting that there was no hard evidence to demonstrate that the growth in the use of reports had led to improvements in the effectiveness of sentencing; nor had it led to any related decrease in the use of custody. The individualisation of sentencing encouraged the use—and potential influence—of reports as they were often used to provide mitigating circumstances. But some of the complications around the issue of how far reports *should* have an impact upon sentencing decisions are put nicely by Davies:

> [It]is easy to see that it is a short step from social inquiry as a means of isolating mitigating factors once the primary [sentencing] decision has been made to social inquiry as a means of helping to determine the primary decision; indeed, in practice, it would be very difficult to distinguish between the two processes. (Davies 1974, p. 23)

The implication here is that sentencers should be making the primary decision (whether the tariff should apply) and that any reports should then be considered in deciding upon which individualised measure should be used, and it is at this stage when probation officers' reports may have an impact.

The situation is further complicated by what Davies sees as three 'extreme' possibilities with regard to the influence of reports. First, where the probation officer knows what the sentencer is going to do and recommends this. Here there is no real influence whatsoever although there is complete agreement between sentencer and probation officer; a situation of symbolic communication according to Davies. Second, where the officer's recommendation is accepted by the magistrate and this might be termed total influence. Finally, a situation of conflict where the officer and the magistrate have different views and the magistrate ignores the former's recommendation. On top of this, there may be very different formal relationships and ways of working between local probation staff and their courts; and there may be personal relationships between sentencers and probation officers so that some officers are trusted more than others by some magistrates (Davies 1974).

Information and Influence

Putting Davies to one side, in an ideal world one can envisage a relatively clear-cut situation where PSRs have an input to sentencing decisions (although exactly what that input comprises may not be a simple matter). The probation officer is acknowledged by the court to be a professional expert (this was easier to postulate when all probation officers were trained social workers; the situation is rather different today) and her authority to comment on certain matters is recognised. Sentencing is a difficult, complex and nuanced process and magistrates and judges have relatively little 'untainted' knowledge of the offender, his/her circumstances, or the context in which the crime has been committed. They are fully aware that defence solicitors will make as positive a case as they can for their clients, exaggerating mitigating circumstances and minimising aggravating factors; on the other hand, prosecutors will do the opposite. It may be possible to imagine the conflicting claims cancelling each other out, but how that would help a judge is unclear.

Into this arena of heavily biased and competing claims, probation staff are understood to be able to provide a more objective appraisal of the offender. They are seen to have a clear role in the provision of information pertinent to the case; information which is more independent than that put forward by defence or prosecution. A PSR will provide 'reliable, comprehensive information relevant to what the court is seeking to do' (Home Office 1961, p. 84); this is very different from what defence or prosecuting solicitors will offer and it is only probation officers (or other specialists) who can take this neutral position.

The information contained in a report is intended to aid the court in deciding what is the most appropriate method of dealing with the offender; what is the most effective sentence. The Streatfeild Committee (Home Office 1961, p. 94) suggested three areas that reports might cover:

(a) Information about the social and domestic background of the offender which is relevant to the court's assessment of his culpability;
(b) Information about the offender and his surroundings which is relevant to the court's consideration of how his criminal career might be checked; and
(c) An opinion as to the likely effect on the offender's criminal career of probation or some other specified form of sentence.

The Report (Home Office 1961, p. 95) then goes on to set out what should usually be included in reports under (a) and (b):

[E]ssential details of the offender's home surroundings, and family background; his attitude to his family and their response to him; his school and work record and spare-time activities; his attitude to his employment; his attitude to the present offence; his attitude and response to previous forms of treatment following any previous convictions; detailed histories about relevant physical and mental conditions; an assessment of personality and character.

Two points might be made about this list: first, it is likely to take some time to collect—weeks rather than days; and second, it is likely to lead to a document of quite a few pages—more than two or three at least. At least one visit to the offender's home would be needed; interviews with family members as well as with the offender; perhaps also with an employer or teacher. A previous probation officer might have to be contacted, and a doctor.

Such information is, no doubt helpful to sentencers and relevant to their sentencing decision but only if punishment is not driven solely by retributive principles. If we simply wish to punish offenders for what they have done with no interest in looking to the future, then there would be little need for any kind of reports. PSRs are well fitted for a system based on rehabilitation; they can be adapted to suit a diversion from custody agenda; but they have little place if sentencing is driven by retribution.

With regard to the question of the input of a PSR to the sentencing decision there are a number of possibilities. It might be ignored or dismissed by a sentencer (for a number of reasons); it might be helpful in a general, rather nebulous, way by supplying some background to the offender which then plays a greater or lesser part in the sentencing decision along with a number of other factors; it might help to encourage the sentencer to choose a sentence that was one of several already being considered; it might push the sentencer to consider and decide upon a sentence that was not under consideration; it might reinforce or help to justify a decision that was already taken although not yet stated in court; or it might lead to a sentence that was being considered being ruled out as possibility.

It is often assumed that concordance between the sentencing proposal made in a report and the sentencing decision is an indication of the influence of PSRs, but this is not necessarily the case. Almost 50 years ago, Carter and Wilkins (1967) noted that there could be four possible explanations: first, sentencers may simply agree with the PSR proposal because they trust the expertise of probation officers; second, the sentence may have been so obvious that both sentencer and probation officer came to the same conclusion independently; third, probation officers might be second-guessing the sentence that they believe is going to be passed; and fourth, sentencers and probation officers might be in complete agreement about the factors that drive the sentencing decision. This, of course, assumes that a clear proposal is actually made in the PSR, but this is not always the case. A number of options may be set out with no clear 'best bet'. If discussing the possibility of a community order or a suspended sentence order, a number of different requirements might be explored in different combinations and this might result in a lack of clarity. And some probation officers have always been opposed to the idea of actively proposing custody (although this is probably not quite so common now as it was in the 1970s and 1980s—the alternatives to custody era) so their PSRs would not make a clear proposal as it was accepted that custody was inevitable.

Ultimately, the key idea behind the PSR is that it will help 'fit' the offender to the most appropriate sentence and that this will lead to reduced reoffending. By 'fitting' offender and sentence, the offender is more likely to react positively to the sentence (to perceive the sentence as legitimate), and thereby more likely to complete the sentence successfully without reoffending. There is no evidence to demonstrate this and it would be difficult to research in practice: offender/sentence 'fit' is a vague concept (and may change over the period of supervision); how could a positive reaction to a sentence be assessed accurately; and while sentence completion is easy to measure, 'successful' completion is another matter and accurately measuring reoffending is almost impossible.

As noted earlier, reports could be several pages in length and because (especially prior to the introduction of National Standards in 1992) probation officers had considerable discretion in how they organised their work and dealt with their various tasks, they could be inconsistent in the details they covered and the interpretation of facts. The quality of reports could, therefore, vary and this would have an impact on justice. Poor reports could lead to an offender being dealt with unfairly. Inconsistent practice was an issue that had dogged the probation service, particularly since the introduction of community service in 1973 and in 1992 the first full set of National Standards were introduced for probation, including a chapter on PSRs (Home Office 1992a). By 1990, the number of PSRs had dropped from the 225,000 noted by Davies in 1971 to almost 200,000; reports were prepared for 10 per cent of all sentences passed by the courts, although this figure varied depending upon sentence with reports prepared on almost 50 per cent of those sentenced to imprisonment, 75 per cent of those sentenced to community service and 82 per cent of those given probation orders. The average number of PSRs completed per maingrade officer in 1990 was 55.8, more than one each week of the year (although it is notable that there was considerable variation between areas with a high of 75.6 in North Yorkshire and a low of 33.1 in Powys). So reports were taking up a significant amount of an officer's time, which in turn meant money and the cost of reports had been increasing (along with probation service expenditure generally; see the 1990 Probation Statistics, Home Office 1992b). The 1992 National Standards noted that PSRs 'should be no more than 2 pages long' (Home Office 1992a, p. 18) yet set out a wide range of information that potentially could be included in a report. By 1999, the number of PSRs prepared had increased to 237,456 (Home Office 2001).

Sentencers' Views

What are the views of sentencers about PSRs? After all, they are the main consumers of court reports; it is their decisions that reports are intended to influence. A series of studies carried out during 1993–2003 offers some information about how sentencers perceived reports. The first of these was part of a major survey commissioned by the Home Office to assess the views of representatives of criminal justice agencies about the 1991 Criminal Justice Act (Mair and May 1995). As Gelsthorpe and Raynor (1995) have argued, PSRs had a key role to play in the Act as their use was expanded. More than nine out of ten magistrates (N = 489) said they found PSRs very or quite useful (93 per cent); interestingly, this figure was slightly higher than the percentage of probation officers (90 per cent) who said they thought sentencers found reports very/quite useful. Respondents were also asked how they would rate the quality of PSRs (without any definition of what quality meant) and 91 per cent of magistrates rated them as very or quite good (probation officers were less likely to rate them as very good: 34 per cent vs. 28 per cent).

The introduction of Key Performance Indicators for the probation service led to the development of what was planned to be a regular survey of courts to measure satisfaction with probation. The pilot study contained a series of questions about PSRs, and the sample included 498 lay magistrates, 28 stipendiary magistrates (now District Judges) and 27 judges. The results were—on the whole—very positive. 93 per cent of lay magistrates, the same percentage of stipendiaries, and 88 per cent of judges considered PSRs to be consistently or usually useful (again, without any definition of what this meant). A majority of lay magistrates (67 per cent) and of stipendiaries (59 per cent) considered proposals for sentence in the two most recent PSRs they had seen to be appropriate (judges were not asked this question). However, a minority (33 per cent of lay magistrates and 19 per cent of stipendiaries) claimed that they might have passed a different sentence in the absence of a report. One possible problem emerged with the finding that two-thirds of both lay and stipendiary magistrates stated that the agreed standard adjournment time for a PSR was 28 days. And it was notable that most of the comments offered about PSRs noted that they were too often unrealistic, naïve, never proposed custody and thereby undermined the credibility of the service (May 1995). The first national survey following the pilot found similar results for the usefulness of reports and the appropriateness of proposals for sentence (May 1997).

Finally, a survey of magistrates' perceptions of the probation service was carried out for the National Probation Directorate in June 2003, with 5716 magistrates responding to a self-completion questionnaire. Three-quarters of respondents rated the overall usefulness of PSRs in reaching sentencing decisions as good; two-thirds viewed the overall quality of reports as good; and 55 per cent rated the appropriateness of proposals for sentence as good. Again, there were signs of some dissatisfaction with the lack of proposals for custody in reports (National Probation Service 2003).

These findings are all—on the surface at least—highly positive about PSRs; but there are a number of points that limit how far we can rely on them. First, they can offer nothing about how PSRs influence the sentencing decision. Reports are seen as useful, presumably on the basis that they provide interesting and relevant information about the offenders, although it should be emphasised that usefulness is not defined. Just how such information is then used to help a sentencing decision to be made remains opaque. Second, what is a good-quality report? Is it one which supplies relevant information; does it make a 'realistic' sentencing proposal; is it well written and easy to understand; is it concise and to-the-point? And finally, there are certainly issues about the length of time that reports take to be prepared, and with 'unrealistic' proposals. The Labour government that took office in 1997 made cutting delays in court cases a key issue and PSRs that took a month to prepare obviously played a part in delays to the delivery of justice. It is notable that by the 2003 survey, a 15 day turnaround policy for PSRs had been introduced.

Unrealistic or naïve proposals seem to be the biggest problem that sentencers tend to have with PSRs. At first sight, this may seem to be an understandable issue: the sentencer(s) has a sentence in mind and the PSR proposes something that has not been? considered as an option. But why should this present a problem? If sentencers are the key authority figures in a court and the sentencing decision is theirs, why should they complain about what they perceive as an unrealistic sentencing proposal in a PSR? Does this represent some kind of threat to their authority? If a proposal is well argued, then why would a sentencer dismiss it as unrealistic simply because he/she did not agree with it? How are the arguments of the defence for a lesser sentence, or those of the prosecution for a more punitive sentence seen by sentencers? Is it that they are recognised to be making biased arguments because of their role and thus any suggestions they make about sentencing are justifiable, while the probation officer is seen as a more objective, independent figure and if the PSR presents an unrealistic proposal this is more of a threat to the process of justice? Sentencers expectations of probation officers are different from those held about defence or prosecution solicitors; probation officers are expected to have a greater understanding of the sentencing process, of the factors that are taken into account in making decisions about sentence.

Tata et al. found that in Scotland 'most sheriffs disliked the idea of report writers proposing a sentence or indeed appearing to be directive or explicitly judgemental' (2008, p. 847). The sheriffs in their study expected report writers to be aware of sentencing patterns in their court and to take full account of this when preparing their report. Thus, an unrealistic report meant that the writer did not understand the court. But, probation officers did not routinely have access to data on sentencing patterns in individual courts and given the degree of sentencing disparity amongst sheriffs it would be difficult to tailor a report to a specific sheriff. Report writers were, therefore, almost doomed to fail to live up to sheriffs' expectations about being realistic.

Why might sentencers be so reluctant to accept an 'unrealistic' sentencing proposal as an honest attempt to make a case for a sentence that might—given the factors discussed in the report—be justifiable? Why is this not simply acknowledged as another factor to be taken into account when sentencing; why are such proposals seen as damaging to the credibility of the probation service? Again, Tata and his colleagues shed some light on this. They argue that sheriffs perceive themselves as the dominant figures in court so their judgements with regard to sentencing were paramount, but probation officers too had a hand in this.

[B]oth social work report writers *and* judges can lay legitimate claim to deciding the allocation of punishment (sentencing). Nearly all sheriffs were sensitive and resistant to any suggestion that their decision process had been or should be 'influenced by' (as opposed to merely 'informed by') reports. (Tata et al. 2008, p. 850, emphasis in original)

It might be argued that probation officers do not have quite the same legitimate claim to deciding upon sentence as sentencers, but the fact that they do have an input is clearly enough to make sentencers feel slightly threatened by this other source of professional expertise. As a result, reports are not perhaps used to the degree that they might be:

The discourse of monopoly judicial ownership of sentencing suggests, on the one hand, that the individual case can only be properly assessed by those schooled in the legal understanding of formal abstract principles. On the other hand, these principles are also said to be largely contingent on the particular circumstances of each individual case. (Tata et al. 2008, p. 851)

Beyens and Scheirs (2010, p. 323) found a similar situation in Belgium where, they argue that:

Judges emphasize the professional ownership of 'their' decision, sticking to their own penal culture which is permeated by values of independence, wide discretion, individualization and neoclassical principles of individual responsibility, retribution and deterrence. The social information, provided in a framework of supervision and guidance and prioritizing community-based sanctions, does not fit into this classical judicial framework, where social reports are still 'strange', endogenous elements.

The Objectives of Reports

PSRs are not neutral tools. Canton (2011) has pointed to two views of reports: as strategic documents or as providing reliable information. Reports are expected to provide the latter, but they cannot escape being the former. In the past, PSRs may have been seen as objective tools but as we have become more sophisticated in the way we interpret texts following the post-structuralist approach to literature, reports now must be understood in a more complex light. Cases are constructed in court with the prosecution and defence contributing to the final picture that leads to a verdict and a sentencing decision. Probation officers too contribute to the construction of a case in PSRs. Their accounts will not shape the verdict, but they can play a part in building up a picture of the offender and the crime that can shape the sentence. If PSRs were not trusted to contain reliable information their usefulness would be seriously compromised and the credibility of the probation service would be undermined. But how reliable can such information be if PSRs are also strategic documents which are aiming for a result which may or may not be fully articulated in the report?

Probation staff are by no means disinterested players in the provision of PSRs. Probation has always had to struggle to be heard in the competing voices that make up the court process. By offering advice to sentencers via PSRs they are basically selling their product to the court; during the life of the service staff may have been pushing different products, but it was all to the same end—to encourage the courts to use the probation service for dealing with offenders. In the early days of the police court missionary, they literally made a plea for mercy for those who could be reclaimed; as professionalism began to take root, they offered a diagnosis that suggested certain treatment would cure the problem; later, they argued for the use of probation-based sentences as alternatives to custody; and today they are carrying out risk assessment in an effort to safeguard public protection. It is with the third and fourth of these that problems emerge.

In arguing for diversion from custody it was almost inevitable that sentencers would begin to question proposals made in PSRs as unrealistic. If a custodial sentence is under consideration, for a probation officer to make a case for a lesser sentence could all too easily be taken by sentencers as an unwelcome plea for a 'soft option'. It is to be presumed that sentencers do not make the decision to impose a custodial sentence lightly; imprisonment is the most severe sentence available to the courts (in the absence of capital punishment) and for a probation officer to argue for what is, by definition, a lighter, less punitive sentence is to invite accusations of naivety and a lack of realism. To compound matters, the probation officer is—as discussed above—a figure of less authority in court, so there is a serious issue here. From the mid-1970s to the end of the

1980s, the probation service was expected to act (in a quasi-official way) to divert offenders from custody thereby setting itself up for accusations of being unrealistic in the sentencing proposals contained in PSRs.

With regard to probation's current focus on risk assessment, the problem is that a defined template is used to assess risk (OASys) and the PSR will not be nearly so personalised and narrative-driven as in the past. This could easily translate into reports being seen by sentencers as mechanistic exercises which do not provide the rich contextual information about the offender that was once the province of the PSR. Taylor and her colleagues found that this could have a negative effect in the case of an Intensive Alternative to Custody (IAC) programme in Greater Manchester:

> Findings suggest that sentencers are at times frustrated by the use of templates and copied formats within PSRs … Although the template has been found to be effective in the early stages of the IAC, its continued use is likely to undermine the credibility of the IAC as an intense order focusing on an individual's specific needs. (Taylor et al. 2013, p. 54)

One particular issue is that PSRs are a way for the probation service to assert its usefulness to the courts. By offering advice (which may or may not be appreciated by sentencers) about sentencing, the service is staking a claim for its presence in court. In the past, reports only commented upon the suitability of the offender for probation supervision but today they are expected to comment upon the appropriateness of any sentence. As a market-place for probation to advertise and sell its products, the PSR is no longer restricted to a handful of probation-based products. There is a real tension here. On the one hand, why should probation not encourage the use of its own products; as Haines and Morgan claim (2007, p. 187), PSRs are '[a]s far as the courts are concerned … the most regular, visible service that probation officers provide'. Report writers would be expected to use this platform to offer realistic, credible advice to the courts so that they would be more likely to make use of probation-based sentences. Lack of confidence by the courts could only lead to less use of probation and this could in turn lead to a spiral of decreasing confidence and fewer probation sentences which might result in serious questions emerging about the viability of the probation service. Thus, a PSR as a vehicle for marketing probation should not be unexpected and perhaps courts were once content with this position and understood its context.

But a PSR is now expected to assess risk and to propose any sentence that might be appropriate. There is plenty of anecdotal evidence to suggest that sentencers believe that PSRs only rarely propose a custodial sentence, and it would not be surprising if they are also unlikely to propose a fine or discharge. If they do so, it is possible that they do not encourage their use to the same degree that they would push for a probation-based sentence. Thus, instead of a marketing opportunity for a probation-based sentence, the PSR is now expected to be a vehicle for assessing the viability of any sentence with the same enthusiasm as that given to probation. Probation staff, therefore, become neutral advisers about the appropriateness of any sentence. They are still in the position of 'experts' but no longer experts in probation; more as professionals in assessing risk and making the appropriate conclusion about a sentencing proposal. Given the research by Tata and his colleagues discussed earlier, it is possible that sentencers do not feel that probation inhabit this new role effectively; they may be experts in risk assessment (although that holds its own threats) but they may not be acknowledged as objective when it comes to making proposals for sentence.

A range of sentences are available to the courts and while judges might be expected to be fully aware of that range, lay magistrates—who are unpaid and untrained in the law, and who only sit for a few half-days in a month—are not likely to bear in mind the full spectrum of what is available to them. The court clerk may be able to fill this role, but clerks are trained in the law and may be unaware of the detail of what certain sentences comprise. Defence and prosecuting solicitors will only be pushing for a specific outcome and may not know exactly what that entails in practice. Probation staff—even taking account of the potential biases discussed above—are knowledgeable about the full range of sentences available and are the only actors in court who have this knowledge. From this point of view, probation as disinterested, expert commentator on the potential sentence that would be most appropriate, noting the relevant pros and cons, would be a significant role. It would also represent a considerable change to the current situation where the PSR is a short, highly condensed report focusing on risk (see Gelsthorpe et al. 2010); and a probation officer is not as likely to be present in court as she would have been in the past in order to discuss options.

Perhaps the key role for reports in the diversion from custody era was to try to persuade the court to refrain from passing a custodial sentence and to use a community penalty instead. If this worked, the prison population would be reduced and more humane and effective sentences would be used. There is no research evidence to suggest that PSRs acted in this way, but that is not to conclude that they therefore failed. The history of alternatives to custody suggests that only around 50 per cent of cases in any initiative would be diversions, but how far the members of this group were diverted as a result of the influence of a PSR is unknown. Conversely, there is the question of how far PSRs might be responsible for the other 50 per cent who were subject to net widening.

Even if reports are not directly influential in avoiding custody, they may have a key role to play indirectly. There can be little argument about the increasingly punitive nature of sentencing in England and Wales in the past 30 years. This is related to a more punitive society generally and it is a development that shows no sign of stabilising far less diminishing. Without probation staff who could make the case for less punitive sentences and for a more considered approach to dealing with offenders? This is a rather different role for PSRs than advocating diversion from custody. Probation has been a civilising influence on the justice system since its creation; this influence may not be as strong as it once was, and its future does not look promising, but it is still all we have. The presence of a criminal justice agency that can consistently advocate a humane approach to sentencing may play a small but not insignificant role in helping to curb the punitive culture that surrounds us.

All of this is rather speculative as research into PSRs and their influence has not been especially popular. And it is difficult to think about how influence works when so many factors are present. We still know little about how sentencers actually read and understand PSRs. The research by Tata and his colleagues (2008, 2010) in Scotland, by Beyens and Scheirs (2010) in Belgium and by Wandall (2010) in Denmark have begun to open up this issue, but much remains to be done. What is clear from their work is that sentencers read reports in different ways to that which the writers intended, that writers encode their messages for various reasons, and that different sentencers read reports differently. Complicating matters further, there are issues of personal trust in probation generally and in individual staff in particular, the question of authority in court, the possibility that a local probation service might wish to encourage the use of a specific sentence, and so on. Thus the question of how probation staff can influence sentencing and promote community sanctions and measures is far more complex than might first appear. It is not (and probably never has been) a simple matter of the writer composing a report that is read and interpreted by sentencers in the way intended and a sentencing decision made accordingly. And if promoting community sanctions is carried out openly by way of a PSR, then the sentencer is quite likely to see the report as biased or unrealistic with obvious negative consequences for credibility in probation.

Current Problems

In England and Wales matters are made even more problematic by two developments that, although chronologically and politically unrelated, are actually closely linked to each other. The first is the huge growth in Fast Delivery Reports, and the second the marketization of the probation service.

Fast Delivery Reports are a response to complaints that courts had to make lengthy and unnecessary adjournments in order to wait while PSRs were being prepared. This was at a time when reports might take several weeks to complete as interviews might be carried out with several individuals besides the offender, and a document of half a dozen pages then written up. Justice is not well served by delays, especially what were perceived as unnecessary delays caused by probation staff who were spending too much time in preparing reports (and it is worth noting that in the early 1990s, the standard agreed adjournment time for a PSR in the magistrates' courts was 21–28 days; May 1995). Delays are also costly. As noted earlier, the first set of National Standards envisaged reports being no longer than two pages, and this was a first effort at trying to cut the time taken to prepare them. By 2000, statistics were being collected on the number of Fast Delivery Reports written and that year 14,971 of the

219,952 reports written were FDRs (7 per cent); by 2006 the number of FDRs had increased to 55,275 (26 per cent of the total). By definition, FDRs cannot go into the detail that traditional PSRs did, so the narrative detail and the context of the offender and offence were minimised, and perhaps also the care taken with the argument for a sentencing proposal.

More disturbing has been the rise of oral FDRs. These are given in court on the same day following a short adjournment and may well be carried out by a Probation Service Officer (who is not a fully qualified probation officer). Oral FDRs were introduced in 2005 and that year a total of 3072 were prepared, the vast majority (97 per cent) of which were—perhaps not surprisingly—for the magistrates' courts. As more serious cases are dealt with at the Crown Court, FDRs—whether oral or written—are unlikely to have much of a role to play there (and in fact only 2314 written FDRS were prepared at Crown Court in 2005—5 per cent of the total). In 2011 the total number of FDRs had risen to 126,423, more than doubling since 2006 and making up more than three out of every ten (62 per cent) of all court reports. By 2014 the total number of court reports had dropped to 141,932 from 204,631 in 2011, but 108,179 of these were FDRs—more than three-quarters (76 per cent) of all reports. Indeed, oral reports made up more than one-third more (36 per cent) of all FDRs, and more than a quarter (28 per cent) of all reports. In the magistrates' courts 82 per cent of reports were FDRs (36 per cent were oral reports). While oral FDRs have made little impact on the Crown Court (there were only 1375 in 2014), written FDRs now make up 56 per cent of Crown Court reports.

The standard written PSR is an endangered species and while FDRs may have speeded up the court process and their brevity may not have any adverse effect on the quality of the report as Gelsthorpe and Raynor (1995) have demonstrated, there may be negative consequences. Short PSRs tend to rely only on information from the offender, thereby exclud-ing information from family members, employers and the like. Nor are they as likely as normal PSRs to discuss a supervision package that might involve added requirements. In the first half of the 1990s when Gelsthorpe and Raynor carried out their research, this latter issue may not have posed too much of a problem as only a single requirement could be added to a probation order. Today when several conditions can be added, this may be a significant issue; in 2014 just over half of all community orders made by the courts (51 per cent) had more than one requirement, while 62 per cent of suspended sentence orders had more than one.

To put together an appropriate package of more than a single requirement for a community or suspended sentence order requires time to contact others (who may or may not be in the probation service) to discuss the options and negotiate an agreed order. It may require more than a single meeting with the offender. This takes time and FDRs—especially oral FDRs—do not permit much time. As already noted, the new orders are made up of added conditions and many of these are organised and operated by voluntary, third or private sector agencies. Therefore, on the one hand the structure of the new orders with a wide range of possible conditions would seem to require a reasonable time to prepare a PSR which can effectively have some influence on sentencing decisions; while on the other, the growth of FDRs rules out the possibility of this happening as successfully as it might. While the overall number of reports has fallen consistently since 2009 (from 216,854 to 141,932 in 2014), the number of FDRs has increased by 4833 (from 103,346 in 2009 to 108,179 in 2014; and it is the growth of oral FDRs which accounts for the overall increase (34,390 in 2009 and 39,159 in 2014).

If the use of FDRs continues to grow, then the opportunity for probation to have an impact in advising on sentencing may continue but PSRs will become essentially instrumental tools rather than expressive accounts. The majority of PSRs continue to propose a community sentence (71 per cent) while almost one in five (19 per cent) propose a suspended sentence order. Only 8 per cent propose custody and 2 per cent a fine. Gelsthorpe et al. (2010, p. 485) have found—albeit on a very small sample—distinct signs in PSRs from the last 50 years of 'a shift towards the language of risk, and at the same time a drift towards more negative presentation'. They conclude that this could lead to sentencers passing more punitive sentences purely as a precautionary measure. They go on:

> Similarly, an approach to assessment that is mechanical, stereotyped, distancing and carried out by an officer who looks at the computer more often than at the offender seems unlikely to promote positive engagement or to elicit positive information. In this way the focus on risk, if imposed on

practitioners through a managerialist process rather than adopted by them as a natural enhancement to their work, might even be unintentionally contributing towards increasingly severe sentencing in England and Wales. (Gelsthorpe et al. 2010, p. 486)

The second development—not unrelated to the development and growth of FDRs—is the marketization of probation. Probation has worked with voluntary agencies throughout its history, but mandatory requirements about partnership began to take effect from the early 1990s. Since then, there has been increasing pressure for probation to work alongside a range of community, voluntary, public and private sector agencies. The two key recommendations of the Carter Report (2003) pulled probation in different directions: the creation of a National Offender Management Service comprising prisons and probation; and the introduction of 'contestability' whereby private and voluntary sector agencies could compete to offer probation work more efficiently, effectively and economically. The first of these was centralising probation while the second would lead to fragmentation. The Labour government accepted Carter's recommendations, but they came to full fruition under the Coalition government of 2010–15. In February 2015 as the culmination of the Coalition's Transforming Rehabilitation programme, the National Probation Service (NPS) lost responsibility for working with medium- and low-risk offenders and this was transferred to eight Community Rehabilitation Companies (CRCs) which covered 21 areas (Sodexo runs six areas and Purple Futures five). These are private sector companies and they will be paid by results. The NPS retains responsibility for high risk offenders (also on a payment by results basis) and—crucially for the purposes of this chapter—for the preparation of PSRs. This arrangement raises some significant issues.

While PSRs remain to advise on sentencing and to promote community penalties, the NPS will be only be promoting itself in respect of the high-risk offenders it will deal with. By definition high-risk offenders will be less likely to be successful and therefore less likely to trigger maximum payment, so when the NPS proposes a community sentence for such offenders it may be condemning itself to less successful outcomes. For other offenders the PSR—prepared by NPS staff—will be promoting the work of a private company which is in the business of profit-making. If the preparation of courts reports was to be handed over to the CRCs themselves there would be clear conflict of interest problems; it would be financially advantageous for a CRC to encourage the use of sentences for which it was responsible as this would be likely to lead to greater profit; and—in the struggle for profit—it might also lead to over-use of these sentences for offenders who could have been given a lesser sentence, as these individuals would be more likely to complete the sentence without reconviction thereby triggering payment (and net widening).

In the past, whether or not the PSR writer ended up as the supervisor of the offender, both were likely to work for the same probation board. Now, where PSRs are prepared on low and medium-risk offenders, the report writer and the offender manager will be working for completely separate organisations which may not be conducive to high quality reports. And to complicate matters, many of the requirements that go to make up a community order or suspended sentence order may be provided by other voluntary or private sector companies. PSRs are no longer proposing community penalties that are coherent entities, nor do they promote a coherent organisation.

Conclusions

If we accept the proposition that community penalties are a good thing—that they are necessary in any sentencing system for a number of reasons—then we must also accept that their use needs to be encouraged. Probation and its numerous related sentences constantly need to be brought to the attention of sentencers. Probation also offers the only chance for a relatively objective assessment of the risks posed by an offender and of the appropriateness of a sentence. The complications around what goes into court reports, how they are read and interpreted by sentencers, what their impact is, does not in any way detract from the importance of the role of probation in preparing reports for the courts. Indeed, it could be argued that this is the key job of probation, as by advising on sentencing and thereby—directly or indirectly—promoting the use of community sanctions it demonstrates regularly what probation can offer.

Currently in England and Wales, this aspect of probation work is under threat. Not only are the bulk of community orders and suspended sentence orders supervised by private companies who do not prepare reports, but there are clear signs that oral FDRs are becoming more prevalent and that written reports are increasingly becoming tick-box exercises. This move from expressive to instrumental reports may be speeding up justice but it is also leading to offenders being dehumanised. Probation has always helped to humanize offenders and it is vital that this remains at the core of its work. To do this work effectively requires credibility with magistrates and judges, and the preparation of reports for the courts is crucial to the establishment and maintenance of probation credibility.

Note

Unless otherwise noted, all figures used in this chapter are taken from Ministry of Justice statistics available at https://www.gov.uk/government/organisations/ministry-of-justice/about/statistics.

References

Beyens, K., & Scheirs, V. (2010). Encounters of a different kind. *Punishment and Society, 12*(3), 309–328.

Canton, R. (2011). *Probation: Working with offenders.* London: Routledge.

Carter, P. (2003). *Managing offenders, reducing crime.* London: Strategy Unit.

Carter, R. M., & Wilkins, L. T. (1967). Some factors in sentencing policy. *Journal of Criminal Law, Criminology and Police Science, 58*(4), 503–514.

Davies, M. (1974). Social inquiry for the courts: An examination of the current position in England and Wales. *British Journal of Criminology, 14*, 1–3.

Gelsthorpe, L., & Raynor, P. (1995). Quality and effectiveness in probation officers' reports to sentencers. *British Journal of Criminology, 35*(2), 188–200.

Gelsthorpe, L., Raynor, P., & Robinson, G. (2010). Pre-sentence reports in England and Wales: Changing discourses of need, risk and quality. In F. McNeill, P. Raynor, & C. Trotter (Eds.), *Offender supervision: New directions in theory, research and practice.* Abingdon: Willan.

Haines, K., & Morgan, R. (2007). Services before trial and sentence: Achievement, decline and potential. In L. Gelsthorpe & R. Morgan (Eds.), *Handbook of probation*. Cullompton: Willan.

Home Office. (1910). *Report of the Departmental Committee on the Probation of Offenders Act, 1907*. London: HMSO.

Home Office. (1961). *Report of the Interdepartmental Committee on the Business of the Criminal Courts*. London: HMSO.

Home Office. (1992a). *National standards for the supervision of offenders in the community*. London: Home Office.

Home Office. (1992b). *Probation statistics England and Wales 1990*. London: Home Office.

Home Office. (2001). *Probation statistics England and Wales 1999*. London: Home Office.

Le Mesurier, L. (Ed.). (1935). *A handbook of probation and social work of the courts*. London: National Association of Probation Officers.

Mair, G., & May, C. (1995). *Practitioners' views of the criminal justice act: A survey of criminal justice agencies* (Research and Planning Unit Paper 91). London: Home Office.

May, C. (1995). *Measuring the satisfaction of courts with the probation service* (Home Office Research Study 144). London: Home Office.

May, C. (1997). *Magistrates' views of the probation service* (RSD Research Findings 48). London: Home Office.

McWilliams, W. (1986). The English probation system and the diagnostic ideal. *Howard Journal, 25*(4), 24–60.

National Probation Service. (2003). *Magistrates' perceptions of the probation service*. London: National Probation Service.

Tata, C. (2010). A sense of justice: The role of pre-sentence reports in the production (and disruption) of guilt and guilty pleas. *Punishment and Society, 12*(3), 23–61.

Tata, C., Burns, N., Halliday, S., Hutton, N., & McNeill, F. (2008). Assisting and advising the sentencing decision process. *British Journal of Criminology, 48*, 835–855.

Taylor, E., Clarke, R., & McArt, D. (2013). The intensive alternative to custody: "Selling" sentences and satisfying judicial concerns. *Probation Journal, 61*(1), 4–9.

Wandall, R. H. (2010). Resisting risk assessment? Pre-sentence reports and individualized sentencing in Denmark. *Punishment and Society, 12*(3), 32–47.

Has Probation Any Impact in Terms of Reparation to Victims and Communities? Complicating a Simple Question

Leo van Garsse

Introduction

In the list of topics and questions addressed with regard to probation, that of reparation cannot be neglected. Indeed, for a couple of decades now, the prominence of reparation and restoration in the list of goals of public intervention in the aftermath of crime has been obvious. The original justification of criminal justice (CJ) as a symbolic re-confirmation of moral order as a 'public good' has tended to give way to a modernist, pragmatic approach. Herein the notion of 'justice' is conceived as a 'function' in a society focussed upon maximising a climate of security, likely to promote an atmosphere of well-being among the citizens. In this line, and more in particular after the Second World War, doing justice was seen more and more as a matter of public service, to be managed as efficiently as possible. In a context of worldwide disintegration of traditional communities, the theme of victims' need for reparation showed up as a matter of political credibility. The individual 'victim' became recognised as the

L. van Garsse (✉)
Department of Social Pedagogy, Ghent University, Ghent, Belgium

© The Editor(s) (if applicable) and The Author(s) 2016
F. McNeill et al. (eds.), *Probation*,
DOI 10.1057/978-1-137-51982-5_5

holder of specific group of civil rights, to be responded to by the state. Moreover, the victim's social surroundings were also to be recognised as an important stakeholder in the provision of criminal justice. Doing justice thereby was seen as, at least partly, an aspect of community-building with prominence given to the role and to the interest of the individual or the communal–collective victim, with both in a position of claiming the right to be properly compensated for the damage done through the offence.

The notion of 'restorative justice', with origins in the USA and Canada from the 1970s onwards (Aertsen 2004) found its way with remarkable ease through the UK and Western Europe to actually become a criminal policy approach that is well known everywhere and respected in circles both of the UN and of the Council of Europe. The general idea is the elaboration of a criminal justice system focussed upon the actual reparation of harm rather than upon retribution of the 'wrong' done (Zehr 1990; Aertsen 2004; Walgrave 2008). The symbolic and the abstract have to give way to the 'real' and the tangible. This is one reason at least to question punishment, as well as its alternatives, on their reparative potential.

In answering the question in the title of this chapter, my point of view is that of a pedagogue and a formal practitioner in victim–offender mediation in all sorts of criminal cases. More in general, I have been—and still am—a promoter of restorative justice in Flanders for more than twenty years. In April 2015 I completed a PhD research project analysing the development in Flanders of '*forensisch welzijnswerk*', a scheme launched in the late 1970s that focuses on every attempt in the sphere of criminal justice to promote the well-being of any person in any way involved, and thus including probation, victim assistance and restorative justice alike.

By practical experience as well as by research I feel strongly stimulated not to isolate CJ development and policies from their historical backgrounds or from their socio-political contexts. To really know what we're talking about, we cannot ignore the dynamics within which all sorts of decisions have been taken and all sorts of practices have appeared worth being considered and put into practice. This makes it difficult to answer the question on the reparative impact of probation, either *in abstracto* or in general.

For starters, it's no secret of course that probation and the notion of 'restorative justice' are both rooted in the no-nonsense, straightforward approach of self-organisation characteristic of the USA in particular and of the Anglo-Saxon countries in general. Reading the work of de Tocqueville (1963 [1835]) today in the surroundings of a country like Belgium, it is still hard not to share, at least partly, some of the fascination of this French aristocrat with the differences between a continental European and an 'overseas' conceptualisation of both democracy and (criminal) justice alike. Moreover, it's still far from difficult to recognise the same 'cultural' differences in discussions that take place today outside official discourses. For similar reasons, seen from a Belgian perspective and taking a position some mental distance from what appears to be actually considered universal 'common sense', the question in the title of this chapter seems very Anglo-Saxon to me. Therefore, in trying to answer it, I'd like to contextualise and somehow develop the terms in which it was formulated.

The Notion of Reparation: Is There Something to Repair?

Literally, 'reparation' as a goal of CJ intervention suggests the reconstruction of the situation, just as it was before the incident. And using instead the word 'restoration' might even sound worse.

We might wonder whether these goals are at all realistic. To the extent that crime is perceived as an intersubjective 'event', some philosophers would see it as something that cannot be undone, and that should, apart from every temptation to dramatise, be appreciated as such in the pursuit of justice (Arendt 2007[1964]; Derrida 2003; Biesta 2009). We might wonder also whether something such as the 'reparation' of the harm done to the victims can be taken care of by a system or some organised procedure, and then result in a predictable an measurable outcome, without stealing it from the parties involved (see Christie 1977). Unless, that is, reparation could actually be reduced to the transfer of an amount of money, objectively determined.

Experience shows that in Belgium at least, victims of crime often perceive the promise of being 'repaired' as an insult. Confronted with this systemic 'goal', they don't feel they have been taken seriously in regard to what they have experienced. This probably is one of the reasons why victims of serious offences would—at first—rather reject 'reparative/ restorative measures' as buying off their right to further complain and as a theft of their place and identity in 'their' case. (Van Garsse 2004)

Advocates of victim's rights might perceive such resistance as an indicator of secondary victimisation caused by the very offer of mediation (The European Forum for Victims' Services 2004). Their plea is for a rigid and careful selection of the few cases that are considered 'safe' enough for a victim–offender dialogue, or 'light' enough to allow for a responsible application of a 'merely reparative' measure. A recent directive of the European Parliament on victims' rights aims to achieve the same protective atmosphere and stresses the right of the victim to refuse to accept formally any attempts at reparation, beyond a unilateral financial transaction (Dir. 2012/29/EU: art. 12).

Other scholars have for quite some been warning of the inherent limitlessness of the victim's right to reparation. They consider it at the least a false, misleading promise within the context of modern judicial proceedings, bound as they are by such principles as equality, legality and proportionality (Fijnaut 1983; Gutwirth and De Hert 2002, 2011). Moreover, the victim might feel forced into the role of 'good victim', so as to be likely to fit expectations of being not only damaged but 'hurt' as well, and therefore 'in need of reparation' (Van Dijk 2008). Many mediators would confirm that having to play the role of the victim, especially in cases of minor crime, can indeed be perceived as a burden: During my work in developing victim-offender mediation in Flanders, I got both surprised and fascinated by the heterogeneity within the group of those identifying with the position of 'victim'. The notion of 'victimship' appeared to be constituted by a broad range of different emotions and expectations. Still, looking closer, in every case one need was present as a prominent constitutive factor: the need the gain some ownership of their situation, to be of influence, not to be overruled (again), even if – paradoxically- the desire was not to be involved any longer (Van Garsse 2004, 2012, 2013).

Inspired by research on 'procedural justice' (Rawls 1999) and by quite some experience in victim–offender mediation, I too would advocate careful use of the word 'reparation' and even 'restoration' as aims for any public intervention in the sphere of formal criminal justice, let alone as criteria for a successful policy. Popular pleas for the victim's right to be repaired tend to formalise, organise and 'instrumentalise' what ought to be respected as aspects of the atmosphere of the personal, the subjective and the unpredictable (Van Garsse 2004; see also Derrida 2003 and Biesta 2006). Maybe we should change our vocabulary from 'reparation' and 'restoration' to 'respectful co-involvement in doing justice' (Derrida 2001, 2003). Thereby the focus shifts from the authoritarian projection of a desired outcome to an open, process-oriented invitation of civic capacity (Van Garsse 2012).

The Notions of 'Community' and/as 'Victim': Between Reality and Projection

In the same line of thinking, even the notions of 'victim' and 'community' are lacking clarity.

On the one hand, the concept of 'victim' can be defined broadly as 'every person/organisation economically, emotionally … affected by the event'. This broad definition includes the families of the offenders, the neighbours, the friends, the school and so on. In a republican view like that of Braithwaite and Pettit (1990), they'd all have a say in the outcome of the case. But what about legal security of the parties involved (Gutwirth and De Hert 2002)?

On the other hand, the notion of 'victim' can also be restricted to those recognised by the judicial authorities as formal stakeholders in a specific file. But then, of course, many concerns among citizens would be neglected and doomed to appear as 'irrelevant' for the case. In this approach, criminal justice risks becoming alienated from social reality and is likely to cause forms of secondary victimisation to citizens not being taken into account by public authorities. This brings us back to the original motifs for the promotion of restorative justice (Christie 1977; Zehr 1990; Aertsen 2004).

Putting the victim and the community on the same line is a common feature of restorative justice literature (Braithwaite and Pettit 1990; Walgrave 2008). But I still have some uneasy feelings about it. The very Anglo-Saxon concept of 'community' does sound rather vague in a very much urbanised, bureaucratised and multi-cultural Belgian society. The term tends to provoke feelings of nostalgia, with reference to the fading of the *'community'* under the still growing pressure of a neo-liberal *'socialisation'* (Bauman 2000; Sachße 2003). Compared with the era of small rural villages where generations of people used to have a strong common sense of values in life, today an average street in a Belgian city is generally characterised by people who are not really connected, unless by merely 'functional' bounds. Of course, even then, communities exist, be it in a fluid and hardly visible form (see Bauman 2000). Placed within the context of the struggling modern welfare states, the notion of community even carries the slight suspicion that it is composed of people looking out for their mutual benefits, even at cost of those of 'the others' (Huyse 1993). Obviously there's a growing difference between 'the community' and 'the collective'. This makes the idea of 'the damaged community in need of reparation', as one of the crucial stake-holders in 'doing justice', far from self-evident. Seen from everyday Belgian reality, the attribution of the victims' role to the community in the context of criminal policy risks being reduced to a cheap justification of—every—public intervention (see Duff 2001). This becomes obvious on looking into the discussions about what kind of activities can be considered *'community* service', and which ones are likely to please only *some* citizens. As we could observe in practice, even the cleaning of a public garden, an offering of community-service applied often, carries an enormous lot of presumptions that only marginally compare to by people's actual experience.

As a result, the popularity of the community service order among the judiciary, be it as an alternative measure or as an autonomous sanction, sharply contrasts with the increasing scarcity of places of work that are ready to collaborate. More and more, one has to *organise* community service, and pay people to provide and supervise it, for the sake of alternative punishment. What are we really talking of here?

One might even say that the call for community involvement in the aftermath of a crime tends to be an attempt at constituting some sort of community rather than actually repairing it. This social-constructivist thinking in terms of the 'function' of handling delinquency comes close to the ideas of Durkheim and others at the beginning of the twentieth century. But can our democracies still afford such a radical modern rationale, after the questioning of this instrumental reasoning by post-war postmodernity? Shouldn't we redefine such a friendly notion as that of community?

Inspired by Hannah Arendt and Jacques Derrida, scholars like Biesta (2006, 2009) and Mouffe (1989, 2005) state that democracy is in great danger of becoming itself a victim of the overall supremacy of a 'needs' approach, linking democracy to the tangible effects of equal distribution of 'satisfaction' and 'contentment' among its citizens. They wonder whether a democratic society can ever be a community unless it is one where the members have nothing in common and where communicating their mutual differences is a source of everlasting political debate and development (Biesta 2006). Like Derrida (2003), they don't see democracy as a way of organising the state, but as a perspective, always 'to come' ('*la démocatie à venir*') throng confrontation with the unexpected of the appearance of the respectable different. In their view, 'doing justice' in a democratic way is not restricted to compensating the community and/or the victim for the harm done. It is about restoring them in their ability to engage in as process of change, proper to democratic dynamics. (Derrida 2003; Biesta 2009).

This line of thought questions the actual widespread popularity of restorative justice as a potential emanation of a merely conservative aspiration to reconstruct existing power balances, amicably but quite effectively disciplining those who oppose. In these terms, there's no clear, everlasting model for democratic justice, neither is there one for the practices and procedures to promote it. And the first question to be asked to a community presenting itself as being in a position to claim the right to be restored cannot be but: 'Who exactly are you?' Put like this, the reparation of the community is not so much a matter of compensating the harm done by the person accountable as a question of the attribution of identity and thus of social pedagogy through political debate (Biesta 1998, 2004, 2006, 2009; Valverde 1999a, b; Derrida 2003).

Anyhow, it seems to be obvious that, from its appearance, the introduction in criminal policy of the concern for 'repairing the victims' has seen an emergence of ideological views, to a certain extent contradicting each other while all having to do with the balance of political power between the presupposed community of citizens and the state (Van Beek 1970; Gutwirth 1993). But to what extend is this type of approach still compatible with a concept and a practice like the one of probation?

The Notion of Probation: Repairing the Community or Testing the Offender?

Looking then not at the effect of probation as such but rather at its socio-political context, what probation offers comes more fully into focus. Therefore, besides the terms 'reparation', 'victim' and 'community', even the notion of probation does not escape contextual contamination. This is obvious when we look at the variety of practices and policies that the umbrella of probation actually covers, some of them focussing on assisting vulnerable ex-offenders to maintain themselves in society, others designed to control and prevent the phenomenon of delinquency as such (Fitzgibbon 2008; McNeill et al. 2009). Probation sometimes aims to prevent a public sanctioning, but sometimes serves, for the deserving offender, as a conditional alternative to a more repressive sanction.

One common feature among all these differences is an obvious link between probation and community. In international circles probation is actually referred to as 'community-oriented sanctions and measures'. But, even this apparent constitutive community involvement does not make clear the nature of the 'community orientation', leaving open whether the offender is addressed *inside, because of, together with,* or rather *by* the community.

Originating in the United States in the middle of the 19th century, the notion of probation goes back to the private sphere, with citizens wanting to contribute to handling deviant behaviour in a context of civil solidarity and mutual care (Verheyden 1975; Peeters 1982). Very much in line with the pragmatic but very nuanced American way of building democracy (Tocqueville 1963), this contribution from the 'community', in its critical dialogue with the state, was able to manifest itself as a valuable and considerable alternative to state intervention. Step by step it provoked wider interest and was given official legal status. In 1925 it was introduced into US federal law, as a way of doing justice to be made concrete in a variety of applications according to local circumstances in one or another American state (Verheyden 1975). In a way, practising probation was a matter rather of pedagogy than of justice, as it provided the offender and the community a perspective on citizenship, seen as a cornerstone of the democratic project (Cornil 1937). From this point of view, the understanding of breaking a rule as damage to the community at the same time appears as a reality and—probably even more—a socio-political construct to be implemented to those applying for full citizenship. As observed by the Belgian scholar Cornil (1937), even in the USA the volunteering by citizens in probation practice was generally symbolic rather than substantial.

Already, during the first half of the 20th century, criminal policy-makers were quite aware of the US practices on probation (Peeters 1982; Verheyden 1975). But at the same time, they were fascinated by the political translation of modernity in Germany, transforming the nation into a 'society' that was directed by firm, goal-oriented central state power and identifying ethical as functional and useful for collective progress (Natorp 1964[1905]; Nohl 1965[1925]; Sachβe 2003; Fijnaut 2014). Moreover, the young and very much industrialised Belgian state was also rooted in a strong liberal rationale.

This interesting intermediate position of Belgium made that country's criminal policy the birthplace of the doctrine of 'social defence'. The idea was to protect the citizens against the disease of social disintegration and delinquency, which was leading to a growing disbelief in the project of a democratic national state (Prins 1910; Cornil 1934; Tulkens 1988). Seeking to reconcile individual responsibility and social determinism, social defence called for a nationwide mobilisation of forces to stimulate people to take a constructive part in society rather than give in to contamination by deviance. Under the medical motto that prevention is always better than cure, some socialist ministers of justice engaged in making the state take the lead in setting up actions to prevent victimisation rather than to make reparation for it.

Education was seen as the strategy *par excellence* to improve the situation of those who on one hand were vulnerable to be affected by delinquency (an offender being in fact also a victim) but also on the other still able to integrate into society. It was seen also as a tool to carefully select those now beyond rescue, against whom society had to be protected, and to preventively isolate them—for always, if necessary. Tulkens (1993) observes that, under the doctrine of social defence, criminal policy tended to distract itself from the criminal, the crime and the problem of punishment and justice. It did so in order to instead address, assist, educate and/or discipline society as a whole.

In the context of social defence the idea of probation was above all promoted as an interesting testing period, starting from the presumed capacity of every human being to take up responsibility. The same promoters of probation problematised the use of repressive detention for being counterproductive from an educational point of view and in fact pointless from a strictly political one (Cornil 1937). After the Second World War however, very much in line with the ideas of the upcoming movement of 'New Social Defence' (Ancel 1965), they were dreaming of making probation the motor of a radical and urgently needed repositioning of 'doing justice' in post-war democratic societies. The idea was to focus upon the collaboration with the offender, approaching him as a citizen, a holder of democratic rights, and upon his meaningful contribution to the debate on how to handle the event. Notwithstanding their well-elaborated pleas, and given the quite promising results of some successive experiments, it took probation in Belgium till 1964 and many years of intensive and long-lasting political debate to be given a legal status. In comparison with its enormous, almost revolutionary potential as a politically motivated concept (Verheyden 1975), the Belgian law on probation carried the smell of resistance and suspicion to what voices of civil society ('the community') could bring to the fore. Peeters (1982) suggests that the preparation of the law lacked sufficient communication with the judiciary. I would suppose, rather, that the post-war Belgian government very much wanted to strengthen the state in order to defend at least the formal unity of a Belgian nation, which was then internally more deeply divided than ever before (see also Huyse 1993).

Be that as may, instead of exploiting the opportunity of a radical repositioning of 'justice', the eventual law on probation rigidly restricted its scope to certain kinds of cases. Notwithstanding the fact that the legislator claimed the embracing of the 'subsidiarity' of traditional punishment was a basic *principle* (Cornil 1964), the application was restricted to a *practice* of special individual treatment for only some cases that were considered too inconsequential to justify 'real' punishment. Instead of restricting repression in the name of subsidiarity, probation ran an enormous risk of becoming a measure of net-widening, with all the ambivalence of a favour (Cornil 1965).

These initial fears were strongly confirmed by practice. After a first period of practice, many voices of probation officers, academics and penal policy-makers expressed disappointment and frustration (Verheyden 1975; Dupont 1980; Peters 1980, 1982; Peeters 1982; Neirinckx 1981).

In 1985 in the Louvain district some local probation officers set up an isolated experimental practice of community service, conceived as a symbolic gesture made by the offender of respect to 'society', and as a means to prevent recidivism (Baeyens 1993). The idea was partly copied from the 1965 law on juvenile protection(!), which provided the possibility of a measure of 'philanthropic' work. It was a promising idea which, however—for decades—was applied merely in some isolated cases and was hardly ever put into practice. Even in the context of probation it would take until the 1990s to have this optional supplement in the package of probation conditions to be more or less generalised. Not by coincidence, this sudden promotion of community service took place as part of a crisis policy in the aftermath of a series of brutal murders. The goal was to demonstrate government's ability to counteract any impression of impunity. In 2002 the measure, given the legal status of an autonomous sanction, suddenly started years of an enormous expansion, suggesting that, notwithstanding the educative and restorative potential, apparently almost all the slightly repressive aspect of a newborn 'sanction' was what public opinion and the judiciary were most interested in (Beyens and Aertsen 2006).

Putting the Victim Back on Stage

The entry into Belgium of victim–offender mediation was the result partly of a discovery, partly of an 'invention'. Belgian practice used to be far from in the lead in spending time and attention on the victim's rights to reparation. In fact, Belgium happens to have been one of only the most recent countries to follow the international recommendations on installing an official fund for victims' financial compensation and to finance, from 1984 on, some specialised professional care for victim assistance (Peters and Goethals 1993).

Compared with Anglo-Saxon countries, until the late 1990s there was no real bottom-up victim's movement in Belgium. Instead, the late development of victim assistance—in the midst of successive episodes of Belgian state reform, consisting of a gradual changing of the Belgian state into a federation of autonomous 'communities' (*Gemeenschappen*)—was, from the very start, an area of intensive ideological as well as strategic debate on where to position and how to justify this new public intervention, which had not arisen in response to any substantial request from citizens.

At the academic level, promoters of social work opposed the view of a group of critical criminologists. The former saw the development of specialised victim assistance as a logical step for the communities in their formal responsibility to promote, by means of a proper policy, a common atmosphere of well-being. Until then, victim assistance was seen as an empathic response to individual needs of a category of citizens, holders of specific civil rights, to be taken care of and—if necessary—to be protected against further harm. These same academics embraced the perspective of a victimology, that was separate from considerations of crime and justice as such. The criminologists opposing them however wanted to address the victim above all as a crucial stakeholder in a process in doing justice, not in a detached, abstract and authoritarian way, but as communication between meaningful approaches to a criminal event. Their view was above all oriented towards changing criminal policy, rather than towards responding to individual needs (Peters and Goethals 1993).

From the beginning of the 1990s onwards, the choice of the Flemish authorities, in search of how to establish a tangible sphere of autonomy for the provision of well-being, was obviously the first of those just outlined. At the same time the federal minister of justice saw his department confronted with a growing crisis in credibility owing to a perceived increase in crime and public insecurity. If (criminal) justice were to be transformed from an archaic symbol into a performant public service, then the (potential) victim obviously was easier to reach and to please than the members of the growing group of offenders. Moreover, in the context of a constant increase in prison overcrowding, the growing policy-investment in responding to victim's needs went also to serve as an implicit justification of the implementation of a more rigid and repressive penal policy (Peters 1993). In this reasoning, we got pretty close to returning to the original doctrine of social defence.

In the very same period, as a member of a small NGO working on alternative and educative measures for juvenile delinquents, I participated in an intuitive development leading towards a restorative approach (Van Garsse 2001, 2013). Starting from the idea of community service, a hitherto unused provision of the 1964 law, we discovered that in fact, given the concrete social context, this measure was rather more likely to stigmatise, shame and discipline than to actually make good any harm. Therefore we decided to include the voice of the victim, presuming that average citizens would be likely to encourage and appreciate 'their' young offender's engagement in some voluntary work for a common good. Interestingly enough, this nice presumption regarding the victim's attitude obviously did not fit the reality. However, victims in general appeared to be very open to the position and the interests of the youngster. Moreover, they were almost always very grateful to be approached and asked for their opinion on 'their' case. But, far from reacting vindictively or selfishly, they above all wanted to be taken seriously by the system. They were afraid that their being abused might be an easy justification for some kind of manipulative concept, like that of the victimised citizen being part of a real 'community', waiting for reparation.

This sobering finding obliged us to radically redraw the whole project, transforming it from an alternative education of a misbehaving youngster into a process of critical communication. Such a process couldn't do without the involvement of the parents and couldn't escape the very pragmatic issues surrounding bills and insurance claims. Finally, it couldn't be blind to the logic of the right of the stakeholder to have at least a say in what should be done next, how and by whom, as well as a proper insight into the reasons behind the eventual decision. Without any in-depth notice on restorative justice or mediation, we were in a way constructing them intuitively, a fascinating and very rich experience, which was observed by some local prosecutors with an increasing scepticism almost leading to a radical refusal to further refer any cases. Indeed, in quite some cases the process resulted in an outcome that nobody could have foreseen, and one not automatically in line with a rigid confirmation of the social rule or with the logic of public intervention as such. To give one example: most victims appeared to be not pleased at all by the apparent signs of net-widening. They then felt somewhat abused by being made cheap excuses for public disciplining. In the same sense they criticised any reference to the suffering of 'the community' as nothing more than an ideological construct. Instead they appeared to claim a certain ownership of their case, without however aspiring to take over the responsibility to judge or punish.

From 1993 onwards I took part in a research project of Louvain Catholic University, on the introduction of pre-trial victim–offender mediation for adults in more serious cases of every sort of crime. Whereas the minister of justice announced the introduction of 'penal mediation' as a modality of 'praetorian probation'—a conditioned dismissal of rather lighter cases at the level of prosecution—the Louvain research explicitly aimed to explore the mutual influence of the communication between on the parties involved, and the judicial process of coming to a decision. Dealing now with cases like severe violence, armed robbery, rape and even murder, it was quite surprising to observe to what an extent our mediation practice confirmed our previous findings with juveniles, and opened up not so much a route to a practice of systematic 'reparation' for the victim as a perspective on a repositioned way of doing justice (Aertsen and Peters 1997; Van Garsse 2012).

In June 2005 the Belgian parliament approved a bill generalising the possibility for victim and offender to request the intervention in their case of a neutral mediator, at any stage of criminal proceedings. It also formally allows judges and prosecutors to take a mediation outcome into account and obliges them to at least mention this in setting out the motivation for their decision on a case. Mediation is now available for cases ranging from a simple insult up to murder. It can be initiated immediately after the event at the level of the police, during court proceedings or even during an offender's imprisonment.

Of course, mediation can also be combined with probation. Moreover, the mediation agreement could inspire the judge or the prosecutor to consider certain probation conditions as an argument to for postponing or suspending imprisonment. In practice, however, such self-evident links between probation and mediation in whatever direction are rather weak.

Like probation, mediation appears to be vulnerable to recuperation by the still dominant repressive culture among the judiciary and policy-makers, as they seek clear-cut solutions rather than running the risk of exposure to critical questioning coming from victim, offender or/and their respective contexts (Van Garsse 2012, 2014). More generally, it cannot be denied that the promise of the legislation on mediation is far from being fulfilled as far as it is reflected in facts and figures, except perhaps in less serious cases (mostly involving young offenders), where the victim–offender dialogue is likely to come down to organising financial compensation to avoid further public intervention. In such circumstances, from the perspective of the judiciary, there is a kind of a logic in not mixing probation and mediation, but rather to use both in parallel way, as instruments to combat the impression of impunity in minor cases, and to preventively ease as a matter of management and routine the victims' voice.

Towards a Conclusion

This chapter has addressed a theme that lies in line with current developments in criminal policy worldwide. In search of arguments to rebuild or reinforce credibility, criminal justice as a whole is likely to present itself as providing a service to citizens, in terms of contributing to a climate of security and respect. The post-war rediscovery of the victim stressed their status as a holder of civil rights, in particular the right to have their interests and personal integrity to be safeguarded. In the logic of the market, paying for justice through taxation requires the satisfaction of the expectations of the 'clients'. The same logic tends to provoke among the different practices in doing justice a kind of competition in doing 'better'. In public debates and even among academics, victim satisfaction is quite an issue in the current evaluation of punishment, let alone of its alternatives. And for those who would still question or resist this development, the popular literature on 'restorative justice' seems to be offering plenty of reasons to cede victory.

However, I haven't got very far in answering the question this chapter started from. Whether probation has any impact on the reparation of victims and communities cannot be answered as such. As a practice of criminal justice, probation is always part of a culture in which its potential weight and its conceptual meaning are in a great part determined by its surroundings. This goes above all for restorative justice and the range of practices of mediation, which are in full development in almost every area where private interests risk collapse in an escalation of conflict. Being a former practitioner and a promoter of victim–offender mediation in Flanders, I have still been unable to resist the temptation to question critically the dynamics behind the current popularity, both of restoration and of repairing the victim, as criteria for successful (criminal) justice in general and probation in particular.

Looked at from a Belgian perspective, my brief overview has led to a sobering finding. However much we strive towards the common goal of discouraging the blind use of imprisonment, and do so by demonstrating, through constructive alternatives, its irrational character, these aren't really joint efforts. This finding is the more surprising when we look at the evident conceptual potential in combining their approaches by allowing victim and offender and their social surroundings to contribute in circumscribing and proposing suitable probation conditions. The other way round, probation could be a way of creating a proper framework to engage in getting victim and offender alike to actually come to a way of 'repairing' that they perceive as fitting the particular circumstances. Going back in history shows even more the communalities between both probation and mediation, as they were received in Belgium. Both appeared as coming from overseas, with some flavour of the exotic. Both practices were balancing two attracting poles, that were likely to provide adversarial ideological standpoints on common ground. On the one hand they opened a perspective of substantially contributing to making the existing criminal justice system more effective and more tangible in its outcomes. On the other hand they both seemed to open a window on a radical repositioning of the existing power balances between the citizens and the state. It a fair to say that the awareness of the latter was at the same time most probably the reason why Belgian probation needed decades of political discussion to obtain a—still very restricting—legal status. And it cannot be denied that the sudden breakthrough in mediation was part of the crisis management of a government suffering a spectacular loss of credibility.

As a last common feature, both probation and the embracement of restorative justice through mediation shared a prominent vulnerability to recuperation as friendly instruments within a commonsensical discourse. Undone from its political connotation as a counterbalance to sovereign state power, the notion of 'community' easily meets that of 'Gemeinschaft'. Probation discourse could never really escape the dominant social-defence rationale under state-responsibility. Undone from its inherently unpredictable outcome, the current emphasis on evaluating restorative justice in terms of degree of 'restoration' and 'reparation' is likely to deprive mediation of its critical potential. Reducing a victim to a person 'in need' and whose 'needs' justify a professional 'service' prevents us from seeing 'harm' as the essence of what the problem of crime is all about. In the current state of the art, probation and mediation services alike on the one hand tend to survive only as friendly social-work practices on the margins of what 'real justice' is all about. There lack of structural connection is making this scenario ever more probable, so that they both become competing fishermen on the restricted lake of minor-case criminal justice that authority usually permits them to obtain their referrals from. On the other hand, in striving to end this dominance by criminal justice, they tend to drown themselves in the seas of subjective needs, becoming pedagogues of reparation and satisfaction, desperately calling for a mandate to 'rightly' choose and select what they do and for whom.

As long as probation is applied by way of a lenient sentence in cases of minor offences committed by youngsters or first-offending adults, it is doomed to be seen as a favour, in reality taking neither the victim's perspective nor the offender's public responsibility seriously.

Obliging (or 'proposing') the offender to reimburse the victim, to engage in mediation, or to do 'something for the community' inevitably presupposes the victim or the community to be carriers of needs and expectations fitting their role in this controlling and vaguely educative approach. This does not mean that the actual application of probation doesn't have any restorative value at all. Undoubtedly in quite some cases it might contribute to satisfactory reparation for victims and their surroundings affected by the event. But these benefits are not capable of compensating for the defensive signal transmitted by the restrictive use of probation's restorative potential within criminal justice. The same goes for mediation tending to focus on individual needs rather than on common issues.

This approach sees probation not as a set of alternative measures to 'real' punishment but as an appeal for civic participation, respecting legal protection and open to public control, in constructing and constantly reconstructing in practice what the notion of 'justice' means in a democratic society. This kind of justice leaves great space for restoration, not as an easy way to get repaired or reimbursed, but as a process of repositioning oneself in relation to the criminal event and its consequences, even in the most serious of crimes (Van Garsse 2004). My point of view doesn't oppose the struggle for victims' rights, but it does oppose the popularity of the humiliating and authoritarian identification of victim assistance with victim protection. It sees probation work and mediation as a common social–pedagogical challenge related to the promotion of human dignity in terms of civic capacity and of democracy as a shared political perspective. As such it is far from abstract. It might suffice to listen carefully to ideas and to identify with reasoning expressed by victims, offenders and communities 'beyond' the roles given to them through routine-based offerings, however unlikely they might sound.

References

Aertsen, I. (2004). *Slachtoffer-dader bemiddeling; Een onderzoek naar de ontwikkeling van een herstelgerichte strafrechtsbedeling.* Leuven: Universitaire Pers Leuven.

Aertsen, I., & Peters, T. (1997). Herstelbemiddeling in slachtofferperspectief. *Tijdschrift voor Criminologie, 4*, 372–383.

Ancel, M. (1965). *Social defence: A modern approach to criminal problems.* London: Routledge & Kegan Paul.

Arendt, H. (2007 [1964]). Arbeiden, werken en handelen. In H. Arendt (Ed.), *Politiek in donkere tijden; Essays over vrijheid en vriendschap* (pp. 25–48). Amsterdam: Boom.

Baeyens, L. (1993). Dienstverlening bij de probatie te Leuven; Voorstelling en evaluatie van een experiment. *Panopticon, 14*(3), 223–233.

Bauman, Z. (2000). *Liquid modernity.* Cambridge, UK: Polity.

Beyens, K., & Aertsen, I. (2006). De autonome werkstraf in België: hoe sterk is het karakter? *Panopticon, 27*(4), 1–6.

Biesta, G. (1998). Pedagogy without humanism. *Interchange, 29*(1), 1–16.

Biesta, G. (2004). Education, accountability, and the ethical demand: Can the democratic potential of accountability be regained? *Educational Theory, 54*(3), 233–250.

Biesta, G. (2006). *Beyond learning: Democratic education for a human future.* London: Paradigm.

Biesta, G. (2009). Deconstruction, justice and the vocation of education. In M. Peters & G. Biesta (Eds.), *Derrida, deconstruction and the politics of pedagogy* (pp. 15–38). New York: Peter Lang.

Braithwaite, J., & Pettit, P. (1990). *Not just deserts: A republican theory of criminal justice.* Oxford: Clarendon.

Christie, N. (1977). Conflicts as property. *British Journal of Criminology, 1*, 1–15.

Cornil, P. (1934). Manifestation Adolphe Prins, 15 décembre 1934. *Revue de l'Université de Bruxelles, 4*(1934–1935), 231–251.

Cornil, P. (1937). L'organisation de la rééducation morale et de la réadaptation sociale des délinquants. *Revue du Droit Pénal, 1937*, 381–395.

Cornil, P. (1964). Probation. *Journal des Tribuneaux, 4467*(Nov. 1964), 683–687.

Cornil, P. (1965). Déclin ou renouveau de la répression pénale. *Revue du Droit Pénal, 1964–1965*, 715–729.

Derrida, J. (2001). *Kracht van de wet; het 'mystieke fundament van het gezag'.* Baarn: Agora.

Derrida, J. (2003). *Voyous.* Paris: Galilée.

Duff, R. A. (2001). *Punishment, communication and community.* Oxford: Oxford University Press.

Dupont, L. (1980). Waarover men niet (meer) spreekt. Een eentonig verhaal over strafrechtelijke hervormingspogingen in België. *Panopticon, 1*, 445–449.

The European Forum for Victim Services. (2004, May). *Statement on the position of the victim within the process of mediation.* Https://d19ylpo4aovc7m.cloudfront.net/fileadmin/howard_league/user/pdf/Commission/Mediation_VS_Europe.pdf.

Fijnaut, C. (1983). Averechtse mobilisatie van slachtoffers. *Delikt en delinkwent, 13*(3), 193–194.

Fijnaut, C. (2014). *Criminologie en strafrechtsbedeling.* Antwerpen and Cambridge: Intersentia.

Fitzgibbon, D. W. (2008). Deconstructing probation: Risk and developments in practice. *Journal of Social Work Practice, 22*(1), 85–101.

Gutwirth, S. (1993). *Waarheidsaanspraken in recht en wetenschap.* Brussel: VUBpress/Maklu.

Gutwirth, S., & De Hert, P. (2002). Grondslagentheoretische variaties op de grens tussen het strafrecht en het burgerlijk recht. Perspectieven op schuld-risico- en strafrechtelijke aansprakelijkheid, slachtofferclaims, buitengerechtelijke afdoening en restorative justice. In K. Boonen, C. P. M. Cleiren, R. Foqué, & T. de Roos (Eds.), *De Weging van 't Hart. Idealen, waarden en taken van het strafrecht* (pp. 121–170). Deventer: Kluwer.

Gutwirth, S., & De Hert, P. (2011). Punir ou réparer? Une fausse alternative. In F. Tulkens, Y. Cartuyvels, & C. Guillain (Eds.), *La peine dans tous ces états* (pp. 67–88). Brussel: Larcier.

Huyse, L. (1993). *De gewapende vrede. Politiek in België na 1945.* Leuven: Kritak.

McNeill, F., Burns, N., Halliday, S., Hutton, N. & Tata, C. (2009), Risk, responsibility and reconfiguration: Penal adaptation and misadaptation, *Punishment and society, 11*(4), 419–442.

Mouffe, C. (1989). Radical democracy: Modern or postmodern? In *Universal abandon? The politics of postmodernism* (pp. 31–45). Durham, NC: Duke University Press.

Mouffe, C. (2005). *Over het politieke.* Kampen: Klement and Pelckmans.

Natorp, P. (1964 [1905]). *Pädagogik und Philosophie.* Paderborn: Schöningh.

Neirinckx, P. (1981). De problemen van de diensten voor Sociale Reïntegratie. Een reactie op een editoriaal. *Panopticon, 2*(4), 375–376.

Nohl, H. (1965 [1925]). Der Sinn der Strafe. In: *Aufgaben und Wege der Sozialpädagogik. Vorträge und Aufsätze vor Herman Nohl* (pp.36–44). Weinheim: Verlag Julius Betz.

Peeters, E. (1982). Het ontstaan van de probatie in België. Een poging tot historische reconstructie. *Panopticon, 3*(2), 99–123.

Peters, T. (1980). De gevangenissen zitten overvol want de alternatieve sancties doen het niet. *Panopticon, 1*(4), 265–270.

Peters, T. (1982). Meningen van maatschappelijk werkers over (wijzigingen in) het strafrechtelijk vooronderzoek. *Panopticon, 3*(3), 329–346.

Peters, T. (1993). Bemiddeling, herstel en strafrechtspleging. *Panopticon, 14*(1), 97–106.

Peters, T., & Goethals, J. (Eds.). (1993). *De achterkant van de criminaliteit.* Deurne: Kluwer Rechtswetenschappen.

Prins, A. (1910). *La défence sociale et les transformations du droit pénal.* Brussels and Paris: Misch et Thron.

Rawls, 1971, *A theory of Justice,* Harvard University Press.

Sachße, C. (2003). *Mütterlichkeit als beruf. Sozialarbeit, Sozialreform und Frauenbewegung 1871–1929.* Weinheim, Basel, and Berlin: Verlagsgruppe Beltz.

Tocqueville, A. (1963). *De la démocatie en Amérique.* Paris: Union générale d'éditions.

Tulkens, F. (1988). Un chapitre de l'histoire des réformateurs. Adolphe Prins et la défence social. In F. Tulkens (Ed.), *Généalogie de la Défence Sociale en Belgique, 1880–1914* (pp. 17–46). Brussels: E. Story—Scientia.

Tulkens, F. (1993). Le droit pénal et la défense social en Belgique à l'aube du XXe siècle. *Panopticon, 14*(6), 485–504.

Valverde, M. (1999a). The personal is the political: Justice and gender in deconstruction. *Economy and Society, 28*(2), 300–311.

Valverde, M. (1999b). Derrida's justice and Foucault's freedom: Ethics, history, and social movements. *Law and Social Inquiry, 24*(3), 655–675.

van Beek, M. M. (1970). The change in the role of the victim of crime. *Tijdschrift voor Strafrecht, 79*, 193–204.

Van Dijk, J. J. M. (2008). *Slachtoffers als zondebokken.* Antwerpen and Apeldoorn: Maklu.

Van Garsse, L. (2001). Praktijk en wetenschap. Drie bedrijven uit de ontwikkelingsgeschiedenis van een bemiddelingspraktijk. In L. Dupont & F. Hutsebaut (Eds.), *Herstelrecht tussen toekomst en verleden* (pp. 515–530). Leuven: Universitaire Pers Leuven.

Van Garsse, L. (2004). Bemiddeling in de Strafrechtelijke context: suggesties voor regelgeving op basis van jaren bemiddelingspraktijk. *Panopticon, 25*(5), 47–63.

Van Garsse, L. (2012). Daders en herstel: tussen plicht, behoefte en capaciteit. In I. Weijers (Ed.), *Slachtoffer-dadergesprekken in de schaduw van het strafproces* (pp. 59–72). The Hague: Boom and Lemma.

Van Garsse, L. (2013). Zwischen Zynismus und Nostalgie. Die Umsetzung von Restorative Justice in Strafsachen in Belgien. *Infodienst. Rundbrief zum Täter-Opfer-Ausgleich, 46*, 43–50.

Van Garsse, L. (2014). Restorative Justice in prisons: "Do not enter without precautions". *Ljetopis socijalnog rada, 22*(1): 15–35

Verheyden, R. (1975). De probatie tussen toekomst en verleden. *Rechtskundig weekblad, Nov. 1975*, 514–559.

Walgrave, L. (2008). *Restorative justice, self-interest and responsible citizenship.* Cullompton: Willan.

Zehr, H. (1990). *Changing lenses: New focus for crime and justice.* Scottdale, PA: Herald.

What Is the Impact of Community Service?

Gill McIvor

Introduction

Unpaid work by offenders—most commonly referred to as community service[1]—is available as a penal measure in many countries worldwide and has become one of the most popular community sentences among the public and the judiciary. This is mainly because it serves numerous purposes and aims—such as diversion from custody, reduced costs to the criminal justice system, reparation and rehabilitation—and because it can be seen to provide tangible benefits for the community. This same diversity, however, means that the effectiveness of community service may be

---

[1] Although unpaid work by offenders is referred to using a variety of terminology—both across jurisdictions and within individual jurisdictions at different points in time—the term 'community service' is widely recognised internationally and is therefore used throughout this chapter except in referring to specific legislative or policy initiatives in which alternative terminology is employed.

G. McIvor (✉)
University of Stirling, Stirling, UK

© The Editor(s) (if applicable) and The Author(s) 2016   **107**
F. McNeill et al. (eds.), *Probation*,
DOI 10.1057/978-1-137-51982-5_6

assessed in a number of ways and its popularity as a penal sanction has also resulted in accusations that it may serve to widen the net of social control.

This chapter will begin by briefly outlining the development of community service as a penal measure across different jurisdictions and at various points of the criminal justice process: as an alternative to prosecution, as an alternative to imprisonment for fine default, as a sentence in its own right, as a direct alternative to a sentence of imprisonment and as a condition of early release from prison. It will then consider the objectives of unpaid work by offenders and how they have tended to shift towards an increasingly retributive emphasis before examining the international evidence regarding the capacity of community service to reduce the use of imprisonment, produce cost savings, provide benefits to the community and reduce the risk of re-offending. The chapter will conclude by discussing developments in the focus of community service in some jurisdictions that can be characterised as placing a greater emphasis upon the re-integrative potential of unpaid work and argue that developments of this kind are more likely than those that forefront punitive objectives and practices to enable a range of other benefits to be achieved.

The Development of Community Service as a Penal Measure

Community service in its varied forms involves offenders undertaking unpaid work for the benefit of the community. It is a penalty that is widely available in Western jurisdictions and can be used at different points in the criminal justice process. While it is most often used as an alternative to a prison sentence or as a community sanction in its own right, in some jurisdictions offenders can be required to undertake unpaid work as an alternative to imprisonment for fine default or as an alternative to prosecution. Work may be undertaken for individual beneficiaries or for third-sector (charitable) organisations and may involve a variety of personal and practical tasks.

While examples of criminal sanctioning with an emphasis on the performance of socially useful work can be identified historically, the first modern community service programme was developed in Alameda County, California in 1966 and involved those convicted of certain road traffic offences performing unpaid work for the community as a requirement by the municipal court. In 1976, the Law Enforcement Assistance Administration in the United States made available funding for the development of community service programmes for adult offenders and in 1978 the Office of Juvenile Justice and Delinquency Prevention provided resources to enable the development of community service programmes for juvenile offenders in eighty-five counties and states. Many programmes ceased when the initial funding ran but others obtained alternative sources of finance, including local and state support (McDonald 1989). The use of community service in the United States has been reported to be widespread, although relatively little is known about its operation. It is usually imposed as a punitive measure in conjunction with other sanctions and often as part of an intensive supervision package which may also include supervision, house arrest, financial restitution and drug testing (Immarigeon 1998).

Community service has now been introduced in most western jurisdictions although, as Harris and Lo (2002) have observed, its broader international spread has been uneven and it is more widely available and used in some countries than in others. Community service orders were first introduced on a *legislated* basis in England and Wales in 1973, with the new orders administered and supervised by the probation service. The Criminal Justice Act 1972 enabled offenders aged 17 years and over who had been convicted of an offence that was punishable by imprisonment to be ordered to undertake between 40 and 240 hours of unpaid work. Community service orders proved to be a popular measure with the courts and, following the introduction and evaluation of pilot schemes, were introduced throughout England and Wales in 1974 (Pease et al. 1975) and in Scotland in 1979 (McIvor 1992).

The formal incorporation of community service into the criminal justice system was watched with interest by other countries and the British experience served as a model for schemes that were subsequently developed elsewhere. During the 1970s community service was introduced in differing formats in several other non-European countries including Australia, Canada and New Zealand and in most of Western Europe (Albrecht and Schädler 1986). Community service was most often introduced, as in Britain, as a direct alternative to short periods of incarceration. In some countries (such as Luxembourg and Norway) it could be substituted for prison as a condition of pardon while in others (such as Germany, Italy and Switzerland) community service orders could be imposed instead of imprisonment for fine default (van Kalmthout and Tak 1988). Some countries initially resisted the addition of community service to their repertoire of criminal sanctions. Sweden, for example, rejected it on the basis that it would have a limited impact on the use of imprisonment and was incompatible with a social structure which regarded work as a privilege, although following an initial pilot in five district courts it was subsequently made available on a national basis.

Community service is therefore now a well-established and popular sanction in many jurisdictions, although there are variations in how it is used and in its penal objectives. In most jurisdictions community service is available as a sanction of the court as a sentence in its own right or as a legislated alternative to a prison sentence at first sentence or following the imposition of a sentence of imprisonment. It may be imposed as a 'stand-alone' option without additional support, as a condition of a supervisory penalty or alongside another order (Harris and Lo 2002). In some jurisdictions community service operates as an alternative to imprisonment for fine default (Dünkel 2004; McIvor et al. 2013), as an alternative to prosecution (Harris and Lo 2002; Richards et al. 2011), as a condition of pre-trial release or as a condition of parole (Harris and Lo 2002).

The Objectives of Community Service

When the option of requiring offenders to undertake unpaid work for the benefit of the community was first introduced in the UK its strength was thought to lie in its ability to appeal to a number of different sentencing aims. The Advisory Council on the Penal System (1970), which recommended the introduction of community service in England and Wales, suggested that community service could serve as a punishment by depriving offenders of their leisure time while enabling them to make reparation for their offence, albeit symbolically to the community rather than to individual victims. The council believed that in some cases community service could also have a 'reforming' influence on offenders by bringing them into contact with other volunteers. In the USA community service is usually considered a form of restitution which holds the offender accountable for his or her actions while compensating victims—or the community more generally—for the harm caused (McIvor 2004a).

Despite the apparent popularity of community service as a sentencing option in various jurisdictions, fundamental concerns have been expressed about its underlying penal philosophy and apparent ability to fulfil simultaneously a number of sentencing aims (Pease 1985). The penal objectives of community service—which will have a bearing on the types of offenders or offences for which it is considered suitable, as well as the nature and range of activities that it may involve—have been subject to much debate and the relative emphasis placed on punishment, reparation and rehabilitation can be seen to vary across jurisdictions and over time within jurisdictions. A recent comparison of community service in four European jurisdictions—Belgium, the Netherlands, Scotland and Spain—found that growing emphasis is being placed on retributive aspects of unpaid work (for example demanding manual work that is 'visible') in an effort to garner public and judicial support while rehabilitative objectives have become more narrowly focused on reducing recidivism (McIvor et al. 2010).

In some jurisdictions, shifts in the relative salience of differing objectives ascribed to community service have been accompanied by changes in terminology. This is particularly evident in relation to England and Wales where community service has undergone important transformations linked to broader penal objectives and related to wider policy concerns. In April 2001, as Home Office rhetoric about criminal justice began to take an increasing punitive slant, the community service order was renamed the community punishment order (CPO) to emphasise its retributive potential. In 2005 the CPO and the community rehabilitation order (previously probation) were replaced by the community order and suspended sentence order to which could be attached an array of requirements including unpaid work, with a renewed emphasis upon 'paying back' to the community. As McIvor (2007) has observed, emphasising the visibility of community punishment had been highlighted in the Carter Report (Carter 2003) and was reflected in the establishment of 'visibility pilots' in six probation areas in July 2005, followed by a national rollout to other probation areas across England and Wales. Visible Unpaid Work was one of three elements of a national strategy for unpaid work aimed at ensuring that the work undertaken by offenders should be recognisable by the local community and was taken forward alongside a Home Office three-year Community Sentences Communication campaign which aimed to 'raise the profile of Community Sentences and promote public confidence that offenders receive demanding punishments which reflect the seriousness of the crime' (National Probation Service 2005, Para. 2). The Visible Unpaid Work campaign promoted unpaid work as a resource to communities that could enhance community safety and well-being. It was accompanied by attempts to encourage greater community involvement in identifying community service projects at the local level through a 'Community Payback Scheme' that was launched November 2005 as part of a wider government initiative to increase the involvement of local communities in the criminal justice system.

As originally conceptualized, the visible unpaid work campaign explicitly ruled out the use of uniforms for offenders 'the intention of which is to humiliate or stigmatise', stressing instead that the emphasis would be on 'badging the work, not the offender' (National Probation Service 2005, Para. 6.i). However, the introduction of uniforms was subsequently raised through the publication of leaked Home Office correspondence in July 2006 that indicated that the new Home Secretary regarded such a move as appropriate to ensure that unpaid work took the form of and was perceived as 'penance and contrition'. This was followed by the publication of a Cabinet Office (2008) report which argued that unpaid work by offenders should be more visible and demanding and renamed 'Community Payback' to reflect this (Thomas and Thompson 2010). High-visibility jackets with a distinctive logo were issued to offenders later that year to make the work carried out by them more visible and 'tough', resulting in some incidents of physical and verbal abuse by members of the public towards those engaged in unpaid work and the refusal to wear them by some offenders who became aggressive towards their supervisors as a result (Thomas and Thompson 2010). A survey of young offenders in England identified high levels of resistance to the wearing of visible jackets on the grounds that they would be embarrassing and would make them the targets of victimisation, and around two-thirds suggested that they would refuse to comply or not turn up for work if required to do so (Pamment and Ellis 2010). As Ahmed et al. (2001) have argued, the process of shaming and its outcomes are complex, and effective 'shame management' is required for the restorative or re-integrative potential of unpaid work to be invoked. It has been argued that the wearing of high-visibility jackets by offenders undertaking community service may actually contribute to communities being less safe because the 'disintegrative shaming' (Braithwaite 1989) that such uniforms promote is likely to result in offenders being further excluded from society and at greater risk of recidivism as a result (Pamment and Ellis 2010).

The Impact of Community Service

Given its varying penal objectives, the impact of community service can be assessed in a number of ways. Later in this chapter efforts to enhance the re-integrative potential of community service to support the process of desistance will be considered. First, however, the success of community service will be discussed in relation to its capacity to divert offenders from sentences of imprisonment and in so doing provide a less costly alternative, the benefits it provides to communities in which the work is carried out (by means of 'symbolic reparation') and the effects upon recidivism of performing unpaid work.

Diversion from Custody and Reduced Criminal Justice System Costs

In most jurisdictions community service is intended to operate as a mechanism to divert offenders from sentences of imprisonment, although from the outset there has been evidence to suggest that it has not always been used consistently to this end. In Scotland, for example, it was estimated that community service orders were used as a direct alternative to imprisonment in 45 % of cases and as an alternative to other non-custodial penalties in the rest (McIvor 1990). The diversionary impact of community service was similar in the pilot schemes in England and Wales (Pease et al. 1975) and in the Netherlands where it was estimated that between 45% and 50% of community service orders had replaced short-term prison sentences (Spaans 1998). Given that breach of a community service order will often result in the offender being required to serve a sentence of imprisonment, it would appear that the likely impact on prison numbers will be limited. Indeed, the apparent popularity of community service with sentencers does not appear in many jurisdictions to have been reflected in a lowered use of imprisonment, with the increased use of community service—and other community-based 'alternatives'—being accompanied by increases in the use of short sentences of imprisonment (Mair and Canton 2007; Beyens 2010; Blay 2010; Boone 2010). As McIvor et al. (2010, p. 95) concluded from their comparative analysis of the use of community service:

> The question of net-widening, relevant from a penological and reductionist point of view, is still unresolved, partly due to the difficulties to demonstrate it with reliable data. From the point of view of net-widening, it becomes however relevant to question the quantitative success of community service. Although we might presume that it can have a certain substitutive effect on imprisonment, its introduction has not led to a shrinking prison population: on the contrary, the growth of unpaid work by offenders has accompanied increase rates of imprisonment, pointing to significant penal expansion.

The existence of net-widening clearly has implications for the cost savings to the criminal justice system that might accrue from the use of community service. Although analyses of the costs of community service compared with other disposals—and particularly prison—are generally favourable, when the indirect costs of community service and imprisonment are taken into account (including the costs of prison sentences imposed in the event of orders being breached) it appears that significant costs savings are only likely to be achieved if community service is used in a relatively high proportion of cases as a direct alternative to imprisonment (Knapp et al. 1992).

Reparation

At an interpersonal level, interaction happens on a daily basis between individuals given community service and people who benefit from the work they carry out, although we still know relatively little about its nature and impact (McIvor et al. 2010). On a directly practical level, the work carried out by offenders on community service can be quantified both financially and in terms of hours completed and it has been documented as providing tangible results such as improvements in local amenities or practical benefits for individual recipients of unpaid work (Schneider 1990; McIvor 1993a).

There is some evidence of the potential 'generative' and re-integrative benefits for offenders of giving something back to their local communities. For example it has been found that offenders appreciate the opportunity to acquire new skills and undertake work that is valued by the beneficiaries. By contrast, offenders have more negative views about work that is mundane, unrewarding and potentially demeaning (McIvor 1992). Work of this nature is unlikely to convey the positive message that those who are undertaking unpaid work have something positive to offer society and their local communities.

Community service can also have a re-integrative impact through enabling offenders to continue working with community organisations on a voluntary (and sometimes paid) capacity after they complete the work they have been ordered to carry out. The re-integrative potential of community service was illustrated by a survey of placement providing agencies in Scotland (McIvor 1993b). Around half of the agencies surveyed indicated that on at least one occasion a community service worker had stayed on in a voluntary (and sometimes paid) capacity after they had completed the work that had been ordered by the court. This was more likely to occur in agencies in which community service workers were better integrated with agency staff and other volunteers and in which they enjoyed direct contact with the service users who would benefit from the work they carried out. An inspection by Her Majesty's Inspectorate of Probation in England and Wales (HMIP 2006) also reported instances of offenders being employed by a beneficiary or continuing to work on a voluntary basis after completing community service, while in Canada it was found that some young people who completed community service were subsequently offered employment by the host organisations (Doob and MacFarlane 1984, cited in Bazemore and Karp 2004).

Studies conducted in a number of jurisdictions including New Zealand (Leibrich et al. 1986) and the USA (Caputo 1999) have also reported high levels of satisfaction among the beneficiaries of community service work. For example, in the Vermont Reparative Project in the USA 94% of agencies were reported to be satisfied with the quality of the work carried out and all were reportedly prepared to have more offenders undertake unpaid work with them as part of their probation programmes (Karp et al. 2002, cited in Bazemore and Karp 2004). In a further survey in Vermont, 88% of reparative board volunteers were of the opinion that community service facilitated probationers' reintegration (Karp et al. 2004).

Recidivism

Community service is often defined as symbolic restitution (or, sometimes, as symbolic reparation) because it is the community that benefits rather than individual victims of crime. It has also been viewed as a fine on the offender's free time (McDonald 1989) and is not necessarily considered to be a sanction with explicitly rehabilitative aims (McIvor 2004b). Yet there is some evidence that the experience of performing unpaid work for the community may bring about positive changes in offenders' attitudes and behaviour. Some studies have found that restitution in general and community service in particular are associated with lower recidivism rates than alternative sanctions such as prison and probation, though other studies have produced contradictory results (Schiff 2003).

With regards to re-offending, comparisons are usually made between community service and imprisonment on the basis that community service is intended to replace short terms of imprisonment. Such comparisons are often limited by the fact that those given prison sentences and community service differ in important ways that in themselves are related to the likelihood of recidivism. There is some evidence, however, that offenders on community service may have lower reconviction rates than would be predicted by their criminal history, age and other relevant characteristics (Lloyd et al. 1995) and when social factors such as unemployment and drug use are taken into account (May 1999). For example, controlling for criminal history, Scottish Government data have identified lower reconviction rates among those given community service than among those receiving prison sentences, particularly among offenders with more extensive criminal histories and with the difference more marked among women than among men (Scottish Government 2012). This latter finding is particularly interesting given the tendency for community service—whether as a disposal or as a condition of a community penalty—to be used disproportionately with young male offenders (Hine 1993; Mair et al. 2007; Patel and Stanley 2008) because it is perceived essentially as a punishment for young men. It has been suggested that women's apparent under-representation on community service may be a result of their caring responsibilities towards children and other dependents being perceived as a barrier to the completion of unpaid work, despite evidence that women may find that undertaking unpaid work is a rewarding and fulfilling experience, particularly if some thought has been given to matching them with suitable types of work (McIvor 2004c).

Evidence that community service outperforms prison has also been found by European researchers. In a study of community service in Switzerland, Killias et al. (2000) recorded fewer re-arrests among offenders given community service than among those given short prison sentences of up to 14 days, although the difference diminished over a longer-term follow-up period (Killias et al. 2010a, b). In the Dutch study by Wermink et al. (2010), which used matched samples of offenders on community service and prisoners serving short sentences of up to six months, a lower rate of recidivism was found in favour of those on community service which was sustained over a period of up to five years. These apparent differences in the sustainability of reductions in recidivism may be related to the length of the prison sentences against which community service was compared, with *very* short sentences being less harmful to offenders in the longer term (Killias et al. 2010a, b).

Other studies have compared recidivism following community service with that following other non-custodial disposals with somewhat mixed results. In a comparison of re-arrests among offenders convicted of driving under the influence and ordered to undertake community service or be fined, Bouffard and Muftić (2007) found lower re-arrest rates among the community service sample measured from the end of the order (although re-arrest rates were higher for the community service sample while they were completing the work). A Dutch study found slightly lower levels of recidivism among offenders given community service compared with a sample who received a suspended prison sentence but the former group also tended to be less serious offenders as indicated by their index offence (Spaans 1998). The study by Killias et al. (2010a, b) involving a comparison of offenders in Switzerland who were randomly allocated to community service or electronic monitoring found that offenders allocated to electronic monitoring re-offended *less* than those ordered to carry out unpaid work. The researchers suggest that this may have been a result of those subject to community service carrying out work in the company of other offenders—and, hence, being exposed to pro-criminal attitudes and negative peer influence—while those given electronic monitoring were more likely to be isolated from the influence of offending peers.

It is also important, however, to take account of qualitative differences in the experiences of offenders who undertake community service and how this may have a bearing on their likelihood of re-offending. A study of community service in Scotland, for example, found some evidence of lower rates of reconviction among offenders who reported their experiences of undertaking unpaid work to be more positive and rewarding: recidivism rates were lower when the work carried out was capable of providing some intrinsic satisfaction and reward and when offenders could readily recognise its worth (McIvor 1992). Perceptions of fairness may also be important in this regard. A study of community service in Switzerland by Killias et al. (2000) found the lowest rates of reconviction to be among offenders given community service who considered their sentence to be fair.

Enhancing the Re-integrative Potential and Effectiveness of Community Service

In the period following the establishment of the first pilot schemes in the UK, there was much debate about the relative merits of different forms of community service work (McIvor 2007). More specifically, discussion focused on the relative advantages and disadvantages of the different contexts in which unpaid work was carried out—whether in community service team settings or in community-based agency placements—and whether it involved practical or personal service tasks. However, an analysis of the operation of community service in Scotland which considered the experiences and outcomes for offenders who carried out different types of work in varied settings produced a much more nuanced picture. Rather than one *type* of placement being more positively regarded than the other, what the placement offered in terms of offenders' experiences seemed to matter most. Offenders regarded carrying out unpaid work as more rewarding if they had contact with the beneficiaries of the work, if their placements afforded them opportunities to acquire new skills and if the work could be readily identified as having some social value (McIvor 1992).

The finding by Killias et al. (2000) of a relationship between the perceived fairness of the sentences offenders received and reconviction suggests that those who regard a community service sentence as 'fair' may be more receptive to re-integrative opportunities that arise when they undertake court-ordered unpaid work (Rex and Gelsthorpe 2002). This points to the possibility that 're-integrative' community service placements may be more likely to encourage desistance than those that are primarily retributive in content and aim. To this end some probation areas in England began to offer accreditation for the skills acquired by offenders on community service—assisted by specialist education, training and employment staff—with the aim of increasing offenders' employability and therefore their likelihood of finding work or undertaking further education or training after completing their community service orders (Rex and Gelsthorpe 2002). Community Punishment Pathfinders were established in England and Wales in 2000 under the Home Office's Crime Reduction Programme focusing on the use of pro-social modelling, skills accreditation and addressing the problems underlying offending behaviour in various combinations. In some projects attempts were also made to improve the quality of work placements to increase their perceived value to offenders. One project focused specifically upon enhancing the integration of the community service and probation elements of combination orders through improved induction and supervision planning (Rex and Gelsthorpe 2002).

The evaluation of the pathfinder project found that short-term outcomes were encouraging, with offenders showing reductions in perceived problems and pro-criminal attitudes, two-thirds being viewed by staff as having undergone positive change and three-quarters being thought by staff to be unlikely to re-offend (possibly because they had a low risk of re-offending in the first place). Importantly, and consistent with McIvor's (1992) research, the features of community service that were most strongly linked with changes in offenders' attitudes were whether they perceived the work to have been of value to themselves and to the beneficiaries (Rex and Gelsthorpe 2002; Gelsthorpe and Rex 2004).

Following the community punishment pathfinders, the 'Enhanced Community Punishment' initiative was launched in October 2003 (Rex et al. 2003). Enhanced Community Punishment built upon the experiences of the pathfinders by focusing upon skill acquisition and attitude change through teaching offenders pro-social attitudes and behaviour and employment-related and problem-solving skills. The aim was to combine elements of reparation and retribution while maximising the rehabilitative potential of community punishment by addressing some offenders' needs to help them avoid offending in the future. Enhanced community punishment was to a large extent evidence-based, incorporating a range of elements including integrated case management, pro-social modelling, cognitive skills modelling, guided skills learning and the use of placements with characteristics—such as contact with the beneficiaries and meaningful work—that would encourage compliance and support the other elements of the disposal. However, a thematic inspection by the Probation Inspectorate for England and Wales indicated that not all projects were providing the intended benefits to offenders and that the quality of case management was very variable (HMIP 2006). Similarly, in a Scottish study which explored the effects of training in pro-social modelling with community service supervisors, some supervisors appeared to value the training and gain some benefit from it—even if was just to confirm what they already regarded as good practice—while it appeared to have no impact on others (McCulloch 2010).

A more recent emphasis upon the re-integrative potential of community service (Glavin 2012) or its potential for generativity (McNeill and Maruna 2007)—described by McIvor (1998, p. 56) as 'gaining the trust, confidence and appreciation of other people and having the opportunity to give something back to them in return'—has some resonance with Bazemore and Maloney's (1994, p. 26) observation that 'offenders are capable of making positive contributions and, having paid their debt, should be allowed to be accepted back into community life.' They made this observation at a time when community service was employed in the USA primarily as a punishment, with little attempt to maximise its potential to support positive changes in the attitudes or behaviour of offenders undertaking unpaid work (Immarigeon 1998). Bazemore and Maloney argued that the increasingly punitive emphasis on community service in the USA appeared to create a disincentive for the development of more imaginative, and arguably more effective, opportunities for offenders to undertake meaningful unpaid work and/or acquire skills while undertaking community service.

Instead, they argued that community service should take a form that would provide added value to offenders and to their communities and that may even serve to strengthen the bond between them to facilitate re-integration. Examples they offered of what they described as 'service on its highest plane' (p. 30) included mentoring; economic development; citizenship and civic participation; helping the disadvantaged; and crime prevention projects. This would, they suggested, require a redefinition of offenders as resources rather than as 'the problem' but would be consistent with strengths-based approaches such as the Good Lives model (Birgden 2002; Ward 2002; Willis and Ward 2013) that place an emphasis upon resilience rather than risk. A competency development strategy, as outlined by Bazemore and Maloney (1994), 'would require that offenders be placed in positive, productive roles in the community which allow them to experience, practice and demonstrate ability to do something well that others value' (p. 29). The work itself would be undertaken in the context of opportunities for learning and personal development, would be of clear value for the community and would entail the offenders and their work being viewed as a positive resource.

This re-integrative form of community service envisaged by Bazemore and Maloney shares many similarities to the 'value added' community service projects that were developed by probation services in the 1990s and subsequently formalised by the establishment of the Community

Punishment Pathfinders in England and Wales. In the United States, the ideas developed by Bazemore and Maloney and elaborated upon by Bazemore and Karp (2004) have seen expression in the creation of 'Civic Justice Corps' in which unpaid work is conceptualised as promoting 'earned redemption' for offenders through work that is visible and useful to individuals and communities, that enables the person performing it to practise and demonstrate competency and reliability, that is clearly directed toward meeting the needs of less fortunate members of the community and that is accompanied by opportunities for the provision of mentoring, advocacy, and social support to those carrying out the work.

In practice, Civic Justice Corps programmes that have been developed have tended to combine unpaid work by offenders with support focused upon preparing participants for employment and work experience. There appears as yet to be very limited outcome data regarding this type of community service. One exception is an evaluation of the New York City Justice Corps (Bauer et al. 2014) which found that there was increased employment among participants compared with a randomised control group referred to 'standard' services, although no differences in educational outcome or recidivism were found. This may be because levels of attrition were relatively high, with only 59% of those referred to the programme completing. Participants themselves were found to be very positive about the programme, especially the community service component of it which they regarded as having enabled them to acquire skills that increased their employability such as communication, leadership and teamwork skills.

Conclusion

Community service is now a well-established and well-used penalty in many jurisdictions, with its popularity arguably deriving from it having the capacity to provide tangible benefits to the community while punishing offenders by imposing a fine upon their free time. Although the core elements of community service have remained largely unchanged since its introduction as a penal sanction—undertaking unpaid work for the benefit of the community—how that work should be conceptualised has evolved in recent years. There is evidence that in some jurisdictions there has been of a shift in emphasis in community service to highlight its punitive potential to assuage media and public criticism that unpaid work by offenders is a 'soft option' and encourage its sustained or increased use as a relatively high tariff penalty (McIvor et al. 2010). The requirement that individuals undertaking unpaid work in England and Wales wear high-visibility jackets that identify them as offenders on community service is one clear example but others can be identified. In Spain, for example, this is reflected in increases in the number of hours or days that offenders are required to work (Blay 2010) while in the Netherlands the types of task that offenders are required to complete have become more demanding (Boone 2010). Even in Scotland, which has largely resisted the 'punitive turn' that has been evident elsewhere, there have been there have been periodic attempts, albeit short-lived, by politicians to enhance the perceived punitiveness of community service and avoid accusation that the government is 'soft on crime' (McIvor 2010).

Developments that aim to forefront the capacity of community service to punish offenders may, however, undermine its potential to bring about other benefits for those carrying out the work and for the communities in which it is undertaken. As the General Secretary of NAPO (the National Association of Probation Officers in England and Wales) remarked in response to proposals to introduce the requirement that offenders be required to wear uniforms that would clearly identify them as performing unpaid work, 'the notion of "penance and contrition" as the cornerstone of unpaid work is extraordinary. Orders need to be seen as purposeful by offenders and raise self-esteem, not severely diminish it' Travis, 2006.

Although there has been less empirical attention to the operation of community service and its impact in recent years, the available evidence points to modest but important benefits. And although community service may be argued to have a limited impact on prison populations—despite this having been a clearly stated intention in most jurisdictions when it was introduced—communities across the world benefit from a significant number of hours of unpaid work which, where such views have been documented, appears to be appreciated by those who directly benefit from it. Moreover, there is some tentative evidence that rates of recidivism are lower following community service than following short sentences and that the quality of offenders' experiences of undertaking unpaid work are important in this respect. Efforts to increase the punitive 'bite' of community service may, therefore, be counterproductive in the longer term. Instead the available evidence would suggest that community service should aim, where possible, both to punish offenders by requiring them to sacrifice their time and at the same time to provide them with experiences and skills that enable them to pay back society in ways that increase their competencies and the likelihood that they will be re-integrated into their communities in turn.

References

Advisory Council on the Penal System. (1970). *Non-custodial and semi-custodial penalties.* London: HMSO.

Ahmed, E., Harris, N., Braithwaite, J., & Braithwaite, V. (2001). *Shame management through reintegration.* Cambridge: Cambridge University Press.

Albrecht, H.-J., & Schädler, W. (1986). Community service in Europe: Concluding remarks. In H.-J. Albrecht & W. Schädler (Eds.), *Community service: A new option in punishing offenders in Europe.* Freiburg: Max Planck Institute for Foreign and International Penal Law.

Bauer, E. L., Crosse, S., McPherson, K., Friedman, J., Zacharia, J., Tapper, D., et al. (2014). *Evaluation of the New York City Justice Corps.* Rockville, MD: Westat.

Bazemore, G., & Karp, D. R. (2004). A Civic Justice Corps: Community service as a means of reintegration. *Justice Policy Journal, 1*(3), 1–37.

Bazemore, G., & Maloney, D. (1994). Rehabilitating community service: Toward restorative service sanctions in a balanced justice system. *Federal Probation, 61*(1), 24–35.

Beyens, K. (2010). From 'community service' to 'autonomous work penalty' in Belgium: What's in a name? *European Journal of Probation, 2*(1), 4–21.

Birgden, A. (2002). Therapeutic jurisprudence and "good lives": A rehabilitation framework for corrections. *Australian Psychologist, 37*(3), 180–186.

Blay, E. (2010). "It could be us": Recent transformations in the use of community service as a punishment in Spain. *European Journal of Probation, 2*(1), 62–81.

Boone, M. (2010). Only for minor offences: Community service in the Netherlands. *European Journal of Probation, 2*(1), 22–40.

Bouffard, J. A., & Muftić, L. R. (2007). The effectiveness of community service sentences compared to traditional fines for low-level offenders. *Prison Journal, 87*(2), 171–194.

Braithwaite, J. (1989). *Crime, shame and re-integration.* Cambridge: Cambridge University Press.

Cabinet Office. (2008). *Engaging communities in fighting crime: A review by Louise Casey.* London: Cabinet Office.

Caputo, G. A. (1999). Why not community service? *Criminal Justice Policy Review, 10*(4), 503–519.

Carter, P. (2003). *Managing offenders, reducing crime: A new approach.* London: Home Office.

Doob, A. N., & MacFarlane, D. P. (1984). *The community service order for youthful offenders: Perceptions and effects.* Toronto: Centre for Criminology, University of Toronto.

Dünkel, F. (2004). Reducing the population of fine defaulters in prison: Experiences with community service in Mecklenburg—Western Pomerania (Germany). In *Crime policy in Europe: Good practices and promising examples.* Strasbourg: Council of Europe.

Gelsthorpe, L., & Rex, S. (2004). Community service as reintegration: Exploring the potential. In G. Mair (Ed.), *What matters in probation?* Cullompton: Willan.

Glavin, M. (2012). Reintegrative community service teams: Developing key practice dimensions of the civic engagement model of offender reentry. *Justice Policy Journal, 9*(2), 1–47.

Harris, R., & Lo, T. W. (2002). Community service: Its use in criminal justice. *International Journal of Offender Therapy and Comparative Criminology, 46*(4), 427–444.

Hine, J. (1993). Access for women: Flexible and friendly? In D. Whitfield & D. Scott (Eds.), *Paying back: Twenty years of community service.* Winchester: Waterside.

HMIP. (2006). *Working to make amends: Inspection findings 1/06.* London: HMIP.

Immarigeon, R. (1998). Sentencing offenders to community service: 30 years of practice, promise and pessimism. *Community Corrections Report, 5*(2), 19–20, 28.

Karp, D. R., Bazemore, G., & Chesire, J. D. (2004). The role and attitudes of Restorative Board members: A case study of volunteers in criminal justice. *Crime and Delinquency, 50*(4), 487–515.

Karp, D. R., Sprayregen, M., & Drakulich, K. (2002). *Vermont reparative probation year 2000 outcome evaluation final report.* Waterbury, VT: Vermont Department of Corrections.

Killias, M., Aebi, M., & Ribeaud, D. (2000). Does community service rehabilitate better than short-term imprisonment? Results of a controlled experiment. *Howard Journal, 39*(1), 40–57.

Killias, M., Gilliéron, G., Kissling, I., & Villetaz, P. (2010a). Community service versus electronic monitoring—What works better?: Results of a randomized trial. *British Journal of Criminology, 50*(6), 1155–1170.

Killias, M., Gilliéron, G., Villard, F., & Poglia, C. (2010b). How damaging is imprisonment in the long-term?: A controlled experiment comparing long-term effects of community service and short custodial sentences on re-offending and social integration. *Journal of Experimental Criminology, 6*, 115–130.

Knapp, M., Robertson, E., & McIvor, G. (1992). The comparative costs of community service and custody in Scotland. *Howard Journal, 31*, 8–30.

Leibrich, J., Galaway, B., & Underhill, Y. (1986). Community service sentencing in New Zealand: A survey of users. *Federal Probation, 50*(1), 55–64.

Lloyd, C., Mair, G., & Hough, M. (1995). *Explaining reconviction rates: A critical analysis* (Home Office Research Study 136). London: Home Office.

Mair, G., & Canton, R. (2007). Sentencing, community penalties and the role of the Probation Service. In L. Gelsthorpe & R. Morgan (Eds.), *Handbook of probation*. Cullompton: Willan.

Mair, G., Cross, N., & Taylor, S. (2007). *The use and impact of the community order and the suspended sentence order*. London: Centre for Crime and Justice Studies.

May, C. (1999). *Explaining reconviction following community sentences: The role of social factors* (Home Office Research Study 192). London: Home Office.

McCulloch, T. (2010). Realising potential: Community service, pro-social modelling and desistance. *European Journal of Probation, 2*(2), 3–22.

McDonald, D. C. (1989). *Punishment without walls: Community service sentences in New York City*. New Brunswick, NJ: Rutgers University Press.

McIvor, G. (1990). Community service and custody in Scotland. *Howard Journal of Criminal Justice, 29*(2), 101–113.

McIvor, G. (1992). *Sentenced to serve: The operation and impact of community service by offenders in Scotland*. Aldershot: Avebury.

McIvor, G. (1993a). Community service by offenders: How much does the community benefit? *Research on Social Work Practice, 3*, 385–403.

McIvor, G. (1993b). Community service by offenders: Agency experiences and attitudes. *Research on Social Work Practice, 3*, 66–82.

McIvor, G. (2004a). Community service and restitution programs. In J. M. Miller & R. A. Wright (Eds.), *Encyclopaedia of criminology*. New York: Routledge.

McIvor, G. (2004b). Reparative and restorative approaches. In A. Bottoms, S. Rex, & G. Robinson (Eds.), *Alternatives to prison: Options for an insecure society*. Cullompton: Willan.

McIvor, G. (2004c). Service with a smile?: Women and community 'punishment'. In G. McIvor (Ed.), *Women who offend* (Research highlights in social work, Vol. 44). London: Jessica Kingsley.

McIvor, G. (2007). Paying back—Unpaid work by offenders. In G. McIvor & P. Raynor (Eds.), *Developments in social work with offenders*. London: Jessica Kingsley.

McIvor, G. (2010). Paying back: 30 years of unpaid work by offenders in Scotland. *European Journal of Probation, 2*(1), 41–61.

McIvor, G., Beyens, K., Blay, E., & Boone, M. (2010). Community service in Belgium, the Netherlands, Scotland and Spain: A comparative perspective. *European Journal of Probation, 2*(1), 82–98.

McIvor, G., Pirnat, C., & Grafl, C. (2013). Unpaid work as an alternative to imprisonment for fine default in Austria and Scotland. *European Journal of Probation, 5*(2), 3–28.

McIvor,G. (1998) 'Prosocial modelling and legitimacy: Lessons from a study of community service', in S. Rex and A. Matravers (eds.) Pro-social Modelling and Legitimacy, Cambridge: University of Cambridge Institute of Criminology.

McNeill, F., & Maruna, S. (2007). Giving up and giving back: Desistance, generativity and social work with offenders. In G. McIvor & P. Raynor (Eds.), *Developments in social work with offenders*. London: Jessica Kingsley.

National Probation Service (2005) Visible Unpaid Work, Probation Circular PC66/2005, London: National Probation Service.

Pamment, N., & Ellis, T. (2010). A retrograde step: The potential impact of high visibility uniforms within youth justice reparation. *Howard Journal, 49*(1), 18–30.

Patel, S., & Stanley, S. (2008). *The use of the community order and the suspended sentence order for women*. London: Centre for Crime and Justice Studies.

Pease, K. (1985). Community service orders. In M. Tonry & N. Morris (Eds.), *Crime and justice: An annual review of research* (Vol. 6). Chicago: University of Chicago Press.

Pease, K., Durkin, P., Earnshaw, I., Payne, D., & Thorpe, J. (1975). *Community service orders* (Home Office Research Study No 29). London: HMSO.

Rex, S., & Gelsthorpe, L. (2002). The role of community service in reducing offending: Evaluating Pathfinder projects in the UK. *Howard Journal, 41*(4), 311–325.

Rex, S., Gelsthorpe, L., Roberts, C., & Jordan, P. (2003). *An evaluation of Community Service Pathfinder projects: Final report 2002.* London: Home Office.

Richards, P., Richards, E., Devon, C., Morris, S., & Mellows-Facer, A. (2011). *Summary justice reform: Evaluation of the fiscal work order pilots.* Edinburgh: Scottish Government Social Research.

Schiff, M. (2003). Models, promises and the promise of restorative justice strategies. In A. Von Hirsch, J. Roberts, A. E. Bottoms, K. Roach, & M. Schiff, (Eds.), *Restorative justice and criminal justice: Competing or reconcilable paradigms?* Oxford: Hart.

Schneider, A. (1990). *Deterrence and juvenile crime: Results from a national policy experiment.* New York: Springer.

Scottish Government. (2012). *Reconviction rates in Scotland: 2009–10 offender cohort.* Edinburgh: Scottish Government.

Spaans, E. C. (1998). Community service in the Netherland: Its effects on recidivism and net-widening. *International Criminal Justice Review, 8,* 1–14.

Thomas, T., & Thompson, D. (2010). Making offenders visible. *Howard Journal, 49*(4), 340–348.

Travis, A. (2006) Reid wants army yo discipline young offenders, The Guardian, 22 July.

van Kalmthout, A. M., & Tak, P. J. P. (1988). *Sanctions-systems in the Member-States of the Council of Europe; Part 1: Deprivation of liberty, community service and other substitutes.* Deventer and Arnhem: Kluwer and Gouda Quint.

Ward, T. (2002). Good lives and the rehabilitation of sexual offenders: Promises and problems. *Aggression and Violent Behavior, 7,* 513–528.

Wermink, H., Blokland, A., Nieuwbeerta, P., Nagin, D., & Tollenaar, N. (2010). Comparing the effects of community service and short-term imprisonment on recidivism: A matched samples approach. *Journal of Experimental Criminology, 6,* 325–349.

Willis, G., & Ward, T. (2013). The good lives model: Evidence that it works. In L. Craig, L. Dixon, & T. A. Gannon (Eds.), *What works in offender rehabilitation: An evidence based approach to assessment and treatment.* Colchester: John Wiley.

What Is Probation's Role in Successful Social Integration (Resettlement) of People Leaving Prison? A Piece in the Jigsaw

Maurice Vanstone

The epithet 'Compassion in the face of evil is no virtue' outside a neo-Baptist church near an American Midwestern prison, which shocked Haney (2005), seems an appropriate symbol for this age in which the number of people being imprisoned, in countries such as America and the United Kingdom, is increasing inexorably while the morality and efficacy of imprisonment remains unchallenged. Primed by what Serin et al. (2010) term a conservative ideology, punish and be damned has become an acceptable political stance on crime by politicians who ostentatiously parade an increased prison population as a measure of their political credentials. Meanwhile, constructive notions such as probation not only face demands to demonstrate their worth but also struggle for survival.

It is against this dispiriting backcloth that this chapter attempts to throw some light on what constitutes the successful resettlement (or re-entry) of ex-prisoners into the community, and what part probation plays, or might play, in this process. It is structured so that a sift

M. Vanstone (✉)
Swansea University, Swansea, UK

© The Editor(s) (if applicable) and The Author(s) 2016
F. McNeill et al. (eds.), *Probation*,
DOI 10.1057/978-1-137-51982-5_7

129

through the evidence relating to the success or promise of resettlement will be preceded by a rehearsal of the practical and moral reasons for state involvement in offering those leaving prison the opportunity to claim a purposeful and constructive role in the community; a brief resumé of the history of rehabilitative work with prisoners; an exploration of the effects of imprisonment; a reminder of what we know about the characteristics of those people who most often end up in prison; and a resumé of the problems that need to be overcome in order to make the successful transition from confinement to freedom. For as Parker (1963, p. 68) so movingly explained, '[the] real difficulties which face men like Charlie Smith when they are free in society, and which face society when they are free among us, only begin to appear in all their desperate complexity, both to him and to those who concern themselves with him, at the point a film might end: when he comes out'.

Some Practical and Moral Issues

So why should society be concerned about the success or otherwise of the resettlement (the preferred term in this chapter) of the ex-prisoner? To begin with, such concern is a manifestation of the compassion singularly lacking in the church sign referred to above: however, compassion is not in itself enough. The question demands both a pragmatic and moral answer; pragmatic because punishment of the individual invariably has unintended negative consequences for the rest of society, and moral because punishment is haphazard and non-specific in its effect. It inflicts pain in unequal measure not just on the perpetrators of crime but on their families and social circles: to put it simply, the scales of justice lack precision. Imprisonment is a deliberate, calculated judicial infliction of pain, on the face of it designed to reduce the harm caused by crime, and it is from that unsettling paradox that the core problems of prisoner resettlement derive. Indeed, it is not difficult to demonstrate that the impact of imprisonment can be counterproductive for society and communities within it. The prison contains a uniquely powerful social environment with a capacity not only to debilitate those serving sentences within it but also to undermine the normative processes vital to the chances of successful resettlement.

This, in itself, provides a compelling reason to redirect the conversation about the impact of imprisonment so that it reflects interest in the social context of criminal behaviour and reinforces unashamedly compassionate values (Liebling and Maruna 2005). It is a conversation that should lead naturally to the conclusion that the amelioration of both the damage caused by imprisonment and the problems carried into the prison by prisoners is essential if they are to be able to lead constructive, crime-free lives and if society is to be afforded protection. However, in addition there must be a moral dimension to this conversation: pragmatism, important as it is, is not enough. As Raynor and Robinson (2009, p. 12) put it, '[T]he moral legitimacy of the state's demand that people refrain from offending is maintained if the state fulfils its duty to ensure that people's basic needs are met.' The legitimacy of criminal justice and penal systems is at stake too. Ward (2009, p. 119) is specific about the concepts of human dignity and rights when he argues that when punishment is imposed it should be done in a way that respects the person's human dignity because it is a 'foundation for human rights protocols and theories' and a cornerstone of rehabilitative effort. Essentially, once people have completed their sentences and served their punishment they have a right 'to be reconciled with the community' after release.

Although probation has an important role to play in this, any examination of that role and its effectiveness, of necessity, has to take account of the many other factors pertinent to the processes of successful resettlement. Moreover, it should be undertaken within the context of wider understanding of the problems faced by prisoners and ex-prisoners and the obvious and less obvious dynamics of the process of change. Pertinently, Raynor and Robinson (2009) ask whether probation can play a central role in rehabilitation for the benefit of potential victims of crime and society as a whole by contributing to welfare and social inclusion. Its future, if indeed it has one, depends on exactly that. Accordingly, the challenge facing probation will figure significantly in this chapter, but appropriately it will be placed alongside an examination of other normative features of resettlement.

A Brief and Partial History

Concern about the deleterious effects of imprisonment and the welfare of prisoners has not been the sole prerogative of probation, and internationally has invariably predated probation. For example, after-care has existed in Japan for centuries and the involvement of probation was not consolidated until as late as the 1950s (Hamai and Ville 1995). Moreover, throughout Europe, North America and Australia efforts to reform prisoners during their sentence and after release existed in various forms throughout the early and mid nineteenth century well before the onset of probation (Durnescu 2011; Durnescu et al. 2010; Forsythe 1987; Glueck 1928; Timasheff 1941; White 1976). Thus, for example, during the first two decades of the nineteenth century in England and Wales there was a particular interest in extending 'reformatory influence after release' for young prisoners by placing them in refuges to undergo industrial, moral and religious training (Forsythe 1987, p. 24). Contemporaneously, charities for discharged prisoners were formed to provide welfare for the general prison population and positioned near local county jails where they put an emphasis on emigration and employment. By the midpoint of the century they had multiplied; several emerged in Birmingham and in 1857 the Discharged Prisoners' Aid Society (DPSA) was established to serve prisoners released from the government prisons in London. Charitable though the latter was, it was not popular with all ex-prisoners because it had a rule by which prisoners deposited their release gratuity with the society so that it would not be squandered on alcohol (Priestley 1985). Nevertheless, they were deemed useful enough by government for legislation to be passed in 1862 to pave the way for cooperation between all societies, and that cooperation flourished to such an extent that by 1871 they were sufficiently organized to hold their first conference (Forsythe 1987; NADPAS 1956).

While voluntary involvement in resettlement continued well into the twentieth century in the United Kingdom and many other countries, the state's interest in the reform and resettlement of prisoners and formal procedures became more pervasive. In England and Wales early release on license was applied to penal servitude after 1857, and while it did not involve supervision it did focus on conditions related to employment and industriousness. Clearly it had an economic imperative because it provided a convenient source of mass labour with large groups of licensees being set to work on projects such as the building of the Broadmoor institution for the criminally insane. During the same period in Ireland, however, supervision was introduced. James Organ, a prominent lecturer of prisoners in Dublin, arranged employment for ex-prisoners and made visits every two weeks to both prisoner and employer (Forsythe 1987). In Romania, in 1874, societies of patronage were created near each prison in order to provide educational services during sentence and help with accommodation and employment after release; and within fifty years training and education were ensconced in the law as cornerstones of rehabilitation (Durnescu 2011). Again, in the United Kingdom, the 1894 Gladstone Report concluded that the responsibility for the rehabilitation of prisoners lay directly with the penal system, so creating an imperative for the government, which had been providing funding for the voluntary societies, to increase its involvement and extend its control (Davies 1974). Of course, this did not diminish voluntary effort, which continued and included the forebears of probation, the police court missionaries whose role was pivotal to the later involvement of probation. From the mid nineteenth century onwards they were engaged actively in work with discharged prisoners establishing prison gate missions, which provided food and spiritual guidance underpinned by pledges to abstain for alcohol, and labour yards which provided employment (Jarvis 1972; McWilliams 1983; Vanstone 2007).

Elsewhere in Europe, state involvement emerged at different times and in various forms (O'Brien 1995). In France, parole, involving early release, conditions and supervision, was applied to juveniles as early as 1830 and consolidated in later legislation. In 1885 it was extended to adults when prisoners were released half way through their sentence to the oversight of state-funded private agencies. Similar systems of parole were established in Portugal (1861), Saxony (1862), Germany (1871) and Denmark (1873). Subsequently, at the International Prison Congress of 1910 parole was legitimised over the whole of Europe, and in general involved supervision and/or oversight by private agencies. The story of resettlement in the Netherlands though, is interestingly different. The

Association for the Moral Reformation of Prisoners, which was formed in 1823, campaigned—in the face of the prevailing punitive consensus—for the right to visit and befriend prisoners, and provide material help and moral guidance via a scheme known as the 'free patron system' (Heijder (1973). At the beginning of the twentieth century in England and Wales, extensive state involvement was personified by the newly created probation officers who began supervising young boys released from the newly created Borstals and Approved Schools. It was a function which was extended by legislation in 1948 which made them responsible for the statutory after-care of prisoners released from preventative detention and corrective training (Bochel 1976; King 1969).

So, what can be learned from this history, and why is it of significance in an examination of the effectiveness of resettlement? To begin with, it demonstrates that this type of work with prisoners and ex-prisoners has always been infused with the ideals of rehabilitation. Traditionally, prisoners, despite the fact that they had transgressed against society, were considered worthy of help, and the slow but inexorable growth of state involvement was indicative of political (often religiously motivated) concerns with human rights, dignity and the uncomfortable moral dubiousness of punishment through the use of prison. On reflection it presents us with not only a sobering, moral counterbalance to the current politics of revenge and punitiveness, but also, perhaps, with some enduring lessons that can be applied to modern resettlement practice and theory. Much of the focus of work with prisoners described above was on building what is now termed social and human capital which as will be demonstrated later in this chapter are crucial to people's attempts to lead crime-free lives. Of course, that is not to deny that punishment was harsh and prison conditions cruel, but the prospect of redemption was always there. The psychology of the individual would become a dominant concern (Rose 1985, 1996), but internationally for much of the nineteenth century the process of resettlement concentrated on personal and social problems (in addition, of course, to the soul), the resolution of which, as will become clear later in the chapter, was deemed important to the success of resettlement. Even in a punitive age there was recognition of the negative impact of imprisonment as well as the problems of prisoners.

The Impact of Imprisonment and the Problems of Prisoners

Darrow (1919) may have been overstating his case when he said to prisoners in a Chicago prison that people are imprisoned because they are poor and in greater numbers when economic conditions are tough, but any examination of the personal and socio-economic problems of people who end up in prison—across time and international borders—lends weight to the general tenor of his argument.

For a period of fifty years or more research, whether in Scandinavia, Romania, the United Kingdom or America, has identified a familiar and consistent litany of problems faced by prisoners. So, in the 1960s in Denmark, Berntsen and Christiansen (1965) classified the problems of prisoners in terms of inadequate upbringing either in dysfunctional families or the care of the state, school difficulties, poor physical and mental health, vagrancy, alcohol abuse, divorce or problematical marriages. At the same time in the United Kingdom, Morris (1965; see also Corden 1983), drawing on interviews with 824 prisoners and 588 wives of prisoners, identified problems associated with poverty, unemployment, mental health, marital breakdown, and accommodation. Nearly a half a century later in America, Petersilia (2004) found imprisoned men to be disconnected from their families, to have significant levels of untreated substance abuse and mental health problems, to be poorly educated, to have low employment eligibility and to be facing legal and practical barriers to employment, housing and welfare. At about the same time in Romania, Durnescu and his colleagues (2002) identified the problems of prisoners as related to such things as accommodation, employment, education, family, addiction, mental health, anger management, poor problem-solving and thinking skills. In addition, research has shown that women experience further problems related to violence from partners, sexual abuse, social isolation and self-harm, and the problems of minority ethnic prisoners compounded by the additional difficulties of victimisation and racism (Carlen and Worrall 2004; Edgar 2007).

Even though it has been updated to some degree by notions of loss of agency, control and power, damage to sexual orientation, uncertainty, indeterminacy, self-government, and psychological assessment (Irwin and

Owen 2005; Crewe 2011), any review of the impact of imprisonment would be deficient without reference to Sykes's (1971) classic description of the pains experienced in a maximum security prison in America, namely deprivation of liberty, goods and services, heterosexual relationships, autonomy and security. The fact that imprisonment not only inflicts pain but also undermines and disrupts 'normative processes' heightens the need to seek further layers of understanding (Maruna 2007), and, as Haney (2005, p. 77) has argued, that additional understanding has to be placed within the context of 'situational, community and structural variables'. This is exactly what Snacken (2010) does in her discussion of her own Belgian studies and a study of women in French prisons, and in so doing sketches out an insightful review of the complexities of the impact of prison and offers some pointers to potential effectiveness (see next section). While acknowledging the continuing relevance of Sykes's analysis, she delineates a range of factors associated with variable effects. Thus, differentials in psycho-social effects are related to entry into prison (typically but not exclusively, self-harm, suicide, and heightened levels of stress); short-term sentences (typically, heightened aggression, deterioration in social and family relationships, and depression); and long-term sentences (typically, institutionalisation, emotional regression, apathy, total dependence, and fear of release). Furthermore, she argues, the type of regime and/or prison culture (for example, instrumentally focused on custody, security and discipline or else humanistically focused on contact, interaction and negotiation) and the personal psychology and social experience of the individual prisoner will invariably add further layers of complexity in terms of reactions and impacts. As Crewe (2011, p. 524) puts it, '[in] leaving prisoners in a state of ontological uncertainty, and in tying them into their own subjection, it resembles the dystopian projections of Orwell and Kafka'. If it was not clear before, that assessment and Snacken's unpicking of the impact of imprisonment demonstrate the potentially deep pitfalls facing any search for success in resettlement effort.

Effectiveness

The starting point of that search has to be clarity about what is meant by effectiveness, and this is helped considerably by the observations of

Farrall and Calverley (2006) and Maruna (2007). In their view, effectiveness is not simply about avoiding offending but incorporates the broader concept of desistance, which within their definition combines a crime-free life with positive living. Maruna (2007, p. 657), in a useful tour of various desistance theories, highlights not their differences but rather their commonality, namely that 'desistance should be associated with the achievement of competence, autonomy and success in the prosocial world (usually in the form of a career) and the development of intimate interpersonal bonds (usually in the form of a family)'. Farrall and Calverley put some flesh on these bones by reference to Farrall's (2002) earlier study of desistance and the results of interviews with fifty-one people in the process of desistance. Their concern is with what they term secondary (permanent) desistance and in setting out the life circumstances of the people in their sample they confirm the importance of the role of good social contexts and resolution of problems in desistance. Whilst not excluding group programmes, they argue for one-to-one, high-quality personal relationships to be the main conduit for achievable and significant change. Crucially, they provide a timely reminder of how slow and incremental change is, and how rarely, if ever, desistance comes from road to Damascus-type epiphanies; instead it emanates from the same factors, experiences, insights, life changes and events that contribute to change experienced by people in general. What might be described as the normality of change is given immediacy by their four phase schema—early hopes, intermediate, penultimate and normalcy—and the emphasis they place on optimism. Motivation begins with aspiration and is bolstered by optimism about the possibility of change, which comes full circle to the idea of citizenship. Farrall and Calverly put stress on the relationship between desistance and what they call citizenship values: in a sense, being viewed as a citizen links to behaving as a citizen. In these terms, resettlement work by agencies such as probation needs to begin with citizenship values and eschew authoritarianism and regulation by reinforcing crucial aspects of informal social controls and engaging with the resolution of relevant, practical problems. Most importantly, each agency such as probation needs to view itself as just one piece in a jigsaw.

Given an acceptance of that claim, what can be said of the positive impact probation work has on resettlement? What do we know? The straight answer to both questions is that, as Petersilia (2004) has pointed out, cumulative research evidence leaves us with uncertainty compounded by the issue of definition and different methodologies (namely, psychology and criminology). Petersilia identifies three problems with the available evidence from both the psychological and the criminological fields: first, there are too few robust and randomised evaluations; second, recidivism is characteristically the sole criterion of effectiveness; and third, many research conclusions do not 'have the appearance of truth and reality' (7) and, therefore, are not believed in by practitioners. More fundamentally, she exposes the lack of a dynamic relationship between research and policy, and argues for the fields to join together to 'produce scientifically credible evaluations of reentry programs that practitioners believe work' (8). Clarifying what might be effective is made even more difficult by Maruna's (2007) reminder that currently there is still no clear theory of how resettlement might work. Maruna et al. (2004, p. 10) put this 'theoretical vacuum' down partly to current day fear of experimentation, failure to ask how and why resettlement might work alongside what works, and a lack of 'cross-fertilization between desistence theory and re-entry practice'. With reference to Prochaska and DiClemente's (1982) cycle of change model, they argue that intervention should concern itself with putting wind in the sails of natural desistance processes. Perhaps, their recycling of past but still potent ideas might be further enriched by reference back to Pincus and Minahan's (1973, p. 62) model of social work practice with its idea of collaborative action systems such as the family of a person with an alcohol-related problem or 'employment office worker, employers, a welfare worker, a teacher at a vocational school, and others' coordinated by a probation officer. This sits more than comfortably alongside the facilitation of natural desistance processes and the realisation that because of the range of problems and the societal, political and organisational factors at work, successful resettlement work is dependent inevitably on multi-agency work. This chapter would be seriously deficient if its focus was on anything else other than the *contribution* of probation to the process of social reintegration alongside other factors.

Farrall (2002, 2004) is particularly helpful on this issue. He looks specifically at how social capital relates to desistance, and drawing on his study of 200 probationers concludes, albeit tentatively, that the particular and dynamic variables of family and employment have a correlation with desistance from crime. This leads naturally to his assessment that strengthening those aspects of social capital (desistance-related as opposed to merely offence-related needs) should be a policy and practice focus of probation. Interestingly, this back-to-the-future theme reminds me of my own experience of what is after all the traditional role of the probation officer in the United Kingdom. While training in 1968, I accompanied a very experienced probation officer on a visit to a terraced house in the Docks area of Cardiff and observed him negotiate an agreement with the parents of a young boy who was on the verge of losing his liberty, and this agreement was self-evidently about bolstering the boy's social capital (although that is not how I conceptualised it at the time). In that small front room I observed practice incorporating cycles of change, action systems, and Farrall's proposed innovations in practice before I had even heard the words treatment intervention let alone social capital, and it left me with an indelible understanding that a probation officer's job was, in essence, to do with offering tangible, relevant help with, among other things, employment, accommodation, parenting and family problems.

Notwithstanding this history and current uncertainty, there remain reasons for optimism. The available evidence does throw some light on aspects of resettlement work that offer promise of success (Clancy et al. 2006; Maguire 2007; Maguire and Raynor 2006; Zamble and Quinsey 1997; Maruna 2002), and these in turn contain pointers for future probation policy and practice. Essentially, at their root lies a clear reminder of the importance of collaborative relationships underpinned not only by empathy, mutual respect, genuineness and concreteness but also the principles of continuity (Robinson 2005). A relatively recent example, the resettlement 'Pathfinder' research of England and Wales, demonstrated a correlation between a continuous relationship between worker and prisoner and lower reconvictions (Clancy et al. 2006): prisoners who did not maintain contact were more likely to go on to further offending. In addition, more positive outcomes were associated with short pre-release programmes plus follow-up contact and provision of resettlement services. In other words, programmes themselves are not enough—a finding that resonates with one of the conclusions of the STOP experiment in Wales that reinforcement of skills and knowledge acquired in the programme was crucial to the transition to a more pro-social way of life and sustained desistance (Raynor and Vanstone 1996). Put simply, positive gains in problem-solving skills need to be sustained in order to maintain a prosocial way of life.

Zamble and Quinsey's (1997) research based on interviews with released male prisoners in Ontario is relevant to this point in as much as it shows that individual reaction to problems is highly pertinent to the consideration of what might lead to the cessation of offending or otherwise. It highlighted the fact that lack of success in dealing with problems, whether practical or personal, reduced optimism about the prospects of change, stimulated negative emotions and thereby triggered a cycle of failure and demotivation. The researchers concluded that there was a strong correlation between recidivism and poor or negative reactions to common problems. This is exactly the kind of complexity inherent in the resettlement process which was identified by Snacken (2010) when she put forward the importance of both the dimension of the individual's coping strategies, motivation and personal resources, and the appropriate responses by services for prisoners before and after release. Interestingly, further light is cast on the nature of the individual's capacity to deal with problems and setbacks by Maruna's (2000) research. His interviews with people who had an offending history suggested that the nature of their self-talk, or what he calls narrative, was key to successful desistance. Those people who felt that they had control over their day-to-day decisions and could influence positively the direction of their lives were more likely to desist from an offending way of life than those who felt that outside factors determined what happened to them. Desisters were optimistic and strategic about their futures, whereas those who continued to offend lacked any sense of where life might take them.

Important and illuminating though these findings are, they are not particularly new. Espousing the importance of self-efficacy (Bandura 1982) and self-disabling talk (Ellis and Dryden 1997) has long and distinguished history, and has been revisited by many researchers and commentators, but in this context it is worth reflecting again on Bandura's musings about self-efficacy:

Self-perceptions of efficacy are not simply inert estimates of future action. Self-appraisals of operative capabilities function as one set of proximal determinants of how people behave, their thought patterns, and the emotional reactions they experience in taxing situations (122–3).

Disabling self-talk has its root in irrational beliefs and as Ellis and Dryden (1997, p. 5) point out, Rational Emotive Behaviour Therapy's 'unique contribution to the field of cognitive-behaviour therapy lies in its distinction between rational and irrational beliefs'. Whereas rational beliefs are flexible and do not hinder the achievement of goals, irrational beliefs are rigid and dogmatic and impede the successful achievement of goals and require challenging through cognitive restructuring.

It seems clear, therefore, that those engaged in resettlement work should concentrate not only on the resolution of problems and the creation of opportunities to change, but also on how people view the possibilities of change and success; and, in so doing, they should support and reinforce positive thinking. The resettlement Pathfinders study (Clancy et al. 2006; Lewis et al. 2007) of projects using the FOR … A Change programme (Fabiano and Porporino 2002) is an interesting example. The overall aim of this thirteen-session programme is to increase participants' motivation and encourage them to set goals for change: the emphasis, therefore, is on self-efficacy, confidence, optimism and self-belief. The group leaders were trained to work in a non-directive way in order to subtly tip the balance away from resistance to change, to establish a collaborative partnership, and to encourage self-direction. With the latter in mind, participants are helped to identify and clarify their current state, establish their desired future state, and formulate an action plan, utilising their own and community resources, which not only works towards that desired state but prepares them to deal with setbacks. The programme has been run within prisons and so provides an ideal way of preparing for release, but it can also be community based.

The strong message, therefore, of cumulative research is that the creation of positive opportunities of change for people without a concomitant and genuine desire for change is likely to lead to failure. Motivation and belief in, and optimism about, capacity to change are fundamental characteristics of people who respond positively to the problems they face, particularly after imprisonment. Resettlement workers, therefore, need to help people make effective use of resettlement services and to encourage ownership of the process of change. Also, as late 20th-century shifts in policy (most recently in Romania) confirm, the removal of all impediments to successful resettlement is dependent, among other things, on reinforcing the connections between the prisoner, the family and the community, and in its various formats around the world probation has always been associated with this kind of work (Durnescu et al. 2010). Usefully, Serin et al. (2010, p. 55) add that successful resettlement 'requires utilizing more systematic assessment, incorporating community intervention, and implementing human services with fidelity and humanity'; they outline a model which incorporates commitment to change, internal change factors (belief in the capacity to change or what they call agency), external change factors (including social capital), and desistance correlates (significant events).

Current research is vital, but as one of the earliest examinations of the impact of resettlement work undertaken by Berntsen and Christiansen (1965 referred to above) attests, lessons from the past should not be forgotten. Using randomised and control methodologies, the researchers compared an experimental group of 126 prisoners with a control group. The programme of help began in the early stage of the sentence and involved an intensive programme which followed various in-depth assessments and the formulation of a treatment plan vetted by the project committee. Help was given with family problems, addictions, emotional difficulties, accommodation, clothing, trade union and health insurance scheme membership, work and contacts with relevant agencies. Emphasis was placed on the development of trusting relationships between helper and helped and support was offered for between one and two years after release. In a follow-up lasting at least six, and for the majority, seven and eight years, 41 per cent of the experimental group reconvicted compared with 58 per cent of the control group. Moreover, those who did reconvict committed less serious offences and offended later than the control group. The researchers also concluded that treatment had most effect with medium-risk prisoners.

All of that said, effectiveness in itself is not the only issue. Just as there is a moral dimension to the justification for providing resettlement services so there is one to consideration of effectiveness, and in this respect *just community theory* as put forward many years ago by Kohlberg et al. (1975) is of particular relevance and worth revisiting. It might simply be a reminder of how far authoritarianism and punitiveness as come in modern corrections, but it might also offer an interesting dimension to the essential components of successful resettlement. Based on the idea of a democratic community (which admittedly might be an unrealistic notion for the general prison population), it might nevertheless contain some principles that might be applied, thus enhancing the potential for successful resettlement. The theory promotes a moral-based approach to prison life founded on fairness, justice and conflict resolution, principles which encompass both rehabilitation and control, and thereby facilitate more human interactions between staff and prisoners. On the one hand, staff eschew roles of detection, authority and punishment, while, on the other hand, prisoners through participation in moral engagements develop self-responsibility and moral character. Furthermore, within relationships founded on loyalty and trust prisoners develop a better understanding of moral issues in society and are more likely to choose different patterns of life outside. It fits with the idea of the imprisoned as citizens as opposed to banished deviants (Priestley and Vanstone 2010) and has some interesting precedents, albeit in the specialist field of psychiatric disturbance (Rawlings 1998). The democratic model survives at Grendon Underwood in England and in small units in Shotts and Peterhead prisons in Scotland, which were established after the closure in 1995 of the Barlinnie Special Unit for what was described as 'regime slippage'. Specialist prisons of this kind exist in Denmark, Finland, Holland, Sweden and Switzerland; and there are 15 socio-therapeutic institutions in Germany. Indeed, the Slovenian prison system is largely based on this model (Rawlings 1998). According to Rawlings, most studies reveal a positive impact on both reconviction and the behaviour of men (and *it is* a predominantly male provision) while in prison. Admittedly, these are effects on a particular section of the prison population but lessons might be drawn from this overall model or approach and applied to prison regimes and resettlement programmes in general.

Snacken's (2010) work on the nature of regimes referred to above is instructive here. She lists four ideal types of relationships between staff and prisoners: formal (characterised by distant relationships); conflict interaction (negative image, lack of mutual respect); negotiated interactions (still hierarchical but mutual respect); and personalised (still unequal

relationships between 'helper' and 'helped' but mutual respect, coopera-
tive). So, if the ideal of democratically based prison regimes is unrealistic in the current socio-political climate, at the very least we should be
guided by evidence that successful re-entry depends on the prison experience approximating life outside and thus encouraging self-responsibility,
participation, motivation for change and preparedness for release.

Conclusion and Discussion

Resettlement work, then, has a long international history involving varied voluntary agencies and latterly services provided by the state, and premised on among other things religious zeal, philanthropic and charitable
ideology, psychological theory, ideals of criminal justice and currently a
number of theories clustered under the term desistance. Gradually, and
particularly during the first half of the twentieth century a role in all this
was carved out for probation in its various forms across the world. It has
played a significant but at times overstated role, and its future involvement will be determined by differing political decisions made at national
level. How probation responds to the challenges presented by resettlement depends on how well it is placed in different countries to deliver a
contribution. Those political decisions will leave it better placed in some
countries than others. In England and Wales its role has been diminished lately by less than friendly governmental policies of privatisation
and marketisation.

Ironically, this has come at a time when research is revealing that
high levels of practitioner skill have a positive impact on probationers'
motivation and commitment to change. One such study, described in
detail in Raynor et al. (2010), involved the observation and assessment of
ninety-five video recordings of normal supervisory interviews. A check-
list designed specifically to identify core correctional practices shown by
research to be aligned closely with the reduction of offending and to be
used post research by practitioners themselves was used for each interview
(Andrews and Kiessling 1980; Dowden and Andrews 2004). Although
scores varied significantly across the observed recordings, the scores for
higher-rated staff were consistent and those staff used a wide range of

skills. Moreover, in a follow-up of seventy-five of those interviewed a comparison was made of the reconviction rates of those interviewed by staff with a higher skill rating against those interviewed by staff with lower ratings, and the former did significantly better than the latter. The implication to be drawn from this is that skills are important, and staff who use a wide range of skills effectively will produce better outcomes. Therefore, high-quality probation supervision can play a significant role in the reduction of offending when it involves, first, the use of relationship skills (such as clear communication, listening attentively, creating an environment conducive to helping, positivity, conveying optimism, empathy, being clear about roles and responsibilities), and, second, the use of structuring skills (such as problem-solving, motivation building, subtle challenging, reflection, supporting self-efficacy, developing discrepancies and rolling with resistance). Interestingly, the majority of probation officers in Jersey had experienced social work training, and what can be inferred from the study's findings is that traditional social work skills within a structure of motivational interviewing, pro-social modelling, problem-solving and cognitive structuring can be a potent ingredient of resettlement work (Miller and Rollnick 2002; Trotter 1993; Fabiano and Porporino 2002; Raynor and Vanstone 2015). The obvious caveat here is that other research makes clear that this contribution has to be informed by more general research findings on what is now termed desistance from offending. As Maruna (2007) points out, effectiveness must relate to the wider notion of desistance which covers positive lifestyle as well as avoidance of crime. Accordingly, in collaboration with significant others, probation should focus on the problems related to offending as well as the behaviour and thinking that led to imprisonment, and promote and stimulate a prisoner-led process of change which pays heed to and recognises the importance of a number of equally important elements in the processes connected to successful resettlement.

In the heyday of the treatment model the individual was seen invariably as the passive recipient of the gift of help from a suitably skilled helper capable of diagnosing the problem, whereas now it is not overstating the core lesson from effectiveness research to say that the success of resettlement, more than anything else, hinges on both the participation of the individual in their own problem-solving processes and the nature and quality of that participation. In turn, that participation is wholly dependant on adherence to notions of collaborative relationships and joint planning of action plans as set out over thirty years ago in the Social Skills and Problem Solving Model (Priestley et al. 1978). Consistent with this kind of approach is McNeill's (2006) desistance paradigm, which puts processes rather than intervention at the fore and stresses the importance of identifying the unique nature of each individual's change process and how its wheels might best be oiled. The worker's role, therefore, is one of being 'an advocate providing a conduit to social capital as well as a "treatment" provider building human capital' (McNeill 2006, p. 57). Moreover, because evidence suggests that negative reactions to everyday problem situations lead to re-offending, workers need to pay specific attention to the individual's ability to deal with the personal and practical problems to be faced; and that ability will be strengthened by the contribution to be made by family or other important members of the person's social network. The effective resettlement worker facilitates the exploitation of those aspects of social capital, encourages and reinforces positivity and optimism about the possibility of change and pays genuine heed to individual rather than general needs and problems.

The building of human and social capital, including both help with the acquisition of a wider and adaptive range of skills and referral to appropriate points of help, is important too in laying the groundwork for relapse prevention strategies, so that setbacks can be dealt with positively within a realistic process of change: realistic because as McNeill (2006, p. 47) affirms, 'desistance itself is not an event (like being cured of a disease) but a *process*' (italics in the original). As stated above, desistance-related change is invariably slow and incremental and the effective worker knows this from their self-reflection and self-awareness. Reflective workers are more likely to enhance the potential for success of the resettlement strategy by developing relationships based on trust and mutual respect, but their capacity to achieve this will be inhibited by structures that hamper continuity in the working relationship and fracture the connection between work within the prison and work undertaken after release. One aspect of bridging work of that kind is direct encouragement of the individual prisoner to make efforts to gain community acceptance by taking responsibility for behaviour and make amends through a strengths-based approach which provides tangible and practical help to members of their community, maybe with the assistance of a mentor (Clancy et al. 2006). However, strength-based approaches, as exemplified by the example of using prisoners as Citizens Advice Bureau volunteers, have to be protected against their vulnerability to counter-productive forces (Burnett and Maruna 2006). Finally, all of these promising ingredients of successful resettlement work whether by probation officers or other key workers depend for their success on the motivation of the individual prisoner. That motivation will vary from person to person and will be influenced by individual experience, cultures within prison, and the social and political environment in which ex-prisoners dwell: exclusion and demonisation demoralise and debilitate. In the face of all this, the ability of probation workers to assist the individual in the process of motivation building has never been more important.

References

Andrews, D. A., & Kiessling, J. J. (1980). Program structure and effective correctional practices: A summary of the CaVIC research. In R. R. Ross & P. Gendreau (Eds.), *Effective correctional treatment*. Toronto: Butterworth.

Bandura, A. (1982). Self-efficacy mechanism in human agency. *American Psychologist, 32*(2), 122–147.

Berntsen, K., & Christiansen, K. (1965). A resocialization experiment with short-term offenders. *Scandinavian Studies in Criminology, 1*, 35–54.

Bochel, D. (1976). *Probation and after-care: Its development in England and Wales*. Edinburgh: Scottish Academic Press.

Burnett, R., & Maruna, S. (2006). The kindness of prisoners: Strengths-based resettlement in theory and in action. *Criminology and Criminal Justice, 6*(1), 83–106.

Carlen, P., & Worrall, A. (2004). *Analysing women's imprisonment*. Cullompton: Willan.

Clancy, A., Hudson, K., Maguire, M., Peake, R., Raynor, P., Vanstone, M., et al. (2006). *Getting out and staying out: Results of the prisoner Resettlement Pathfinders* (Researching criminal justice series). Bristol: University of Bristol and Policy Press.

Corden, J. (1983). Persistent petty offenders: Problems and patterns of multiple disadvantage. *Howard Journal of Criminal Justice, XXII*, 69–90.

Crewe, B. (2011). Depth, weight and tightness: Revisiting the pains of imprisonment. *Punishment and Society, 13*(5), 509–529.

Darrow, C. (1919). *Address to the prisoners in the Chicago Jail*. Chicago: Charles Kerr.

Davies, M. (1974). *Prisoners of society: Attitudes and after-care*. London: Routledge and Kegan Paul.

Dowden, C., & Andrews, D. A. (2004). The importance of staff practice in delivering effective correctional treatment: A meta-analytic review of core correctional practice. *International Journal of Offender Therapy and Comparative Criminology, 48*(2), 203–214.

Durnescu, I. (2011). *Resettlement research and practices. An international perspective*. A report commissioned by the European Organisation for Probation Confederation of European Probation. Uthecht.

Durnescu, I., Dobrica, P. M., & Bejan, C. (2010). Prison rehabilitation in Romania. *Journal of Criminal Justice and Security, 2*, 181–195.

Durnescu, I., Lazar, C., & Shaw, R. (2002). Incidence and characteristics of Roma men in Romanian prisons. *Howard Journal of Criminal Justice, 41*(3), 237–244.

Edgar, K. (2007). Black and minority ethnic prisoners. In Y. Jewkes (Ed.), *Handbook of prisons*. Cullompton: Willan.

Ellis, A., & Dryden, W. (1997). *The practice of rational emotive behavior therapy* (2nd ed.). New York: Springer.

Fabiano, E., & Porporino, F. (2002). *Focus on resettlement—A change*. Ottawa, ON: T3 Associates.

Farrall, S. (2002). *Rethinking what works with offenders*. Cullompton: Willan.

Farrall, S. (2004). Social capital and offender reintegration: Making probation desistance focused. In S. Maruna & R. Immarigeon (Eds.), *After crime and punishment*. Cullompton: Willan.

Farrall, S., & Calverley, A. (2006). *Understanding desistance from crime: Theoretical directions in resettlement and rehabilitation*. Maidenhead: Open University Press.

Forsythe, W. J. (1987). *The reform of prisoners 830–1900*. London: Croom Helm.

Glueck, S. (1928). Principles of a rational code. *Harvard Law Review, 41*, 453–482.

Hamai, K., & Ville, R. (1995). Origins and purpose of probation. In K. Hamai, R. Ville, R. Harris, M. Hough, & U. Zveki (Eds.), *Probation round the world*. London: Routledge.

Haney, C. (2005). The contextual revolution in psychology and the question of prison effects. In A. Liebling & S. Maruna (Eds.), *The effects of imprisonment*. Cullompton: Willan.

Heijder, A. (1973). Some aspects of the Dutch Probation System: A search for identity. *International Journal of Offender Therapy and Comparative Criminology, 17*, 106–110.

Irwin, J., & Owen, B. (2005). Harm and the contemporary prison. In A. Liebling & S. Maruna (Eds.), *The effects of imprisonment*. Cullompton: Willan.

Jarvis, F. (1972). *Advise, assist and befriend: A history of the probation and after-care service*. London: National Association of Probation Officers.

King, J. (1969). *The probation and after-care service* (3rd ed.). London: Butterworth.

Kohlberg, L., Kauffman, K., Scharf, P., & Hickey, J. (1975). The just community approach to corrections: A theory. *Journal of Moral Education, 4*(3), 243–260.

Lewis, S., Maguire, M., Raynor, P., Vanstone, M., & Vennard, J. (2007). What works in resettlement? Findings from seven Pathfinders for short-term prisoners in England and Wales. *Criminology and Criminal Justice, 7*(1), 33–53.

Liebling, A., & Maruna, S. (2005). *The effects of imprisonment*. Cullompton: Willan.

Maguire, M. (2007). The resettlement of ex-prisoners. In L. Gelsthorpe & R. Morgan (Eds.), *Handbook of probation*. Cullompton: Willan.

Maguire, M., & Raynor, P. (2006). How the resettlement of prisoners promotes desistence from crime: Or does it? *Criminology and Criminal Justice, 6*(1), 17–36.

Maruna, S. (2000). *Making good: How ex-convicts reform and rebuild their lives*. Washington, DC: American Psychological Association.

Maruna, S. (2007). After prison, what? The ex-prisoner's struggle to desist from crime. In Y. Jewkes (Ed.), *Handbook of prison*. Cullompton: Willan.

Maruna, S., Immarigeon, R., & LeBel, T. P. (2004). Ex-offender reintegration: Theory and practice. In S. Maruna & R. Immarigeon (Eds.), *After crime and punishment*. Cullompton: Willan.

McNeill, F. (2006). A desistance paradigm for offender management. *Criminology and Criminal Justice, 6*(1), 39–62.

McWilliams, W. (1983). The mission to the English Police Courts 1876–1936. *Howard Journal of Criminal Justice, 22*, 129–147.

Miller, W. R., & Rollnick, S. (2002). *Motivational interviewing: Preparing people for change* (2nd ed.). New York: Guildford.

Morris, P. (1965). *Prisoners and their families*. London: Allen and Unwin.

NADPAS. (1956). *Handbook of the National Association of Discharged Prisoners' Societies*. London: NADPAS.

O'Brien, P. (1995). The prison on the continent: Europe 1865–1965. In N. Morris & D. Rothman (Eds.), *The Oxford history of the prison: The practice of punishment in western society*. Oxford: Oxford University Press.

Parker, T. (1963). *The unknown citizen*. London: Hutchinson.

Petersilia, J. (2004). What works in prisoner reentry? *Federal Probation, 68*(2), 4–8.

Pincus, A., & Minahan, A. (1973). *Social work practice: Model and method*. Itasca, IL: F. E. Peacock.

Priestley, P. (1985). *Victorian prison lives: English prison biography 1830–1914*. London: Methuen.

Priestley, P., McGuire, J., Flegg, D., Hemsley, V., & Welham, D. (1978). *Social skills and personal problem solving: A Handbook of Methods*. London: Tavistock.

Priestley, P., & Vanstone, M. (2010). *Offenders or citizens? Readings in rehabilitation*. Cullompton: Willan.

Prochaska, J. O., & DiClemente, C. C. (1982). Transtheoretical therapy: Toward a more integrative model of change. *Psychotherapy: Theory, Research and Practice, 19*, 276–288.

Rawlings, B. (1998). *Research on Therapeutic Communities in prisons: A review of the literature*. Produced for the Prison Service. University of Manchu.

Raynor, P., & Robinson, G. J. (2009). Why help offenders? Arguments for rehabilitation as a penal strategy. *European Journal of Probation, 1*(1), 3–20.

Raynor, P., Ugwudike, P., & Vanstone, M. (2010). Skills and strategies in probation supervision: The Jersey study. In F. McNeill, P. Raynor, & C. Trotter (Eds.), *Offender supervision: New directions in theory, research and practice*. Willan: Cullompton.

Raynor, P., & Vanstone, M. (1996). Reasoning and rehabilitation in Britain: The results of the Straight Thinking On Probation (STOP) programme. *International Journal of Offender Therapy and Comparative Criminology, 40*, 279–291.

Raynor, P., & Vanstone, M. (2015). Moving away from social work and half way back again: New research on skills in probation. *British Journal of Social Work*, First published online February 12.

Robinson, G. J. (2005). What works in offender management. *Howard Journal of Criminal Justice, 44*(3), 307–318.

Rose, N. (1985). *The psychological complex: Psychology, politics and society in England 1869–1939*. London: Routledge and Kegan Paul.

Rose, N. (1996). Psychiatry as a political science: Advanced liberalism and the administration of risk. *History of the Human Sciences, 9*(2), 1–23.

Serin, R. C., Lloyd, C. D., & Hanby, L. J. (2010). Enhancing offender re-entry: An integrated model for enhancing offender re-entry. *European Journal of Probation, 2*(2), 53–75.

Snacken, S. (2010). The effects of imprisonment. In M. Herzog-Evans (Ed.), *Transnational criminology manual* (Vol. 3). Nijmegan: Wolf Legal.

Sykes, G. M. (1971). *The society of captives: A study of a maximum security prison.* Princeton, NJ: Princeton University Press.

Timasheff, N. S. (1941). *One hundred years of probation 1841–1941, Part One: Probation in the United States, England and the British Commonwealth of Nations.* New York: Fordham University Press.

Trotter, C. (1993). *The supervision of offenders—What Works? A study undertaken in community based corrections, Victoria.* Melbourne: Social Work Department, Monash University and the Victoria Department of Justice.

Vanstone, M. (2007). *Supervising offenders in the community: A history of probation theory and practice* (Paperback ed.). Aldershot: Ashgate.

Ward, T. (2009). Dignity and human rights in correctional practice. *European Journal of Probation, 1*(2), 112–127.

White, S. (1976). Alexander Maconochie and the development of parole. *Journal of Criminal Law and Criminology, 67*(1), 72–88.

Zamble, E., & Quinsey, V. (1997). *The criminal recidivism process.* Cambridge: Cambridge University Press.

What Is the Impact of Probation on Satisfying the Public's Desire for Justice or Punishment?

Rob Allen

Introduction

In the Netherlands in 2007, a television documentary alleged that community sanctions were being used for very serious crimes such as homicide and rape. There was an extremely negative public response. An academic study showed that the actual behaviour involved in the 'very serious crimes' was much less serious than their label might have suggested, and that a period in prison had in most cases been imposed alongside the community supervision. But as a result, recidivists and serious cases were excluded from community sanctions and the assumed lack of public acceptance of them has resulted in continued efforts to stress their punitive nature (Boon and van Swaaningen 2013, p. 18).

This experience of mistaken public perceptions influencing the development of probation may be extreme but is not unique. The era of late modernity has brought with it a need for political responsiveness to pub-

R. Allen (✉)
Justice and Prisons, London, UK

© The Editor(s) (if applicable) and The Author(s) 2016
F. McNeill et al. (eds.), *Probation*,
DOI 10.1057/978-1-137-51982-5_8

153

lic and media pressure across a range of policy areas, but particularly strongly in the crime field. Penal populism has had a major impact on probation, whose underpinnings look to have been eroded as faith in rehabilitation and the welfare state have weakened.

Many of the developments—whether it is increasingly inflexible rates of breach for non-compliance with orders, the requirement that all community orders have a punitive element or the wearing of orange bibs while doing community payback—bear the hallmarks of electoral advantage taking precedence over penal effectiveness and a simplistic set of responses to a complex set of problems.

Yet it is neither desirable nor possible for probation to operate in a vacuum, insulated from media, political or public discourse. Increasing public understanding about and confidence in the work of probation services has been recognised as an explicit goal in many countries in recent years. Indeed the Council of Europe Probation Rules include as a key principle that 'the competent authorities and the probation agencies shall inform the media and the general public about the work of probation agencies in order to encourage a better understanding of their role and value in society' (Council of Europe 2010).

Probation must go some way towards meeting the public's desire for justice for four main reasons.

First, a great deal of probation work forms part of the sentencing arrangements in particular jurisdictions. The sentencing of offenders of course plays an important role in upholding social norms and responding to people who breach them. As a sentencing review carried out in England and Wales put it in 2001.

> The public, as a result, can legitimately be expected to uphold and observe the law, and not to take it into their own hands. To achieve this, there must be confidence in the justice of the outcomes, as well as in their effectiveness. Achieving a satisfactory level of public confidence is therefore an important goal of sentencing, and the framework for sentencing needs to support that goal. (Halliday 2001, p. 1)

While it may be possible to think that a criminal justice system could operate with little regard to detailed public concerns (Maruna and King 2008), public opinion being seen to justify and legitimise sentencing and other initiatives in the field 'constitutes a general trend in modern penal policy', in most Western countries at any rate (Ryberg and Roberts 2014, p. 3). Even in Denmark, usually seen as moderate in its criminal policy 'the claim that punishment should reflect public opinion has driven all penal reforms over the last decade' (ibid., p. 3).

Second, pragmatically, if law and policy in respect of community-based sentences are significantly out of step with public opinion, courts will find it harder to make use of such sentences and probation could wither on the vine. Research has found that 'it is particularly in the area of community penalties that judges are most likely to be apprehensive of public hostility' (Roberts 2002) and this may be more the case in jurisdictions in which the public are involved in sentencing. In England and Wales most criminal cases are sentenced by lay magistrates, who number well over 20,000 and see themselves as members of the public albeit with particular powers. A review of literature relating to conditional sentences concluded that 'if the public is (perceived to be) strongly opposed to suspended sentences, then over the course of time, they may fall into disfavour with the judiciary as well.' (Armstrong et al. 2013).

The third reason for the public to be concerned about probation relates to the specific work which probation services do to supervise convicted offenders in the community, whether they are serving community-based orders or have been released from prison. While crime has fallen in most Western countries over the last twenty years and is generally of much less concern as an issue to the public than it has been, the public continue to have legitimate expectations about what the authorities do to prevent it and how they supervise those who have broken the law—particularly those convicted of sexual and violent offences who are seen as a threat to public safety. It is not unreasonable for the public to expect whatever requirements have been imposed by the courts on offenders to be effectively implemented and that the full range of work with offenders—including that which aims to help them to desist from crime or make reparations to their victims or the community—to be carried out as assiduously and effectively as possible.

As the former Chief Inspector of Probation in England and Wales has put it,

> [T]he safety of the public in general, and of children in particular, are hugely sensitive areas of public concern. The Inspectorate has taken a

leading role in emphasising that risk to the public cannot be eliminated, but it is right to expect the relevant authorities to do their job properly. (Bridges 2010)

High-profile failures on the part of the probation service may have elicited a disproportionate response from governments, for example in England and Wales in the mid 2000s, and rightly or wrongly 'a relentless media focus had made matters of public protection a vital litmus test for the perceived competence of government (Silverman 2012).

Finally, as a largely taxpayer-funded service, probation along with other public services requires and deserves some level of scrutiny not only in respect of the tasks it undertakes on behalf of the community but also as to how it is organised and managed and the way resources are used to fund its activities. In England and Wales a recent and highly controversial reorganisation has placed 70 % of probation work in the hands of private companies. Anyone who read the Labour Party's crime manifesto before the 2015 election will have seen their view that the reckless privatisation of probation means dangerous offenders are more likely to be monitored by companies with no track record of success, putting public safety at risk (Labour Party 2015). A series of scandals involving private companies in criminal justice mean that their involvement in probation work is likely to be subject to particularly close scrutiny. The chair of the Magistrates Association in England and Wales told a parliamentary investigation that sentencers must have confidence that the sentence would be properly and effectively delivered and that it did not 'believe it should be driven by profit' (Justice Committee 2011).

Yet while there was a case to be made that probation should broadly reflect public sentiments about the kinds of cases which are suitable for its caseload, the effectiveness of its work and its mode of organisation, that is not to say that developments should be 'driven before the wind' of apparent public mood, regardless of the principles that need to govern it.[1]

This is particularly important because studies of public attitudes to justice are notoriously hard to interpret. Survey results, upon which

---

[1] The phrase was used in regard to sentencing in Halliday (2001), p. ii.

policy-makers and commentators rely in order to gauge the public mood, are highly dependent on the specific wording of the questions being asked.

A 2011 UK survey found that four-fifths of the public said they considered community sentences a soft punishment (Ashcroft 2011). Yet the vast majority of the respondents will have been unfamiliar with what such sentences entail. Without any explanation of the obligations they impose, the way they are enforced and their effects on those made subject to them, an uninformed public view is a highly unreliable talisman for the development of policy (as indeed it would be in health, education, defence or any other area).

Research suggests that increasing the public's understanding about community penalties makes them more acceptable. While a number of efforts have been made in this direction, rather more have been put into satisfying an uninformed public's desire for justice and punishment rather than trying to modify that desire through information, education and opportunities for participation.

The aim of this chapter is to look at the evidence about what the public think about probation and community penalties and draw out some of the possible implications for probation organisations and policy-makers. It broadens and updates the review carried out by Allen and Hough in 2007.

Following this introduction, we start by summarising the ways that probation activities address key dimensions of justice and punishment. Next we look at the broader context of public knowledge and understanding in the field of criminal justice before focussing specifically on probation. The penultimate section considers the drivers of public attitudes, while finally we look at how probation has responded to the challenge of satisfying public demands. The chapter concludes with some brief reflections.

Much of the evidence is taken from the United Kingdom, where, according to a recent study, 'more research has been undertaken into public attitudes to sentencing … than any other' (Hough et al. 2013, p. 16). But many of the trends, initiatives and challenges described have some at least resonance in other jurisdictions, or are likely to do so as probation work becomes better established.

Probation, Punishment and Justice

While the core of probation work in almost all countries involves the supervision of convicted offenders on court orders, probation agencies conduct a range of other tasks the precise combination of which varies from country to country.

These include the supervision of released prisoners and work inside penitentiaries. In addition probation plays an important role in providing reports to courts to assist in the sentencing process and in some countries works with defendants before trial. In some jurisdictions probation agencies work with the victims of crime, on wider crime prevention tasks and on a variety of miscellaneous activities such as the provision of support to the families of offenders, coordinating volunteer prison visitors and enforcing fines. How do these functions map onto the different dimensions of justice and punishment?

This is not the place to summarise the voluminous literature on the purposes of justice and the role of punishment within it but before assessing the impact which probation has on public views in this field it is important to consider briefly what, as a set of activities, probation can and cannot be expected to do.

In England and Wales, the law specifies five purposes of sentencing—the punishment of offenders, the reduction of crime (including its reduction by deterrence), the reform and rehabilitation of offenders, the protection of the public, and the making of reparation by offenders to persons affected by their offences. Probation can arguably make a contribution to all five of these purposes.

A recent analysis of how probation has managed not only to survive but also to thrive following a period of existential threat has identified its contribution to punitive, reparative, rehabilitative and managerial sanctions—the last referring to the way probation works to meet the needs of the criminal justice system by for example taking pressure off an overcrowded prison system (Robinson et al. 2013).

It is the reform and rehabilitation of offenders (and the reduction of crime—though until recently not by deterrence) that has historically been at the heart of probation and arguably still is. The first principle of the

European rules states that 'Probation agencies shall aim to reduce reoffending by establishing positive relationships with offenders in order to supervise (including control where necessary), guide and assist them and to promote their successful social inclusion (Council of Europe 2010).

Alongside, reform, rehabilitation and the reduction of crime, the now widespread availability of community service and the growing development of restorative justice in several countries give probation a central role in respect of reparation.

More problematic for probation are the remaining two purposes. The reference in the Probation Rules to 'control' and both the increasing practice of partnership work with the police and use of technology mean that probation can claim to play a role in the protection of the public. Making such claims is not without risks of course; failures by the London probation service in the supervision of serious offenders did immense damage to its reputation (Allen and Hough 2008) and, compared with imprisonment, community-based supervision can never guarantee public safety in the way some members of the public would appear to like. But the increasingly sophisticated multi-agency work to monitor the behaviour of serious offenders combined with efforts to tackle beliefs, attitudes and behaviour can comprise more effective protection packages than repeated spells of imprisonment alone.

The larger problem is perhaps provided by the first of the purposes—the punishment of offenders. There is of course a long-running debate about whether probation should be a punishment or an alternative to punishment—and whether indeed there is a third way in which probation can provide a 'useful' rather than 'punitive' punishment. It is true of course that probation's supervision of community orders places obligations and restrictions on freedom. Failure to comply with them can and does result in imprisonment. For our concerns in this chapter, the question is whether the punishment inherent in probation and community sentences is seen by the public as sufficient.

This is particularly important because in England and Wales at any rate, punishment is seen as particularly important by the public. Research carried out in 2009 found that 'in keeping with findings from surveys conducted in other jurisdictions, the public move towards the more punitive objectives of punishment and deterrence when considering the sentencing of serious crimes of violence'. (Hough et al. 2009). In this study, while participants in focus groups viewed all five purposes of sentencing as highly important, they 'seemed to place particular weight on punishment, and valued reparation somewhat less than the others'.

There seems to be considerable variation between different countries in respect of the public's desire for justice and punishment. When asked in an international survey about the appropriate sentence for a recidivist burglar, 34% of respondents from 16 countries preferred prison with a range from 56% in the USA to 7% in Catalonia. (Van Kesteren et al. 2014). A majority of respondents opted for community service, though not in the UK.

Public Knowledge and Attitudes About Criminal Justice and Probation: The Context of Crime and Criminal Justice

Research over the last twenty years has consistently shown that in general the public is not very well informed about matters relating to crime, the criminal justice system and sentencing—the contextual field in which attitudes to probation are grown.

In the UK, most people think that crime has been rising or been flat when according to police recorded data, victim surveys and expert views, there have been substantial and sustained falls since the mid 1990s. Mistaken though it is, a view that crime problem is getting worse (or at least no better) brings with it the corollary that current approaches to the problem are not working and a change in law, policy or practice is required.

One of the specific areas which is consistently seen to be failing is sentencing. In the UK a large majority of people say they want harsher punishments than those currently imposed. In 2011, in a typical poll, four out of five of respondents to an opinion poll thought that sentencing of convicted offenders was too lenient (Ashcroft 2011). In the same poll, three quarters believed 'offenders often commit further crimes while serving community sentences' and that 'community sentences are often given to offenders who ought to go to prison'. (ibid.).

In telephone or online surveys such as this, public views are sought in the absence of any real knowledge about existing levels of sentence severity or the use and practice of community sentencing. Respondents were asked their opinion on the basis of 'what you have heard' (ibid.).

While the public may say the system is too soft, we know from other research that in the UK at least most people underestimate sentencing severity, sometimes substantially so. When they are made aware of the actual use of custody, not surprisingly far fewer say that the courts are 'much too lenient'. We also know that when asked about sentencing actual cases, public opinion is generally in line with, and sometimes more lenient than actual sentencing practice.

A Punitive Public?

So perhaps the idea of a punitive public demanding tougher and tougher responses is something of a myth. Well yes and no. The simplistic view that the public want more punishment is certainly challenged by various pieces of evidence.

There are many surveys which show that while punishment is much more commonly preferred for violent crimes, there is considerable support for rehabilitation too. A recent UK study found that 'support for rehabilitating offenders remained high, even for those convicted of serious crimes of violence'. (Hough et al. 2009). It is not clear whether people have in mind rehabilitation within a custodial setting but the apparently widespread belief that people should be offered the opportunity to change is consistent with the principles of probation.

Other polls suggest reasonable levels of support for the principles underlying community penalties. A month after the 2011 riots in English cities, more than nine out of ten of those surveyed supported opportunities for offenders who had committed offences such as theft and vandalism to do unpaid work to pay back for what they had done. (Prison Reform Trust 2011) Again, it is possible that some at least may have had in mind this activity in addition to imprisonment rather than instead of it, but it is evidence of a more nuanced approach than is often appreciated.

Support for community penalties appears reasonable too when people who favour imprisoning an offender are asked about the acceptability of a community order. Substantial numbers find a community order to be acceptable once they are given details about what this would involve. For example, in Hough et al.'s (2009) study, over one-third of respondents who initially favoured imposition of custody for a case of assault found a community penalty to constitute an appropriate alternative sanction. The acceptability of a non-custodial sanction depended upon the seriousness of the offence, and whether the offender has previous convictions.

What this suggests is that when informed about what probation involves, more of the public will see its value. But there remain concerns about how these are put into practice.

The 2010–11 Crime survey in England and Wales found that less than a quarter of respondents were confident that the probation service 'is effective at preventing re-offending', and more than a quarter not at all confident. (Hough et al. 2013). While symptomatic of the fact that the public in all surveys tend to express less confidence in criminal justice agencies at the later stages of the criminal justice process—courts, probation and prisons—than they do in the police and prosecutors—because probation is associated with leniency and liberty it is perhaps especially vulnerable to public concern about its performance. In the 2011 UK poll, only 19 % of the public believed 'community sentences are effective at stopping offenders from reoffending'. As with opinions about the use of probation, attitudes to probation practice may not be well informed but it is clear that there are concerns—whether well founded or not—about the practice of probation as well as its use which need to be addressed.

An analysis of reports provided to the COST project on Offender Supervision in Europe concluded that 'there seems to exist an openness to and support for supervision in some countries, whereas public opinion is less positive in others. The general impression is that there is significant public support for community based sanctions where they can achieve constructive outcomes' (Durnescu et al. 2013). This conclusion mirrors a finding from a poll of victims of crime in the UK which found that 'effective community sentences offer the kind of justice victims want but they are not confident it can be delivered in practice (Victim Support 2012).

If nothing else the complex and contradictory nature of these findings suggest that much more sophisticated ways of analysing public attitudes to sentencing are needed. Methods such as deliberative panels and interviews show people's perceptions to be more sophisticated and flexible than is apparent from surveys.

Yet it is the results of surveys of an uniformed public to which policy makers generally give attention. They consider that people's default position is that sentencing is too lenient, that the wrong people are placed on community sentences and that supervision is not carried out effectively. Much evidence suggests that the more information a person has about a particular case and about a particular sanction, the more likely they are to support community sentences and make similar sentencing choices as would courts. Unfortunately, information about probation and community is often lacking.

A Little Knowledge Is a Dangerous Thing

According to the Commentary on the 2010 Council of Europe Rules on Probation,[2]

> while probation is not easy to define simply or precisely, it is a familiar term understood widely and internationally to refer to arrangements for the supervision of offenders in the community and to the organisations (probation agencies, probation services) responsible for this work. (Council of Europe 2010)

This is almost certainly an overstatement. A recent study found the word 'probation' is widely used in Europe but conveys vastly different meanings in each one of fifteen countries (Herzog-Evans 2013).

In many countries, while probation may be a familiar concept to most (but not all) of those who work in the criminal justice system, members of the general public tend to know very little about what probation

---

[2] Recommendation CM/Rec(2010)1 of the Committee of Ministers to member states on the Council of Europe Probation Rules (Adopted by the Committee of Ministers on 20 January 2010 at the 1075th meeting of the Ministers' Deputies).

involves. In some countries even the term means little. A 2008 survey of 200 participants from 13 cities and 32 villages in Slovakia found that 84 % of respondents answered 'no' to the question 'Have you ever met with a word "probation?"'(Lulei 2012). Only 8 % of surveyed university students described probation correctly in 2012 (Uzelac and Zakman-Ban 2012).

While this may be understandable in countries where probation was introduced only recently, there are similar findings from countries with longer established services. Roberts (2002) found that 'even probation, the most widely used and oldest community sentence in most countries is little known to large numbers of people'. A Mori survey carried out in 2002 found that seven percent claimed to know a lot about what the probation service did in England and Wales, two in five (43 %) said they knew a little while half said they knew hardly anything (35 %) or nothing at all (15 %) (MORI 2002).

The broader concept of community sentences also leaves many people confused. Focus groups carried out in Scotland in 2007 found that the terms 'community sentencing' and 'community penalties' were not familiar or fully understood. 'Community sentencing is assumed to be "the latest government jargon" for community service, while the term "community penalties" is somewhat misleading, since for some it suggests financial penalties' (TNS System Three 2007).

The low visibility of community sentences was confirmed by work undertaken for the Esmee Fairbairn Foundation Rethinking Crime and Punishment initiative. The Decision to Imprison (Hough et al. 2003) found that some sentencers, let alone members of the public, were poorly informed about the full range of community penalties and about their benefits.

Lack of knowledge about community sentences within a context of unwarranted cynicism about sentencing in general combine to produce headline findings which are critical of probation. Community penalties do not have a strong public profile, and are frequently equated with leniency. Before looking at ways in which probation activities conditions can be made more meaningful to the public, it is important to discuss what drives public attitudes and helps to create the false consciousness described above.

Drivers of Public Attitudes

A large body of literature has sought to identify correlates and causes of punitive attitudes. At a national level, while the wealth of a country plays no part in determining either harsh or lenient attitudes towards punishment, differences in income as measured by the Gini coefficient do. The most recent reports of the International Crime and Victim Survey (ICVS) found that 'in countries with large differences in income, the general public is more punitive' (Van Kesteren et al. 2014). The country-level variable of being anglophone which appeared in earlier reports to be associated with greater punitiveness did not turn out to be relevant once income inequality and national crime levels were controlled for.

At the individual level, research has generally found that men tend to be more punitive than women and better educated people less punitive than poorly educated. The ICVS surprisingly found that a younger age was correlated with punitiveness in contrast to other studies which found older people to have harsher views.

It is not possible to summarise all of the research in this area, but there are three consistent findings which have implications for probation efforts to address public concerns.

Crime and Punishment

The first of these concerns the link between crime and punitive attitudes. At a national level, the ICVS analysis found that in countries with higher crime rates, the public is more punitive, even though actual victims are not so and more generally the study found that those recently victimised by common crime are on average no more punitive than others (Van Kesteren et al. 2014). An American survey found that 'crime salience, especially fear and concern about crime consistently predict punitiveness and the study found some aspects of an "angry white male" phenomenon, particularly to the extent that those negative sentiments have a racial focus' (Costelloe et al. 2009). A Canadian study also found an important role in relation to anger (Hartnagel and Templeton 2012). Those with the highest levels of fear about crime or concern that crime is a major problem in society also tend to have the most punitive attitudes.

How to address this is not straightforward. The ICVS found that low satisfaction with the performance of the police in controlling crime is a variable which has an impact on punitiveness at the individual level and this may point towards probation emphasising the work which they do to assist the police to prevent and reduce crime and detect offending. Evidence from the UK suggests that this role is underappreciated by the public. When asked in 2002, who could help to reduce crime only 2% in a British poll mentioned the probation service compared to 13% who mentioned schools and more than three quarters who mentioned the police.

More recently Probation agencies raised concerns to a parliamentary inquiry about widespread public misunderstanding about the extent to which they are responsible for all the services that contribute to reducing re-offending. But the partnership work which probation increasingly plays with other criminal justice agencies—what has been called in a rather uninspiring way 'managerial sanctions'—provides an opportunity for the work to be more clearly located within a crime reduction narrative. While the European prison rules open by declaring that one aim of probation is to contribute to public safety by preventing and reducing the occurrence of offences, there is considerable argument (which is touched on in the next section) about whether this should be the central narrative and if so the extent to which probation should adapt its work to the priorities of other agencies, particularly the police. McNeill for example argues that 'probation agencies and services need to engage much more deeply and urgently with their roles as justice services, rather than as "mere" crime reduction agencies' (McNeill 2011).

Redeemability

The second set of findings relate to how punitive views are linked to broader beliefs and attitudes about individual responsibility and capacity for change. Maruna and King (2009) have identified a belief in redeemability—that people can and do change—as an important variable.

The least punitive people are those who both believe that crime has social origins and that people can change. The most punitive are those who believe that crime is a choice and yet that people who choose crime cannot change their ways. Maruna and King are sceptical about whether educating the public about positivist criminology and social science will reduce punitive opinions, but suggest that 'exposure to "success stories" of those who have been involved in crime, but have since successfully desisted, may have an impact in this regard' (pp. 20–21). This seems particularly relevant to probation.

The Influence of the Media

The third set of findings concern the media. Findings from several countries show a correlation between tabloid consumption and punitiveness (Demker et al. 2008), while in the US the more hours of television are watched, irrespective of genre, the more likely respondents are to support punishment, deterrence, or incapacitation rather than rehabilitation (Rosenberger and Callanan 2011).

There are a range of ways that the media influence attitudes (Rethinking Crime and Punishment 2003). Some are very direct. Tabloid (and even broadsheet) newspapers have run campaigns directed at securing specific changes (such as the introduction of sex offender notification scheme), and more general changes of approach (an end to soft sentencing). In the UK one editor of a daily paper described his newspaper's role in the 1990s as being 'to articulate the concern of its readers and thereby harden the response from the Tory administration' (Dacre, cited in Windlesham 1996). In countries which have introduced probation, the extent to which the media represent the innovation accurately or else seek to distort it can make a difference to its acceptance at large (Canton 2009).

The way the media cover grave offences committed by people under probation supervision can also impact on attitudes, particularly if dramatic events are reported without context. They may be more heavily reliant on the media and have no way of judging whether a probation 'bad news story' is typical. (Justice Committee 2011, p. 62). Unlike other public services such as health and education, where most people have a general knowledge from their own experience of what they are like, views are not anchored in any kind of first-hand experience. The quality of user experience cannot act as a buffer to media messages.

In England and Wales a series of murders committed from 2003 onwards by offenders under probation supervision threw the probation service under the political spotlight, and sensitised politicians further to public opinion about its work. In March 2006 the minister responsible for probation reportedly described it as 'the dagger at the heart of the criminal justice system, undermining public confidence in criminal justice as a whole' (Daily Telegraph 2006). Eight months later his successor made it clear that 'the probation service is letting people down, and needs fundamental reform' (Reid J 2006), arguably sowing the seeds for the changes which saw the eventual dismantling of the public probation service in 2014.

While the media has every right, and indeed duty, to report on the failings of probation and indeed of any other service, the consequences can be serious. Following one of the tragedies, the Home Secretary made reforms to the Parole Board designed to reduce the risk of dangerous offenders being released. The release rate fell from 23 % to 10 % over four years 'as probation staff became increasingly nervous of public and political reaction to another error' (Silverman 2012, p. 45). A judge who later became the Parole Board chair argued that 'we have to look carefully to make sure that the 24 hour seven day a week coverage is not distorting our decision-making'.

It is not just disasters that can damage probation. Negative attitudes towards community punishment were more than twice as prevalent as positive ones in a recent study of English newspapers, suggesting an ingrained hostility. A study in Ireland found the majority of the coverage of probation was either positive or neutral, but noted a recent shift towards a more negative tone (Maguire and Carr 2013).

Responding to the Challenge

The analysis above suggests that efforts to improve the impact of probation on satisfying the public's desire for justice or punishment can take one of two basic forms. The first is to seek to influence those desires to somehow bring them further into line with the principles and values of probation. The second is to accept that that the public, misinformed about much that they may be, need to be confident in community sentencing and supervision and that this may require substantive change in what probation entails.

Moderating Desires for Punishment

In previous work I have looked at ways of moderating attitudes to young offenders (Allen 2002) and efforts to build confidence in community penalties (Allen 2008). In the first I proposed strategies based on informing, influencing and involving the public. What has been the recent experience?

The evidence about the effectiveness of cognitive strategies to change attitudes to punishment has been mixed (Maruna and King 2008). Dutch research found that providing more information about suspended sentences did not change people's general level of punitiveness, but more information did change people's views about the effectiveness of suspended sentences, increasing support for them (Van Gelder et al. 2011).

A recent UK experiment has shown that effective presentation of national and local crime statistics and other information in a booklet can have a positive impact on public confidence by narrowing the gap between actual performance by justice agencies and perceptions of it (Singer and Cooper 2009). This did not include specific information about probation however. It is not known how long any impact lasts and there are questions about how such a method could be taken to scale.

Another more interactive way of providing information is the website *You Be The Judge*, which aims to show users how judges and magistrates decide on the sentences they pass. It explains the decision-making process and gives users the opportunity to pass sentence in scenarios based on real-life cases. After giving their current view of sentencing, users hear evidence about the case and decide on the sentence they would give. They are then informed of the sentence the judge would have given to that offender, and are then finally invited to give their view of sentencing again after completing the case.

An evaluation found that of the 74,000 members of the public who used the website between 2010 and 2012, 52 per cent start with the view that sentencing is 'about right', and 72 per cent finish with the view that sentencing is 'about right'. Three of the cases involve community sentences (Cuthbertson 2013).

It has been proposed that the government should ensure that data about community sentences and work undertaken in the community is widely available, that schools teach about the criminal justice system as part of citizenship education and venues such as doctors' surgeries are used to disseminate information (Coulsfield 2004; Singer and Cooper 2009). There is no reason why areas where community work has been undertaken could not be added to the crime maps which are increasingly available on line—the website *Police. UK* allows people to nominate sites for removing graffiti, clearing litter and rubbish from public areas, repairing and decorating public buildings such as community centres, and working on other projects which benefit the environment.

There is a growing recognition that changing attitudes requires more than information. For probation, there is a case for the positive promotion of its underlying values and engaging with the emotional as well as cognitive side of attitudes. Importantly, statistical arguments about the effectiveness of non-custodial sentences tend to have less impact than arguments about the values and principles underlying them: paying back, making good and learning 'how good people live' resonated strongly in some research (RCP 2002). But as a witness put it to a Parliamentary inquiry: 'How do you get across the complexity of changing people's behaviour? It does not sound like a punishment' (Justice Committee 2011).

There are positive examples of initiatives which seek to do this. In the Local Crime Community Sentence (LCCS) programme a magistrate and probation representative make presentations to local community groups. While similar to the You Be the Judge methodology, LCCS audiences are given a news-style piece that gives the 'headlines' of the case as they might be read in a tabloid newspaper. After reading this—and on the basis of that information alone—participants make a decision about the appropriate sentence. They are then given information about the case and possible responses of the type provided to courts in a pre-sentence report and invited to review their decision. In the evaluation of the programme, over half of those who initially chose the prison option changed their minds after the report presentation and discussion (Grimshaw and Oliveira 2008).

A further way of seeking to moderate attitudes is to increase opportunities for public involvement in probation work. It has been argued that criminal justice institutions tend to repel public examination and participation. 'Courses on life skills, anger management and the like are held in mirrored glass or blasé concrete block buildings sometimes lacking exterior signs communicating what happens inside (Dzur 2014). As well as being physically removed, probation is part of a criminal justice system which is not only bewilderingly complex but performs and characterises tasks in ways which neutralise the public's role in its work.

Notwithstanding this, a survey carried out for the UK government in 2008 found that 58 % of the public wanted to have a say in the type of work that should be undertaken by those subject to community payback and, of those, 71 % said they would attend a meeting to influence this. It is not clear to what extent that online opportunities for the first of these are taken up. A review of the role played by volunteers in Circles of Support and Accountability (COSA) to create supportive monitoring frameworks around sex offenders following their release from prison has argued that they perform a symbolically important role as representatives of the wider community in taking ownership of offender management practices on behalf of the wider society (Almond 2015).

Of course probation has considerable contact with other agencies in the criminal justice system whose opinions can carry particular influence. It is perhaps of concern in the 2011 UK poll quoted above that 90 % of police officers thought offenders saw such sentences as a soft punishment and 86 % believed "offenders often commit further crimes while serving community sentences". This can be contrasted with the recently reported views of the Finnish police on the proposed introduction of prison sentences for petty offenders (Uuitset 2015).

While judges and magistrates are generally thought to have a more positive view of probation, work is needed to ensure that they too are fully aware of what is involved. Pilot projects conducted by Rethinking Crime and Punishment in England showed an impact on sentencers. The then Chief Justice also spent a day doing community service work along-side offenders in order to promote the punishment among his judicial colleagues and the wider public.

Modifying Probation

As well as initiatives to improve understanding of probation, a variety of measures have been taken to make probation more appealing to the public. In England and Wales the report Engaging Communities to Fight Crime has been influential, using findings from surveys to argue for a tougher approach (Casey 2008). Successive governments have accepted its argument that community sentences have not won public confidence as a punishment, citing 'too many cases where community orders require only "supervision" by a probation officer—perhaps one meeting a fort-night (Ministry of Justice 2011). Community sentences have been over-hauled with an intention of offenders serving longer hours, carrying out community work over the course of a working week of at least four days, with more use of electronic tagging, longer curfews and orange jackets for those undertaking community work. Some form of punitive compo-nent must now be included in all orders—a fine, a punitive community order or electronic monitoring—whether or not these will help to reduce re-offending.

Indeed the government accepted that delivering a clear punitive ele-ment to every community order may cause the primarily rehabilitative requirements to be substituted for primarily punitive ones. There is a risk that some of the rehabilitative benefits of current Community Orders could be lost, with adverse implications for the re-offending rate of those offenders subject to community orders.

The intention is in part to signal to society that wrongdoing will not be tolerated. But whether public confidence will really be boosted by an initiative which creates additional visible punishment while increasing re-offending remains to be seen.

Such an approach might have been necessary in order to make com-munity sentences a replacement for short prison sentences. But the gov-ernment made it clear that this is not the case. Instead, on the basis of very little evidence, tougher community punishments are to 'help stop offenders in their tracks earlier to stop them committing more crime' (Ministry of Justice 2011).

There is now a good deal of interest in taking matters further by introducing the model of swift and certain punishment which has apparently been successful in the USA. There are of course a wide range of arguments about the desirability of such an approach and the point at which probation activities become so punitive that they cease to count as probation.

A recent American study of California parole officers has argued that their 'tough love' approach that emphasises surveillance, sanctioning perceived misconduct, and utilising (or threatening to utilise) reimprisonment does not entail the abandonment of the goal of offender assistance, but rather keeps rehabilitation present through folding it within a web of punitive regulation (Werth 2013). Others take a different view (McNeill 2011; Senior 2013). For our purposes it is enough to quote the way in which In England and Wales the Parliamentary Justice Committee said they had

> identified risks in a sentencing policy based on what we regarded as 'misconceptions' about what the public 'wants' and, over the longer term, we feared that resources will be diverted away from a sentencing framework that is genuinely effective in contributing towards the reduction of reoffending. (Justice Committee 2010)

During the 1990s, probation was seen as an endangered species, with American experts arguing that the brand should be retired and enormous pressure on the service in England and Wales. Yet despite political, media, public and even academic criticism it has survived and is expanding into new jurisdictions and within existing ones. Probation reform is a key part of efforts to reduce prison populations in some US states (Allen 2014).

The price which probation may turn out to have paid cannot be discussed here. But we can certainly identify lessons for the future. There are perhaps three overarching ones.

In terms of attitudes to sentencing in general, there is a need to find a way out of the "comedy of errors" in which policy and practice is not developed on the basis of a proper understanding of public opinion and the same opinion is not based on a proper understanding of policy and practice (Allen 2002). Public education in the broadest sense is key.

But so is a more responsible politics of punishment. This is not only a matter for western countries. The European Commission has been unhappy about the way that Bulgarian government ministers have criticised 'soft judgements' by the courts, apparently taking their lead from the prime minister who when head of police was well known for using the phrase, 'We catch them, the judges let them free' (Gounev 2013).

More positively probation needs champions. The truth is that the public in most countries are ambivalent about its role and can be persuaded of its value. But many will look to authorities—opinion formers who will stand up for the values which probation espouses and the institutions which give effect to them. The recent history of probation in England and Wales suggest they may be few and far between.

References

Allen, R. (2002). There must be some way of dealing with kids. *Youth Justice, 2*(1), 3–13.

Allen, R. (2008, December). Changing public attitudes to crime and punishment: Building confidence in community penalties. *Probation Journal, 55*(4), 389–400.

Allen, R. (2014). *Justice reinvestment: Empty slogan or sustainable future for penal policy?* London: Transform Justice.

Allen, R., & Hough, M. (2007). Community penalties, sentencers, the media and public opinion. In R. Morgan & L. Gelsthorpe (Eds.), *The handbook of probation*. Cullompton: Devon.

Allen, R., & Hough, M. (2008). Does it matter? Reflections of the effectiveness of institutionalised public participation in the development of sentencing policy. In A. Freiberg & K. Gelb (Eds.), *Penal populism, sentencing councils and sentencing policy* (pp. 224–239). Cullompton and Devon: Willan.

Almond, P. (2015, Spring). Circles of support and accountability: Criminal justice volunteers as deliberative public. *British Journal of Community Justice, 13*(1), 25–39.

Armstrong, S., McIvor, G., McNeill, F. & McGuinness, P. (2013) International Evidence Review of Conditional (Suspended) Sentences, SCCJR Research

Report No. 01/2013 Retrieved from http://www.sccjr.ac.uk/publications/international-evidence-review-of-conditional-suspended-sentences/

Ashcroft, Lord (2011) Crime, Punishment & The People Public opinion and the criminal justice debate. Retrieved from http://lordashcroftpolls.com/wp-content/uploads/2011/12/crime-punishment-and-the-people.pdf

Boon, M., & van Swaaningen, R. (2013). Regression to the mean: Punishment in the Netherlands. In V. Ruggiero & M. Ryan (Eds.), *Punishment in Europe*. Palgrave Macmillan: Basingstoke.

Bridges, A. (2010). *History of HMI probation*. Retrieved June 25, 2015, from https://www.justiceinspectorates.gov.uk/hmiprobation/about-hmi-probation/statement-of/#.VYuUpPlVhHx

Canton, R. (2009). Taking probation abroad. *European Journal of Probation. University of Bucharest, 1*(1), 66–78.

Casey, L (2008). Engaging communities in fighting crime: A review by Louise Casey. London: Cabinet Office.

Costelloe, M., Chiricos, T., & Gertz, M. (2009, January). Punitive attitudes toward criminals Exploring the relevance of crime salience and economic insecurity. *Punishment & Society, 11*(1), 25–49.

Coulsfield, L. (2004). *Crime, courts and confidence: Report of an independent inquiry into alternatives to prison*. London: Esmee Fairbairn Foundation.

Council of Europe. (2010). *Recommendation CM/Rec (2010) 1 of the Committee of Ministers to member states on the Council of Europe Probation Rules* (Adopted by the Committee of Ministers on 20 January 2010 at the 1075th meeting of the Ministers' Deputies) Strasbourg.

Cuthbertson, S. (2013). *Analysis of complete 'You be the Judge' website experiences*. Analytical Summary May 2013. London Ministry of Justice.

Daily Telegraph. (2006, March 21). Regrets not enough if probation service cannot cope.

Demker, M., Towns, A., Duus-Otterstrom, G., & Sebring, J. (2008, July). Fear and punishment in Sweden: Exploring penal attitudes. *Punishment & Society, 10* (3), 319–332.

Durnescu, I., Enengl, C., & Grafl, C. (2013). Experiencing supervision. In F. McNeill & K. Beyens (Eds.), *Offender supervision in Europe*. Basingstoke Palgrave Macmillan.

Dzur, A. (2014). Repellent institutions and the absentee public. In Ryberg, J, & Roberts, J. (2014). Exploring the normative significance of public opinion for state punishment. In J. Ryberg & J. Roberts (Eds.), Popular punishment. New York: Oxford University Press.

Gounev, P. (2013). Soft and harsh penalties in Bulgaria. In V. Ruggiero & M. Ryan (Eds.), *Punishment in Europe*. Basingstoke Palgrave Macmillan.

Grimshaw, R. & Oliveira, M. (2008). *Independent evaluation of the fourth year of LCCS: July 2007–June 2008*. Report on the national results Centre for Crime and Justice Studies.

Halliday, J. (2001). *Making punishments work*. London: Home Office.

Hartnagel, T., & Templeton, L. (2012, October). Emotions about crime and attitudes to punishment. *Punishment & Society, 14*(4), 452–474.

Herzog-Evans, M. (2013). What's in a Name? Penological and Institutional connotations of probation officers' labelling in Europe. *Eurovista, 2*(3), 121–133.

Hough, M., Bradford, B., Jackson, J., & Roberts, J. (2013). *Attitudes to sentencing and trust in justice exploring trends from the crime survey for England and Wales*. London: Ministry of Justice.

Hough, M., Jacobsen, J., & Millie, A. (2003). *The decision to imprison*. London: Prison Reform Trust.

Hough, M., Roberts, J., Jacobson, J., Moon, N., & Steel, N. (2009). *Public attitudes to the principles of sentencing*. London: ICPR.

Justice Committee. (2010). *Cutting crime: The case for justice reinvestment*. HMSO.

Justice Committee. (2011). *The role of the probation service*. London HMSO.

Labour Party. (2015). *A better plan to secure safer communities* London Labour Party.

Lulei, M. (2012). *Experiencing and practising offenders supervision in Slovakia*. Retrieved from http://www.offendersupervision.eu/wp-content/uploads/2012/11/Practising-OS-in-Slovakia-Sept-2012.pdf

Maguire, N., & Carr, N. (2013). Changing shape and shifting boundaries. *European Journal of Probation, 5*(3), 3–23.

Maruna, S., & King, A. (2008). Selling the public on probation. *Probation Journal, 55*(4), 337–353.

Maruna, S., & King, A. (2009). Once a criminal, always a criminal? 'Redeemability' and the psychology of punitive public attitude. *European Journal on Criminal Policy and Research, 15*, 7–24.

McNeill, F. (2011, March). Probation, credibility and justice. *Probation Journal, 58*(1), 9–22.

Ministry of Justice. (2011). *Breaking the cycle response*. London HMSO.

MORI (2002) Perceptions of the National Probation Service: Research study conducted for National Probation Service Home Office London

Prison Reform Trust. (2011 September). Public want offenders to make amends London Prison. Reform Trust Retrieved from http://www.prisonreformtrust.org.uk/Portals/0/Documents/public%20want%20offenders%20to%20make%20amends.pdf

RCP. (2002). *What do the public really feel about non-custodial penalties?* London: Esmee Fairbairn Foundation.

Reid J (2006). Probation Review non-negotiable Unpublished Speech. Retrieved from http://www.crimlinks.com/News2006/Nov72006.html.

Rethinking Crime and Punishment. (2003). *Media and the shaping of public knowledge and attitudes towards crime and punishment*, London Esmee Fairbairn Foundation.

Roberts, J. (2002). Public opinion and the nature of community penalties: International findings. In J. Roberts & M. Hough (Eds.), *Changing attitudes to punishment: Public opinion, crime and justice*. Cullompton: Willan.

Robinson, G. McNeill, F. & Maruna, S. (2013). Punishment in society: The improbable persistence of probation and other community sanctions and measures. In Simon & Sparks (Eds.), *The Sage handbook of punishment and society*.

Robinson, G., McNeill, F., & Maruna, S. (2013). Punishment in society: The improbable persistence of community sanctions. In J. Simon & R. Sparks (Eds.), The Sage handbook of punishment and society. London and New York: Sage.

Rosenberger, J. & Callanan, V. (2011, December). The influence of media on penal attitudes. *Criminal Justice Review, 36*(4), 435–455.

Ryberg, J, & Roberts, J. (2014). Exploring the normative significance of public opinion for state punishment. In J. Ryberg & J. Roberts (Eds.), *Popular punishment*. New York: Oxford University Press.

Senior, P. (2013, September). Community engagement: Innovation; past, present and future. *Probation Journal, 60*, 242–258.

Silverman, J. (2012). *Crime policy and the media*. the shaping of criminal justice, 1989–2010. Abingdon: Routledge.

Singer, L., & Cooper, S. (2009, December). Improving public confidence in the criminal justice system: An evaluation of a communication activity. *Howard Journal of Criminal Justice* 48(5) 485–500.

TNS System Three. (2007). *Community sentencing: Public perceptions and attitudes* (Summary Research Report). Scottish Executive Social Research. Retrieved from http://www.scotland.gov.uk/Publications/2007/11/15102229/6

Uutitset, (24 June 2015). Police blast return of prison sentences for low-level crime. Retrieved from http://yle.fi/uutiset/police_blast_return_of_prison_sentences_for_low-level_crime/8101719

Uzelac, S. & Zakman-Ban, V. (2012). *Attitudes of Croatian public towards probation*. Unpublished paper quoted in Durnescu et al (2013).

Van Gelder, J.-L., Aarten, P., Lamet, W., & van der Laan, P. (2011). Unknown, unloved? Public opinion on and knowledge of suspended sentences in the Netherland. *Crime and Delinquency*. Retrieved from http://cad.sagepub.com/content/early/2011/11/16/0011128711426537.full.pdf

Van Kesteren, J., Van Diijk, J., & Mayhew, P. (2014). The international crime victims surveys: A retrospective. *International Review of Victimology, 20*(1), 49–69.

Victim Support (and Make Justice Work). (2012). *Out in the open: What victims really think about community sentencing.* London: Victim Support.

Werth, R. (2013, July). The construction and stewardship of responsible yet precarious subjects: Punitive ideology, rehabilitation, and 'tough love' among parole personnel. *Punishment& Society, 15*, 219–246.

Windlesham, D. (1996). *Response to crime* (Vol. 3). Oxford: OUP.

What Are the Costs and Benefits of Probation?

Faye S. Taxman and Stephanie Maass

Probation is an elastic sanction, and one that occurs in the community. The elasticity of the sanction means that it can be tailored to an individual based on the risk and need factors, as well as the severity of the offense. Probation, unlike incarceration which is defined by total restrictions of liberty, can use the tools of supervision to achieve various degrees of liberty restriction. The flexibility of the sanction is a benefit but the costs related to supervision depend on the degree to which the program features are proportional to the offense, are parsimonious, reinforce citizenship, and affect social justice. This chapter reviews the costs and benefits of community sanctions that affect the justice system, the individual probationer, and the community. In total, probation has a number of attributes, but the consideration of these costs and benefits is important as systems are further developed and probation emerges as a preferred sanction.

As a community-based vehicle for sanctioning offenders, probation offers a three-pronged arena of impact: to the justice system, to the

F.S. Taxman (✉) • S. Maass
Center for Advancing Correctional Excellence (ACE!)
George Mason University, Fairfax, VA, USA

© The Editor(s) (if applicable) and The Author(s) 2016
F. McNeill et al. (eds.), *Probation*,
DOI 10.1057/978-1-137-51982-5_9

individual offender, and to the community at large. Costs and benefits are incurred in each domain, and sometimes the costs and/or benefits in one arena may have a counter-impact on another. It is critical to consider each domain separately, but also their collective impact in terms of the proportionality of the punishment, the parsimoniousness of the punishment, the impact on the citizenship rights and roles of the individual, and social justice. These are the financial and human costs and benefits associated with probation. The competing demands between costs and benefits support the expansion and use of probation. The fiscal costs are generally lower than facility-based punishment systems (i.e. prison and jail which require 24-hour services, food, residence, etc.). The human costs to the individual and the family are also reduced compared with facility-based punishments. This is not to say that there is not a cost to providing probation services, but the types of costs vary from other punishments. The same is true for benefits.

Probation is practiced differently around the world, which reflects another type of elasticity. Probation is compatible with restorative justice, rehabilitation, alternatives to incarceration, retribution, and incapacitation. In some jurisdictions, it is viewed as either enforcement (monitoring conditions assigned by the court) or social work (service provisions), or something between these divergent positions. Or it can be considered as an opportunity to address the harms from the crime through either restorative justice or reparations. The flexible nature of probation means that the sentence may vary within a jurisdiction, but will certainly differ between jurisdictions. For example, in Sweden the emphasis is on community service for many offenders whereas in Scotland probation officers operate under a social work framework.

The favorite framework for probation now encompasses the Risk-Need-Responsivity (RNR) model, which is a hybrid approach. The RNR framework seeks to tailor responses to the risks to public safety from an individual while addressing the criminogenic factors that drive offending behavior or destabilizing factors or life situations that affect one's stability in the community. This approach blends the enforcement and social-work approaches with greater attention to individualized needs. Under the RNR framework, the role of the probation officer is to focus on cognitive restructuring as part of the probation process. This allows for greater attention to achieving the sentencing goals and the requirements of supervision. The RNR supervision framework has considerable flexibility in being shaped to an individual person and their individual circumstances, which permits this model to be practiced in various ways (see Taxman 2008; Drake 2012).

In the United States, the National Research Council (2014) established a set of principles that should be considered in thinking about the appropriateness of penal severity. These principles are that sanctions should be proportional to the offense, that they should be parsimonious to address the offense and the characteristics of the individual, that they should promote continued citizenship (for moral rehabilitation), and that they should address social justice. Taxman and Rhine (2015) developed five markers that define the probation sentence to assess the key features of sentences and to provide a comparable way to describe probation sentences. In this chapter, we will use the NRC principles and Taxman and Rhine's markers as a means of articulating the costs and benefits of a probation sentence to the justice system, the individual, and the community (society) at large. Assessing the value of probation across these domains is important in appreciating the potential that can occur from shifting our focus from incarceration as the preferred sanction onto community sanctions such as probation.

The following discussion of costs and benefits of probation must acknowledge the tremendous range in how probation is practiced. It must recognize that there are both fiscal and human costs and benefits that will differ depending on how probation is practiced. Our discussion below will identify the factors that weigh into considering costs and benefits given the versatility of probation. The goal of this chapter, however, is to illustrate the costs and benefits under various scenarios in order to further highlight how probation can achieve different sentencing goals and societal purposes, and be a valid sanction.

The Costs and Benefits to the Justice System

Probation is principally elastic. As a sentence, probation occurs in the community, under varying periods of time and requirements. Probation is ordered by the sentencing judge or court, with the conditions and requirements determined by the judge. It is assumed that the sentencing goals—rehabilitation, retribution, deterrence, or incapacitation—define the nature of these conditions and requirements. With the concern about citizenship and social justice, the integration of the RNR framework into punishment goals positions sentencing to facilitate the process of transitioning a justice-involved individual into a non-offender status by reintegrating the individual into society as a contributing, law-abiding citizen. Desistance restores both the individual and the community. The conditions that are attached to probation articulate the judge's punishment preference. However, it is important to realize that the experience of probation comingles the sentencing goals and the many requirements of probation embedded in the agency administering probation. For example, if a sentencing judge focuses on incapacitation but the probation agency uses community service (restorative justice or payback), this may or may not be consistent with the judge's goals for the sentence. These discrepancies are part of the problem of probation being a court-ordered sentenced punishment but one administered by agencies that may have different goals. Overall, it is important to consider probation as a frame that can be adjusted to fit the individual, the convicted offense, and the needs of the community.

The justice system can use probation to foster goals of desistance by focusing probation conditions around factors that will allow the offender to repay society, address factors that contribute to offending, and allow the offender to obtain new skills (i.e. education, employment, parenting, etc.) to contribute to society. The flexibility of the probation sanction—as either a stand-alone sentence or as a platform (frame) to add components pertinent to the factors that affect offending behavior and can expedite desistance from a life of crime—is an asset. Taxman and Rhine (2015) identified five markers that define the probation sentence, and this framework provides the means to assess benefits and/or costs to the justice system: (1) the mission and goals of probation within a framework for various purposes of sentences and punishment; (2) the length of supervision terms; (3) the intensity and restrictiveness of conditions of supervision; (4) the extent to which formal treatment programming is coercive rather than voluntary; and (5) the consequences of breaches or violations of probation. Each marker has associated benefits and costs.

The elasticity of probation is both a blessing and curse. The blessing is that it can be molded to individual needs and situations, and it can reflect the sentencing judge's perception of the goals of punishment. Punishment, and its various intrusions and restrictions, should never be greater than the offender's culpability and the gravity of the offense (Tonry 2006). This earmark of proportionality and parsimony that defines legal principles is a guiding post not only for the mission and goals of a sanction for a criminal offense, but also for the administration of probation. Probation, by definition, should reflect these legal principles, which means that the conditions of probation should be constrained to only address liberty restrictions that are needed to appropriately punish the person, regardless of whether the goal of punishment is for rehabilitation, retribution, incapacitation, or deterrence. These various forms of punishment do not justify increasing the harshness of probation, but they do demand that the sentencing goals be articulated through probation (and therefore the components of punishment). The challenge in most probation systems is to be parsimonious but also purposeful—to ensure that the sentencing goals are appropriately achieved.

McNeill (2012) recognizes that it is difficult to disentangle the goals of punishment and rehabilitation; both operate under various disguises, and can be considered from various angles—psychological, judicial, social, and moral rehabilitation—which demonstrates that rehabilitation is similar to punishment in various different ways. Psychological rehabilitation refers to the typical correctional rehabilitation where the emphasis is on changing and/or restoring the offender for the purpose of addressing deficits or problems. Judicial rehabilitation refers to offsetting the criminal record with efforts to reintegrate the person back to society. Moral rehabilitation refers to addressing the harm done to the victim (community) to assume a "restored" position in society. Building on these other forms of rehabilitation is the social recognition and acceptance of the reformed, corrected person back into the folds of society. This analysis of rehabilitation as a goal of sentencing illustrates how intertwined the goals of sentencing are in terms of maximizing the benefits of community sanction. But it also shows the various forms that rehabilitation can take, some of which are similar to other goals of punishment.

Length of Supervision In practice, probation varies considerably around the globe. As mentioned earlier, a major factor that defines probation is the length of the time under state control. The probation sentence is flexible—generally defined by the court but sometimes defined by administrative procedures. The length of time under supervision is considered a marker for a more onerous sentence—shorter periods are typically reserved for less-serious offenders and/or offenses while longer periods signal that the individual, owing to the nature of their offense and/or their history, is deserving of longer terms of control by the state. The length of supervision is usually reflective of overall sentencing practices within a jurisdiction, region, or country. In some countries the length of supervision may be defined by legislative bodies, while in others the length of supervision is up to the sentencing judge. As a marker of individual "costs," the length of supervision is the degree to which the state maintains control over an individual. The benefits from this time under social control are that the individual can make progress on personal goals, and that they can benefit from the services and requirements of probation. A community sanction does not affect the citizenship rights or responsibilities of the individual, which is the earmark of an important punishment system (National Research Council 2014).

Probation Frame as Determined by the Intensity and Restrictiveness of Conditions of Supervision Probation is essentially an open frame where unlimited restrictions can be placed on an individual. This creates a flexibility to tailor the community sanction to the individual, but it also creates a challenge regarding the degree to which the requirements are onerous. The cornerstone of the requirements is the face-to-face contact between the officer and the individual probationer. This is the main cost of being on probation—having an officer to report to—but it can also be a benefit if the two individuals have a mutual and trusting working relationship. Liberty restrictions are basically the degree to which the demands for supervision affect the physical movement, financial resources, and psychological demands on the individual. Over the last three decades, sophisticated technological tools became a larger part of the landscape of probation strategies, contributing to increased monitoring, surveillance, and individual control. The emergence of these tools reflected the need to have more evidentiary and objective data to document the probationer's progress, while simultaneously expanding the use of technological (and non-officer-based) tools to restrict the liberties of individuals. The application of different technologies has provided the ability to expand supervision "outside the office" or beyond physical walls. It has also used persuasive strategies to impact individual behavior.

Examples of the technological tools include drug testing (biological), electronic monitors (geographic or spatial), and treatment interventions (psychological). Drug testing, which requires a physical sample of urine, blood, saliva, or sweat to detect any drug use, emerged in the late 1980s as a technology that probation and parole agencies could use to obtain evidence on whether the individual is engaged in the use of illicit substances. Drug testing policies vary considerably across agencies, especially as the technology for drug testing continues to evolve. Some agency policies require the court to specify the conditions under which an offender can be drug-tested, yet others allow the probation agency to freely use the technology without the permission of the court. Many agencies drug test on a set schedule, while others use random testing procedures. Another area associated with the increased adoption of technology for enforcement purposes is the reliance on electronic monitoring, or geographical positioning satellite (GPS) devices, which can either restrict offenders to a given area close to the monitor or track the path of their movement. The geographical tools create "walls" for the individual given the restrictions. Since they are visible (i.e. the person must wear the anklet), the status is known.

The growing reliance on the imposition of financial penalties as a condition of supervision presents not just a punitive dimension, but a liberty restriction too. Alongside the requirement to pay restitution to the victim or a general fund for victims, it is not uncommon for some agencies or punishment systems to levy a supervision fee for being on probation. For some organizations, additional costs can include fees for drug testing, electronic monitoring or GPS, treatment participation, or other mandated conditions of release. In addition, the use of probation fees (as a revenue source) essentially requires that offenders pay for their punishment. This is qualitatively different from the concept of restitution that is directed at repairing the harm caused by the crime that was committed. Instead, probation fees exact a restriction on the individual by limiting their "disposable" income when on probation and imposing a strain on the individuals affected.

Use of Formal Programming Whether Coercive or Voluntary   Another feature of supervision that is attractive to judicial systems and punishment systems is the use of educational and treatment programming (as part of personal rehabilitation) and community service (as moral rehabilitation). In some systems, a condition of supervision frequently requires individuals to participate in a myriad of community service and/or treatment programs. Associated with efforts to hold offenders more accountable, community service requirements have increased as part of efforts to repay the victim or the community. Community service focuses on the offender repaying the community for the offense by "giving back" through manual labor to correct a community-based problem such as cleaning parks, painting public areas, working in a nonprofit agency, and other similar venues. More traditional, treatment-type activities include drug or alcohol treatment, mental health treatment, sexual offending counseling, and provision for other types of services. Within the evidence-based treatment field, certain types of treatment programming are recognized to be more likely to facilitate reductions in recidivism. This includes therapeutic communities, cognitive behavioral therapy, contingency management (incentivizing the individual), and behavioral management. Some of the programming is geared to address the risk and need factors that individuals present. Educational programs are designed to address general education deficits (e.g. reading, writing, science) while the individual is under supervision.

Many of these programs feature both rehabilitation-type services as well as accountability. And, over the last two decades, more technological tools of drug testing and monitors are used within programming to ensure that the individual is maintaining the requirements of the sentence, such as being drug- and alcohol-free, attending programs, making clinical progress, and so on. The coupling of treatment and control to define a correctional program is built on the premise that a formalized program structure will define the sanction in a manner that differs from standard face-to-face probation contacts or referral to services in the community. This way treatment and sanctioning are intertwined. This places an additional burden on the individual because the probation officer is more keenly aware of their progress, but it has the added benefit of ensuring that treatment is part of the requirements. These efforts, which at their core represent coerced treatment models, embrace the "spirit" of confinement and accountability by imposing a greater breadth of penalties and structure, signaling that the individual is being punished (as compared with treated). The benefits of programming are that it provides the opportunities to address deficits or to advance individuals' skills, but the costs are the potential psychological drain that occurs from knowing the consequences of program failure.

Consequences of Breaches or Violations of Probation   An important component of the impact of community sanctions is how breaches or violations are addressed in the system. The failure to meet judicially ordered conditions is a violation of the sanction, and therefore systems need to have some means to address these breaches. Many jurisdictions pursue revocations to address violations of the conditions of supervision. The failure to comply with mandated judicial conditions is often viewed as being as severe as a new crime event. Probation agencies, as well as the judiciary, see such violations or breaches as willful disobedience to abide by the law. More importantly, since probationers are viewed as "wards of the state," the failure to comply with the orders is considered serious because it undermines the credibility of probation. A major theme is that the responses to these breaches need to be swift and certain, and that this will enhance compliance. Probation officers have been steadfast in reinforcing the need for the judiciary to be more punitive in responding to supervision violations, mainly as a means to reinforce understanding that being on probation is a sanction and a privilege. When the privilege is perceived as being abused (by non-compliance), the probation officers often seek the ultimate penalty of incarceration. A true consequence of the community sanction is the possibility of being further punished if the individual probationer does not fulfill the requirements of the sanction. This adds to the costs of the community sanction because the individual knows that the stakes are higher—failure in the community can result in more punishment and maybe even reinstatement of the original sentence of incarceration. This places a high burden on community sanctions.

In summary, the costs of probation are as diverse as the benefits. A lot depends on the nature of the individual and the characteristics of the sanction. It is important to recognize that the probation components drive the costs and benefits, and a lot of the benefits derive from the perception of the individual probationer as to the value they place on the components of the sanction. If the benefits appear worthwhile—the individual feels that the programming and requirements add value—then the costs are diminished. If the components are perceived as intrusive, useless, or even out of balance with the intent of the sanction or the severity of the offense, then the human costs may be considered too great. That is, if the "pains of punishment" (see Durnescu 2011) are excessive, then the benefits will not be as appreciated.

While in this chapter we do not discuss the operational costs associated with probation in terms of the overarching purpose of community supervision, it is important to note that these costs exist in addition to the costs discussed here. The probation personnel are cheaper than prison cells given that there is no need to pay for personnel that operate twenty-four hours a day or provide secure physical space to detain an offender. However, overloading the probation personnel with high caseloads can artificially reduce the actual costs of probation. The higher the caseload, the less likely are probation personnel to be able to employ effective practices such as risk management, working alliances to create trust and fairness, case management and service referral, and service provision—and therefore the less likely they are to achieve the goals of the community sanction. That is, probation officers can achieve many of the goals of a sanction if they have sufficient time to address the criminogenic risk and needs of probationers. Other related costs of probation are related to service provision to address the substance-abuse and mental-health issues of probationers, as well as their employment, educational, and other unmet needs. The cost of probation is entirely related to the size of the caseload, and the degree to which the probation officers link offenders to community-based services. The costs are sometimes offset by the related financial penalties such as fines, probation fees, drug testing fees, restitution, and any other court-related costs.

Probation is a penalty that can benefit the justice system without overextending the system in terms of resources. But the system can undermine the ability of probation by overextending the resources available to probation, placing such a burden on probationers that it exceeds the principles of parsimony and proportionality, and by stacking conditions on probationers that intensify the sanction.

Costs and Benefits to the Individual Under Justice Control

For the individual offender, a probation sentence is one that is served in the community. In most instances, the person can live in their own residence with their loved ones. Rarely, probation may require specialized housing such as a sober living environment or halfway house, a short term in jail, or some specialized housing. Being in the community means that the individual has a greater opportunity to fully participate in civic responsibilities such as employment, being a family member, and being part of the community. These civic responsibilities mean essentially that the person does not need to be stripped of their identity or personal responsibilities for their families or network. A clear benefit of the community sanction is that the individual remains in the community and remains active in their own life. They stay in the community while repaying society and/or being punished, thus retaining employment that would be otherwise disrupted by even a short incarceration sentence, continuing to be part of a community social network, and keeping their family intact. Also, the state is not responsible for the basic needs of the individual such as housing, food, clothing, etc.

A community sanction is less stigmatizing to the individual, and offers the potential for them to maintain their own identity. The social identity of an individual is part of their personhood, their definition of their self. Incarceration can have an impact on the individual's identity since it removes the opportunity to be a spouse, parent, child, friend, and so on that are part of a person's identity. However, the ability to be in the community and maintain normal activities allows the individual to maintain the identity of a functioning individual that contributes to the well-being of those around them. This identity lays the foundation for an individual to stay connected to the community, which has an even greater ability to reduce the negative consequences of identifying with being an "outlaw" or a second-class citizen. The maintenance of one's identity reduces narratives of condemnation which present barriers to integration and desistance, and has the potential to increase redemption narratives (Maruna 2001).

Being in the community gives the individual probationer the opportunity to stay connected with traditional and natural community resources for addressing cognitive restructuring, substance abuse and mental health, and providing employment, housing, and/or educational services that could benefit the person. The ability to participate in community resources, many of which may not be offered by the justice system but instead are offered by the health, educational, or vocational systems, reinforces the individual's being part of the community. While these services may be needed to address criminogenic needs, for the most part they will also be needed by other citizens too. This reduces the barriers to asking for "help" or to using community resources to reinforce an individual's role in the community. Assistance to the individual in linking with and/or participating in services that will improve their quality of life has the added benefit of assisting them to be a better citizen, and to fulfill their role in the normal community. More importantly, while these services may or may not be provided as part of probation (as mandated conditions) they nonetheless offer definite opportunities to the individual.

The benefits of residing in the community, being able to resume "normal" activities, and becoming engaged in community resources are all well recognized. But the crux of the probation process is the face-to-face relationship with the officer. The officer has discretion regarding how performance on supervision is assessed, and the criteria by which an individual can be considered compliant or non-compliant. Having a probation officer, even if it is a layman as in some countries or a social worker as in others, has both positive and negative aspects. The positive stem from the fact that the individual has an "advocate" or someone they can rely upon for assistance. This relationship can enhance someone's quality of life by giving access to needed services or making available resources that may not be at an individual's disposal.

However, an implicit cost in the probation process is this discretion that officers have regarding their role in supervising the individual. Officers and individuals may have different perceptions regarding progress on supervision. For example, an officer may suggest that a person pursue a high-school diploma as a way to improve their life. While this may not be "mandated," the mere suggestion may set an expectation for the individual. If the individual struggles with other conditions of supervision or cannot find a job, this implicit expectation could get in the way of the demands placed on them for supervision. This amounts essentially to an implicit form of coercion, since the probation officer may, with the authority of the state, make a recommendation to the individual that is similar to an implicit requirement. This is the Achilles heel of supervision, and it is such concerns that are associated with being under supervision.

Another cost of supervision lies in the "pains of punishment." The nature and type of conditions of supervision may be onerous to the individual, to an extent that will depend on the characteristics of the probation sentence, and the degree to which the sentence includes a number of requirements or conditions. In the United States, it is not uncommon for individuals on supervision to have a series of standard conditions (i.e., do not move without permission from the probation officer, do not associate with others on supervision, do not own a gun, etc.), special conditions (i.e., drug treatment, employment, mental-health services), or fines or fees. Taxman (2012) has referred to such conditions and requirements as forms of liberty restrictions in that they place demands on a person's physical and financial liberties—they are restrictive. Petersilia and Deschenes (1994), in the mid 1990s, conducted a survey of offenders and found that one-third would prefer incarceration as compared with community punishments because the potential conditions, and the uncertainty of the behavior of probation officers, may have an impact on their degree of success under supervision.

Costs and Benefits to the Community at Large

Probation is a community resource, and in many communities across the globe probation interacts and intersects with other community organizations. The relationships among these organizations is part of the support network in the community since they provide resources to the community's members. Probation services typically rely on community resources and can contribute to building community-based organizations that meet the broader needs of the community such as behavioral health services, somatic healthcare, gang prevention and resistance efforts, housing supports, employment or vocational services, and social support networks.

Strong probation agencies work hand in hand with other community organizations. These partnerships are designed to increase the resources available to the community and to address some of the lifestyle factors that may affect involvement in criminal behavior. Probation systems that rely upon community organizations, that build the available community services, or that facilitate the community services for probationers are cornerstones to stronger communities that can meet the needs of their citizens. The community organizations range widely from government agencies to nonprofit organizations including a broad array of natural community organizations such as religious, civic, arts, and community groups. Inclusion of the natural community organizations serves to focus attention on bolstering the individual probationer's recognition that there are resources available in the community to address basic human needs (i.e. food, shelter, employment, etc.). Essentially, the services can provide support to assist probationers to avoid being part of the justice system.

The probationer can play a part in the community through paying fines and probation fees, and through restitution and contribution to other financial resources. These financial contributions are another resource for the community, and may provide additional funding for probation and for services for the victim, as well as more generally. They may be of assistance to the probationer but may also be available to the community at-large. Many community sanctions include community service or other restorative justice components to reduce the harm from criminal behavior (generally to the community but sometimes to the specific victim). Community service programs generally require the probationer to "pay back" for their offending by performing some type of service to an organization in the community. For example, some community service programs require the individual probationer to participate in removing debris or rubbish from parks, beaches, or community common areas, repairing community neighborhoods (i.e., painting, repairing fences, etc.), or in building houses or community centers. While the individuals provide needed labor for these projects, the labor supports the communities by providing resources that may not be otherwise available. In many ways, community service will transform a community by allowing the justice system to contribute to the community. The inclusion of community service as part of probation sentences is to recognize the value of the labor and contributions that individuals can make to address the harms to the community done through criminal behavior.

Community service also illustrates that individuals can positively impact the community through various actions and behaviors that are contributory, and also that these actions and behaviors have the collateral benefits of assisting others. In fact, the inclusion of community service in probation sentences reinforces an individual's role in the community and their identity as a member of the community that provides a valuable resource. Community organizations, both government and nonprofit, are important resources both for the probation service and for probationers since they assist probationers to repay society through community service work.

Probation serves another benefit to the community by providing employment. Probation agencies generally require professional staff that have at least a college degree, and some agencies require a master's degree or specialized certifications (i.e. social work, counseling, etc.). When probation offices are distributed across communities, they provide local employment for professional staff as well as support staff. The probation offices can be used as a local resource for community meetings (such as self-help groups) or the offices can be used to facilitate other government and/or nonprofit resources in an area. When probation agencies are located in areas of high crime or crime concentration, they can serve as part of the crime control strategy. The probation agencies then become a resource for the community as well as a catalyst for other efforts to reduce crime-producing factors.

There is also a cost to communities that have probation agencies in them. The offices can be areas where individuals congregate, which may be undesirable to community residents. This is a part of the "Not In My Back Yard" mentality, with residents fearing that increases in crime rates and plummeting property values will accompany the addition of correctional supervision and treatment agencies in their community (Piat 2000). While residents need in fact have no fears about such agencies bringing with them increases in crime (Boyd et al. 2012), it is difficult to place probation offices in some communities. This cost is driven by the knowledge that a probation or treatment agency is located in a particular community and residents' perceptions that the presence of these agencies will have a negative effect on the community. However, the building of social capital in such an area may also be viewed as a benefit.

Conclusion

In many systems, probation is considered a sanction "in lieu of" incarceration. This essentially means probation is considered an opportunity afforded to an individual or a chance for them to make amends. But it also means that probation is not considered as legitimate a punishment as incarceration. This perception categorizes probation as an inferior sentence. However, given the elasticity of probation, along with the growth in technology and the add-ons of programming to the probation frame, it is possible that probation may actually be the preferred sanction. It is preferred because it has the greatest potential to limit state control over individuals, to be shaped in a manner that is consistent with the severity of the offense and the characteristics of the offender, and to be less costly to the individual, the justice system, and society overall. Assessing the value of probation through the lens of proportionality, parsimony, citizenship, and social justice can assist us to shift our focus on incarceration as the preferred sanction over community sanctions such as probation.

The costs and benefits of probation depend heavily on the nature of the actual probation sentence for an individual. It is clear that the benefits can achieve a greater purpose for the sanction than merely incapacitation—probation does more to promote citizenship and social justice than incarceration. Individuals remain in the community with the same civic responsibilities that they had before the sanction. The individual is less of a drain on society, and their family and community suffer less, with the person maintaining their citizenship and performing in the roles of parent, spouse, and civic member. During the period of supervision, the features of rehabilitation articulated by McNeill (2012)—personal, judicial, psychological, and social—can be accomplished. Each effect on the individual, their role in society, the community and the justice system can be accomplished through probation supervision. The costs to the individual arise from failure to comply with the requirements of supervision and/or to meet its stated (and often unstated) expectations. Some of the costs are attributable to the probation officers who have discretion over the outcome of supervision, depending on the compliance of the individual probationer. The officer could make favorable or unfavorable determinations about the individual and these assessments have an impact on the outcomes from supervision. While we tend to undervalue the pains of sanctions (see Crewe 2012) and the impact on the individual (Haney 2005), it is the physical and human costs that should be considered in the determination of the value of probation.

Collectively, probation has value as a sanction all to itself. Once it is recognized as a legitimate sanction, the benefits will also multiply in value. The difficulty at present is that probation, in the eyes of the system and the community, is not appreciated. Until it is respected in the same light as incarceration, its benefits will be slow to accrue. These benefits will be to extend the degree to which the justice system and the community obtain more value from supervision—and then individuals on supervision will have a different experience from one of merely managing conditions and instead appreciate the various types of rehabilitation that can be derived from facility-based punishments. The citizenship and social justice features associated with community supervision are more likely to yield greater benefits over time.

References

Boyd, S. J., Fang, L. J., Medoff, D. R., Dixon, L. B., & Gorelick, D. A. (2012). Use of a "microecological technique" to study crime incidents around methadone maintenance treatment centers. *Addiction, 107*(9), 1632–1638. Retrieved from http://doi.org/10.1111/j.1360-0443.2012.03872.x

Crewe, B. (2012). Depth, weight, tightness: Revisiting the pains of imprisonment. *Punishment and Society, 13*(5), 509–529.

Drake, E. K. (2012). *"What works" in community supervision: Interim report* (Document No. 11-12-1201). Olympia: Washington State Institute for Public Policy. Retrieved from http://www.wsipp.wa.gov/ReportFile/1094

Durnescu, I. (2011). Pains of probation: Effective practice and human rights. *International Journal of Offender Therapy and Comparative Criminology, 55,* 530–545.

Haney, C. (2005). *Reforming punishment: The psychological limits to the pains of punishment.* Washington, DC: American Psychological Association.

Maruna, S. (2001). *Making good.* Washington, DC: American Psychological Association.

McNeill, F. (2012). Four forms of supervision: Towards an interdisciplinary perspective. *Legal and Criminological Psychology, 17*(1), 18–36.

National Research Council. (2014). The growth of incarceration in the United States: Exploring causes and consequences. In Committee on Causes and Consequences of High Rates of Incarceration, J. Travis, B. Western, & S. Redburn (Eds.). *Committee on Law and Justice, Division of Behavioral and Social Sciences and Education.* Washington, DC: National Academies Press.

Petersilia, J., & Deschenes, E. (1994). Perceptions of punishment: Inmates and staff rank the severity of prison versus intermediate sanctions. *Prison Journal, 74*(3), 306–328.

Piat, M. (2000). Becoming the victim: A study on community reactions towards group homes. *Psychiatric Rehabilitation Journal, 24*(2), 108–116.

Taxman, F. S. (2008). No illusions: Offender and organizational change in Maryland's Proactive Community Supervision efforts. *Criminology & Public Policy, 7*(2), 275–302.

Taxman, F. S. (2012). Probation, intermediate sanctions, and community-based corrections. In J. Petersilia & K. Reitz (Eds.), *The Oxford handbook of sentencing and corrections* (pp. 363–385). New York: Oxford University Press.

Taxman, F. S. & Rhine, E. (2015). *Markers of probation: Exploring measures of supervision.* Los Angeles, CA: 2nd World Congress.

Tonry, M. (2006). Purposes and functions of sentencing. In M. Tonry (Ed.), *Crime and justice: A review of research* (Vol. 34). Chicago: University of Chicago Press.

Experiencing Supervision: From 'Sparing the First Offenders' to 'Punishment in the Community' and Repairing the Harm Done

Ioan Durnescu

Introduction

By supervision we understand here all activities associated with the implementation of the community sanctions and measures that have a surveillance component which is implemented in the community: probation orders, community service orders, conditional sentences, suspended sentences, deferred sentences and so on.

When suspended sentencing ('sursis') was first introduced in Europe at the end of the nineteenth century the main rationale was 'sparing the worthy first offender from the demoralizing influences of imprisonment and [saving] him from recidivism' (Cornil 1933, cited in Vanstone 2008, p. 5). Indeed, in the context of an increased awareness of the 'contaminating' role of imprisonment and more serious debates

---

Some ideas are further developed in Durnescu et al. (2013) Experiencing Supervision in McNeill, F. and Beyens, K. (eds) *Offender Supervision in Europe*. Palgrave Macmillan.

I. Durnescu (✉)
Faculty of Sociology, University of Bucharest, Bucharest, Romania

© The Editor(s) (if applicable) and The Author(s) 2016
F. McNeill et al. (eds.), *Probation*,
DOI 10.1057/978-1-137-51982-5_10

regarding proportionality, the European legislators agreed to introduce in the national sanctioning systems options that were in between imprisonment and fines. In most cases, the suspended sentence involved no other penal message than that of a warning. For example, the laws of both Lejeune (in Belgium) and Berenger (in France) claimed that there was no need for supervision or patronage because the offenders would reform themselves given the opportunity (for more see Vanstone 2008). For many years therefore, suspended sentences remained only a warning with no other punitive component.

After the Second World War almost everywhere in Europe the suspended sentence came to be supplemented with the element of supervision or control for 'those unable to reform unaided' (Harris 1995, p. 46). In the coming years, suspended-sentence or probation orders were made more and more demanding for the offenders: increasing the minimum probation period or adding more and more requirements (e.g. to attend or reside in different sorts of treatment centres). In the sixties, in the context of a massive industrialization and increased drug use, yet more obligations were attached in order to allow suspended sentences to become more credible alternatives to incarceration but also to respond to the needs of a new penal population. In the seventies and eighties community service was introduced in many European jurisdictions. Later, as victims started to be viewed as playing a more central role in the criminal procedure, still other obligations were added to the suspended-sentence device—e.g. reparation orders, mediation, compensation and so on. More recently, more technology-based obligations have been developed and attached to suspended or conditional sentences—e.g. electronic monitoring, drug testing and so on.

The expansion of offender supervision and the diversity of its forms have been well documented elsewhere (see McNeill 2014; Durnescu 2013), but what it is striking even nowadays is that in the public imagination supervision is still perceived somehow as a 'judicial favour' (Dianu 1997, p. 59), an easy option, a non-punishment or only a pat on the offender's shoulder. This kind of attitude was reflected to a certain extent also in the research field. It is only recently that scholars have started to scrutinize more carefully how supervisees live the supervision experience. Some studies have looked at supervision as a general experience while others have focused more on how particular obligations attached to supervision are experienced. A few studies have also looked at how offenders experience meeting with the victim. In the next sections of this chapter we will examine these studies in an attempt to understand how supervisees perceive the supervision experience.

Supervision as a General Activity

One of the first scholars who looked into the meaning of punishment from the offender's point of view was Davies (1979). As part of the staff development programme, Davies (1979) asked 14 probation officers to select up to five probationers. These subjects were interviewed and asked several questions that are highly relevant for our review. When asked to compare the probation officer with another professional, most of the respondents identified the probation officer most closely with social workers. One quarter of the probationers viewed probation officers as more akin to the teaching profession. Somewhat consistently with these associations, 67% of those interviewed by Davies believed that the purpose of probation was to prevent reoffending, 49% thought it was to provide some practical help and 22% saw it as a form of counselling. According to probationers' accounts, interventions were on a one-to-one basis and the discussions were mainly around use of leisure time, employment prospects and home circumstances. Two-thirds of those interviewed believed that being on probation made a positive impact on their lives.

A later study conducted in 1983 by Day in England discovered that probation supervision was perceived as constructive as long as the advice given by the probation officers was helpful and positive. Most of the respondents described the probation officer in positive terms and one-third of them reported positive changes in their behaviours and attitudes towards others.

Allen (1985) asked his respondents two questions: what they believed the purpose of probation was and what they believed its purpose should be. One of the surprises of this study—not in line with Davies's (1979) observations—was that 78% of his respondents agreed that the main purpose of probation was surveillance and not rehabilitation. That said, 69 % believed that the latter objective *should be* the main aim of probation.

The same expectations were expressed by Rex's (1999) participants. She interviewed 21 probation officers and 60 of their probationers and found that supervision was successful where the probation officer combined 'an appeal to a sense of responsibility with a demonstration of concern and respect for the person' (p. 377). Almost a quarter of the participants were women and half were over 30 years old. Most of them attributed their desistance from crime to probation supervision. Engagement and desistance were facilitated by the personal and professional commitment of the probation officer. The probation officer's reasonableness, fairness and encouragement seemed to spawn a sense of personal loyalty among probationers. Of the probationers, 87 % mentioned that the probation officer needed to show empathy and 65 % of them stated that the probation officer needed to have the ability to listen, show interest and understanding and help them talk. Moreover, 58 % of the participants wanted to be treated with respect and not be judged or patronized by the probation staff. Interestingly, most of the probationers mentioned that these skills needed to be balanced against more formal aspects of probation supervision.

In terms of what they hoped for from the supervision process, the probationers interviewed by Rex (1999) stated that they would appreciate help in solving practical problems in areas like accommodation and debts. They would also expect the probation officer to help them develop some insight into the difficulties they have with relationships and with addiction. They did not expect the probation officer to solve their problems for them but appreciated any assistance to do so themselves.

The same focus on the problem-solving approach was emphasized in Farrall's study (2002). After interviewing 199 probationers, Farrall (2002) found that the most important areas of help needed by the probationers were employment and mending damaged family relationships. However, he concluded that neither of these areas was an important area of intervention for the probation officers. As he sadly concluded, desistance could be attributed to probation interventions in only a few cases. But after a fifth sweep of interviews that took place in 2013 with the same probationers, Farrall et al. (2014) nuanced his earlier findings and concluded that probation supervision seems to produce a delayed positive effect on the lives of probationers. Many ex-probationers acknowledged the constructive influence of probation supervision but after many years.

In an attempt to capture a more detailed perception of the supervision experience, based on in-depth interviews, Durnescu (2011) identified eight pains of probation as described by people under probation supervision in Romania. These were grouped into six areas: deprivation of autonomy, deprivation of time, financial costs, stigmatization effects, forced return to the offence and life under tremendous threat. The first pain—the deprivation of autonomy—was divided into two main deprivations: pain of reorganizing the daily routine around the sanction and the deprivation of private family life. More recently, Hayes (2015) interviewed nine offenders subject to community and suspended-sentence orders in England. Based on these interviews he identified six major groups of pains: pains of rehabilitation (the more requirements the more painful the experience is), pains of liberty deprivation (punishment through breach), penal welfare issues (the more vulnerability one has the more painful the supervision is), pains of external agency interventions (the more agencies are involved the more difficult the supervision process is perceived), process pains ('the process is the punishment': see Feeley and Simon 1992) and stigma. Shame as one of the pains of rehabilitation seemed to be one of the most powerful pains. Interestingly however, Hayes (2015) argues that shame can contribute to rehabilitation under certain circumstances.

As can be noted, although these two studies were conducted in two different jurisdictions most of these pains are shared in common by the probationers. The differences (e.g. the pains of rehabilitation) may be explained by the different ways of configuring the sanctions or the practices around them. This is also the point made by Hayes (2015), who argues that some pains are intensified by the supervisory relationship (e.g. pains of rehabilitation and pains of liberty deprivation). Some other can be ameliorated by the supervisory relationship (e.g. penal welfare issues) or are not affected by this relationship (e.g. pains of the process or stigma).

Comparing these pains with those identified in prison research (see Sykes 1968; Cohen and Taylor 1972; Crewe 2011 etc.) one can observe that some of them are quite close to the prison experience. In fact, most of the studies seem to suggest that the place of implementation is one of the most important factors that made the probation experience differ from the prison. Both sanctions seem to be difficult to negotiate for offenders. Some studies have suggested that some actively prefer the simplicity and predictability of the prison sentence rather than the intrusions and complexities of the supervision. In this respect, many offenders mentioned the fear of a more severe sanction as a result of violating conditions (May and Wood 2010; Payne and Gainey 1998). Intensive probation programs are perceived by offenders to be more punitive than short prison terms (Petersilia and Turner 1993). The same was found in Crouch's (1993) study where almost one-third of the inmates stated that they preferred 1 year in prison to 3 years on probation. This was also the observation of Armstrong and Weaver (2010), who found that although community sanctions and measures are considered by offenders more constructive than prison, they are also more demanding. However, contrary to prior research they found that nearly everyone would prefer community-based sentences to a prison sentence, largely to preserve family and work ties. This preference was not apparent among those with severe addiction problems, who seemed to favour a short-term prison sentence. Most probably, the reasons behind this option are to do with the accessibility of services while in prison and also to the incapacitating effect of the prison in relation to drug use.

How Do Different Supervision Obligations and Practices Impact on the Experience?

Parts of the supervision process or different supervision practices seem to trigger different reactions among probationers. For example, some research seems to suggest that risk assessment is infuriatingly passive—something that it is done to you and not with you. Prisoners and ex-prisoners interviewed by Attrill and Liell (2007) emphasized this frustration many times in their accounts. The lack of control and the excessive focus on the past offending behaviour seem to create frustration and disappointment among parolees. As suggested by Maruna (2010), these risk assessment practices interfere in a negative way with the symbolic message of the rite of passage. Fitzgibbon (2011) continues this idea and argues that the ascendancy of public protection over rehabilitation legitimizes the deconstruction of the client into a bundle of risks (2011, p. 140).

The rise of 'what works' literature and its impact on probation practice were also scrutinized by some researchers. In most cases, researchers found that probation officers required to adhere to these principles usually enjoy less discretion than previously (Canton 2011) and that the involvement of the offenders in their own treatment has become less and less important. Supervision is framed as something that it is done *to* offenders rather than *with* them (Burke and Collett 2010).

One of the most critical groups of offenders is recalled prisoners. Padfield (2012) found the recalled prisoners have little impact on the licence conditions and those who have failed to comply often display a lack of understanding of these restrictions. In spite of the negative consequences on their lives, the recalled prisoners are not routinely asked about their experience or expectations. Several prisoners felt that they were 'set up to fail' by unreasonable parole conditions and many felt 'let down' by their supervisors. Only a few of them felt sympathy for the probation officers for the difficult decisions they have to make and many thought probation officers have too much power (Padfield 2013). Digard (2010) interviewed 20 recalled prisoners and found that some of them were recalled for minor violations or even for highly subjective reasons. Many of them saw their offender managers as being responsible for their re-imprisonment and therefore developed a deep mistrust of them. Almost half of them developed animosity towards their offender manager.

Mixed accounts are also reported by offenders under electronic monitoring (EM). While most offenders acknowledge the opportunity to avoid prison and live a similar to normal life (Hammerschick and Neuman 2008), and also the help to keep away from their criminal friends and spend more time with the family, some complain about the pressure put on them by electronic monitoring in terms of stress, fear and temptation. As Hucklesby (2009) notes, one of the strengths of electronic monitoring is the certainty and speed of the non-compliance detection. As a consequence, this puts a lot of pressure on the offender's self-discipline (Stassart et al. 2000), prevents parents on EM from taking part in some of the children's activities (e.g. evening parties) (Jorgensen 2011) and weighs heavily on the offender's social life, as well as causing stigmatization (Vander Beken and Vanhaelemeesch 2012). Vander Beken and Vanhaelemeesch (2012) also found that the electronic monitoring has a strong impact on third parties (partners/spouses, children etc.). Hucklesby (2009) examined the factors associated with compliance and non-compliance and found that they are complex and inter-related. In most cases they are associated with procedural justice, individual motivations and attachment to significant others.

Community service seems to trigger more or less the same kind of reactions among probationers. Most of those subject to community service seem to evaluate the community service experience as worthwhile and useful in terms of acquiring new skills or enhancing the prospects for a new job (McIvor 1992; Bramberger 2009; Dantinne et al. 2009; van den Dorpel et al. 2010). Another benefit of community service can be the useful opportunity it provides for some offenders to form good relationships and increase self-esteem (Beyens 2010). The 'dark side' of this sanction was also stressed by some offenders. The fact that the sanction requires commitment and offers no payment for labour is hard to accept for some offenders. In Van den Dorpel et al.'s (2010) study, half of the probationers described community service as boring and one-third of them defined it as dirty.

More positive perceptions were described by participants in Mair and Mills's (2009) study. Almost all interviewees stated that the probation officer was easy to talk to, understanding and helpful with their problems. Moreover, some of them were even surprised how supportive and helpful the probation officer was, even when issues of compliance were discussed. It seems that they appreciated the effort of the probation officers to go the extra mile in order to help with their problems.

One of the merits of Mair and Mills's study is that they focused on the impact of different requirements on the lived experience of supervision. Although the drug rehabilitation requirement was perceived as helpful, one respondent found it difficult to keep the appointments (out of 16 participants in the study). All the others perceived this experience as positive. The same was with the community service, which was found by some respondents to be inconvenient. Four participants were required to attend an accredited programme. While no issues were raised regarding the content of the programme, they stated that they were quite reluctant to talk about their past at the beginning of the programme. They were also critical about the frequent changes in the group composition in the first week and the fact that missing one session resulted in re-sitting the whole module. Van de Bunt et al. (2011) interviewed four sex offenders attending groupwork programmes and concluded they felt that probation officers were helpful and provided a safe environment where they could talk freely. However, they also expressed fear of their neighbours finding out about their offence. This question raises again the important issue of confidentiality in a group setting.

In the context of 'what work' agendas, some probation services in Europe work very closely with other agencies in order to provide comprehensive services. In this case, offenders seem to enjoy working alongside 'normal' people (Gibbs 1999) but also express fear and anxiety about probation officers disclosing too much confidential information to partners (Huisman and Aanen 2006; Moerings et al. 2006).

As can be noted, different configurations of punishments can be associated with different sets of reactions. Some of the pains of probation may be deliberate (as observed by Mair and Mills 2009) but that does not necessarily make them understandable and legitimate from the perspective of offenders. Some other consequences of punishment may not be intentional (defined as 'incidental punishment' by Walker 1991) or may affect third parties (defined as 'obiter punishment' by Walker 1991). It is of utmost importance that researchers engage with these issues in order to make the impacts of punishments more transparent and legitimate.

Differential Treatment of Supervision

In the context of anti-discriminatory and anti-oppressive practice movements of the 80s in social work, researchers started to pay more attention to minority groups and their experiences of intervention. One of the first studies in this area was the one conducted by Calverley et al. (2006) on 483 black and Asian offenders across 17 probation areas in England and Wales. The vast majority of offenders (86%) stated that they were fairly treated by their supervisors and with respect. Moreover, the majority of them had had sight of the supervision plan and felt their views had been taken into account when the plan was drafted. The majority of the respondents were more likely to favour a minority ethnic supervisor, but only 3 % defined a good supervisor in terms of ethnicity. What seemed important was that the supervisor should be a good listener, understanding and sympathetic with their problems.

The experiences of women subject to supervision started to receive more attention from researchers after 2000. In their recent review, Malloch and McIvor (2011) found that the quality of the relationship and the focus on self-esteem were the critical elements of a positive experience of women on community service. They also noted that women faced particular barriers in complying with community service owing to gender-based roles and responsibilities. For instance, having childcare responsibilities made it difficult for some women to attend appointments or provide unpaid work at different times of the day. Costs of transport might also be a significant problem for some women.

These findings were further developed by Hedderman et al. (2011), who concluded that women on supervision tended to have developed more complex and severe problems than men on supervision. In this context, probation officers needed to develop long-term relationships with these clients and not treat them as standard cases. The belief that supervisors were genuinely interested in their welfare led the women to feel that visits, reminders or telephone calls were helpful rather than feeling like a form of surveillance.

Supervision and the Victims

At the beginning of the 80s a new movement made its way into the criminal justice system—the victims' rights movement. This movement was supported by late modern views on justice (based on the attitude that 'if we cannot prevent crimes at least we can compensate the victims') and also by some powerful media campaigns following some tragic cases (see the Megan[1] case, the Jenna case and so on).

---

[1] The murder of Megan Kanka occurred in New Jersey, USA. The seven-year-old was raped and murdered by her neighbour. The murder attracted a lot of media attention and subsequently led to the adoption of 'Megan's Law', which requires law-enforcement authorities to disclose detailed information about the location of sex offenders. Visit this website, for example: http://www.megan-slaw.ca.gov/search_main.aspx?searchBy=county&county=los%20angeles&lang=ENGLISH.

Victims' rights become more and more important for criminal justice systems across the world and they were regulated in different transnational bodies including the United Nations (United Nation Declaration on Basic Principles of Justice for Victims of Crime and Abuse of Power 1985), the Council of Europe (Council Recommendation R 1985 on the position of the victim within the framework of the criminal law) and the European Parliament together with the Council of the European Union (European Union Directive 2012/29/EU 2012 on establishing minimum standards on the right, support and protection of victims of crime, and replacing Council Framework Decision 2001/220/JHA). Although they stem from different bodies, there is a great deal of overlap between these international instruments in suggesting ways by which the victims should enjoy rights, such as to be informed, to be consulted, to receive advice, to be accompanied, to receive compensation and so on. Most of these rights had been translated into criminal or criminal procedure codes, and new procedures or requirements were introduced, such as reparation, restitution, compensation, victim–offender mediation and so on.

The question of how victims engage with these new sanctions and with what sorts of outcomes has been asked many times in the literature (see MORI 2004; Hammerschick et al. 1994; Aertsen 1993; Lemonne et al. 2007 etc.). Based on these studies, victims need to be heard and recognized. If they are well informed about mediation, for instance, they tend to agree to take part in it and are very satisfied or satisfied with the process of mediation and its outcome. As shown by Van Ness and Strong (2002), restorative justice processes contribute to victim recovery through redress, vindication and healing. However, critical authors argue that victims do not need to be 'repaired', and that the language of 'reparation' and 'restoration' should be replaced with 'respectful co-involvement in doing justice' (see Derrida 2001; also van Garsse, this volume).

As far as the focus of this chapter is concerned, we are more interested in how offenders experience different forms of restorative justice (e.g. victim–offender mediation, family conferencing, community reparative boards, circle sentencing etc.). In this respect research is quite limited. Most of the studies and the meta-analyses have focused on the impact of restorative justice schemes on recidivism (see Bonta et al. 2002; Latimer et al. 2005; Bradshaw and Rosenborough 2005 etc.). Indeed, the vast majority of these studies demonstrated varying degrees of programme success in this direction.

Other studies have focused more on the impact of restorative justice on different groups of offenders. Some studies found an improved recidivism rate for violent offenders taking part in restorative justice programme but not for the property offenders (see McCold and Wachtel 1998; Sherman et al. 2000; Hayes 2005). Sherman et al. (2000) provide some possible explanations for this somehow counter-intuitive finding. They argue that involving violent offenders in a restorative process offers a different emotional climate and basis for the legitimacy of subsequent interventions. In other words, taking part in a restorative justice process offers the offender the opportunity to apologize, express remorse and empathy for the victim. This can work in reducing the likelihood of recidivism even among violent offenders. Other studies looked at the differential effectiveness of restorative justice according to some individual (age, gender, ethnicity) or community related factors (level of poverty). In spite the fact that these studies show contradictory results, it seems that restorative justice programmes work well with any kind of offender in any kind of context. It may be that restorative justice works better for young offenders and for those with a short criminal history, but research is clear in demonstrating that some impact is also visible among the other subgroups of offenders.

But restorative justice programmes have potentially more offender-focused—and indeed victim-focused—objectives than just reducing reoffending. They can provide more legitimacy to the justice system's interventions and therefore increase compliance. They can provide an 'opportunity to facilitate a desire, or consolidate a decision, to desist' (Robinson and Shapland 2008, p. 352). They can increase victim awareness and community involvement, and so on.

These possible outcomes are not very well explored in the literature. Instead there are a few studies that look at the offenders' satisfaction. In their meta-analysis, Latimer et al. (2005) found that offenders participating in restorative justice programmes displayed higher satisfaction with the process compared with those offenders who did not take part in such a programme. However, the difference was not statistically significant. In terms of compliance with restitution agreements, the same review concluded that offenders taking part in restorative justice programmes were significantly more likely to comply completely with the restitution agreements than those who followed the traditional route.

Limits of the Existing Research

One of the most common limits of the existing studies is that they often look at supervision as if this is a monolithic structure or a homogeneous phenomenon. But as we have seen in some later studies, the supervision experience is influenced by many factors, such as the legal structure, the obligations attached to supervision, the skills and the attitude of the supervisor, and sometimes by external factors from supervision (e.g. childcare responsibilities, health issues etc.). Personal factors such as gender and ethnicity play also in important role in defining the lived experience of supervision.

All these aspects lead us to believe that supervision is a complex process that involves the sanction, the probationer, the supervisor, the probation agency context, the probationer's environment and so on. This complexity requires a more sophisticated qualitative research methodology. Unfortunately, we cannot simplify a reality that is tremendously complex without running the risk of producing mere glimpses of it that are fragmented and distorted.

As most of these studies are based on small numbers of subjects and sometimes on self-selected samples (see the restorative justice example), the conclusions might reflect the views of only a limited number of offenders and most often not of the ones most hard to reach (e.g. non-compliant ones, hostile offenders, homeless offenders, recalled prisoners etc.).

Conclusions

Bearing in mind the limitations described in the previous section, we could suggest that research seems to argue that the more that the probation officer is perceived by offenders as a helpful figure, the more positive outcomes are reported by the supervision recipients. If the supervisor is described as close to a social worker in approach, if s/he is reasonable, genuine, empathic and understanding, then supervisees appear to be more engaged and involved in the process of rehabilitation and change.

On the contrary, if the supervision process is inflated with requirements, if the process is perceived as intrusive and lacks legitimacy, then probationers seem to be dissatisfied and less engaged with the process of supervision. Simply put, the more demanding the community sanction is, the more likely the person will be found to breach the conditions (see also Hucklesby 1994, 2002). As noted in the literature, most probationers acknowledge the formality of the supervision process and even accept its demanding nature. As long as they perceive the sanction as fair and the probation officer as reasonable, respectful and helpful, they tend to engage with the supervision process in a constructive manner. Of course, supervision is perceived as harsher by some subgroups of offenders than by others: the former include those subject to electronic monitoring, women with childcare responsibilities and drug users with hectic lifestyle. These observations are in particular important as they stress the fact that the experience of the probationers is deeply shaped not only by the political choices and the concrete supervision practices but also by factors that are outside the criminal justice system.

The lived experience of supervision is also situated at the intersection of personal factors such as gender, ethnicity etc. and social-ecological ones such as childcare responsibilities and distances to travel. The literature seems also to suggest the existence of a very strong relational component in the supervision process. This dimension is not only about the relationship between the probation officer and the offender, but also about the relationship of the offender with significant others (e.g. peers, family etc.). The quality of the probation-officer–probationer relationship and the genuine interest in the client's well-being seem here to be of paramount importance in producing a positive supervision experience. It is for future research to scrutinize whether, in the context of these ingredients, probationers tend to interpret even the most intrusive surveillance practices as helpful and constructive.

This complexity may be the reason the lived experience of supervision is so difficult to capture in simple observational terms. In this context, the question should be not 'how is supervision experienced?' but rather 'how do different people experience distinct forms of supervision in different socio-economic-cultural and legal contexts?'

Of course, these conclusions should be treated with caution as they are solely based on the offenders' accounts, and those accounts must reflect certain partialities. We do not know whether probationers always mean what they say (Rex 1999) or whether what supervisors call 'care' is perceived as such by the probationers (Canton 2011, p. 24). Moreover, it is not clear yet how these perceptions interact with specific outcomes of supervision when the supervised population is so diverse in terms of gender, ethnicity, criminal history, social background etc. Legitimacy and compliance research might shed some further light on these questions.

References

Aertsen, I. (1993). Slachtoffers van crimineel geweld: een kwalitatief-fenomenologische analyse [Victimis of criminal violence: A qualitative-phenomenological analysis]. In T. Peters & J. Goethals (Eds.), *De achterkant van de criminaliteit: Over victimilogie, slachtofferhulp en strafrechtsbedeling* [The backdoor of criminality: About victimology, victim care and law] (pp. 117–217). Antwerp: Kluwer Rechtswetenschappen Belgie.

Allen, G. F. (1985). The probationers speak: Analysis of probationer's experiences and attitudes. *Federal Probation, 49*(3), 67–75.

Attrill, G., & Liell, G. (2007). Offenders views on risk assessment. In N. Padfield (Ed.), *Who to release? Parole, fairness and criminal justice* (pp. 191–201). Cullompton: Willan.

Beyens, K. (2010). From "community service" to "autonomous work penalty" in Belgium. What's in a name? *European Journal of Probation, 2*(1), 4–21.

Bonta, J., Wallace-Capretta, S., Rooney, J., & McAnoy, K. (2002). An outcome evaluation of a restorative justice alternative to incarceration. *Justice Review, 5*(4), 319–338.

Bradshaw, W., & Rosenborough, D. (2005, December). Restorative justice dialogue: The impact of mediation and conferencing on juvenile recidivism. *Federal Probation, 69*(2), 15–21, 52.

Bramberger, L. (2009). *Und was hat es gebracht? Personlicher und altruisticher Nutzen der Erbringung gemeinnutziger Leistung aus Sicht der Klienten der Bewahrungshilfe* [What good did it do? Personal and altruistic value of

community service orders from the probation service's clients' point of view].
Diploma thesis, University of Innsbruck, Austria.

Burke, L., & Collett, S. (2010, September). People are not things: What new labour has done to probation. *Probation Journal, 57,* 232–249. Sage.

Calverley, A., Cole, B., Kaur, G., Lewis, S., Raynor, P., Sadeghi, S., et al. (2006). Black and Asian probationers: Implications of the Home Office study. *Probation Journal, 53*(1), 24–37.

Canton, R. (2011). *Probation: Working with offenders.* Abingdon: Routledge.

Cohen, S., & Taylor, L. (1972). *Psychological Survival.* Harmondsworth: Penguin.

Council Recommendation R 11. (1985). Retrieved from http://www.coe.int/t/dghl/standardsetting/victims/recR_85_11e.pdf

Crewe, B. (2011). Depth, weight, tightness: Revisiting the pains of imprisonment. *Punishment and Society, 13*(5), 509–529.

Crouch, B. (1993). Is incarceration really worse? Analysis of offenders' preferences for prison over probation. *Justice Quarterly, 10*(1), 67–88.

Dantinne, M., Duchêne, J., Lauwaert, K., Aertsen, I., Bogaerts, S., Goethals, J., et al. (2009). *Peine de travail et vécu du condamné. Beleving van de veroordeelde tot een werkstraf* (unpublished report). Liège and Leuven: Université de Liège and Katholieke Universiteit Leuven.

Davies, M. (1979). Through the eyes of the probationer. *Probation Journal, 26,* 84–88. Sage.

Day, P. (1983). Consumer and supervisor perspectives on probation. *Probation Journal, 30,* 61–63. Sage.

Derrida, J. (2001). *Cosmopolitanism and forgiveness* (M. Dooley & M. Hughes, Trans.). London: Routledge.

Dianu, T. (1997). *Non-custodial sanctions: Alternative models for post-communist societies.* New York: Nova Science.

Digard, L. (2010). When legitimacy is denied: Offender perceptions of the prison recall system. *Probation Journal, 57*(1), 160–163. Sage.

Durnescu, I. (2011). Pains of probation: Effective practice and human rights. *International Journal of Offender Therapy and Comparative Criminology, 55,* 530–545.

Durnescu, I. (2013). Probation skills between education and professional socialization. *European Journal of Criminology.* doi:10.1177/1477370813504162

European Commission, Directive 2012/29/EU. (2012). Retrieved from http://ec.europa.eu/justice/criminal/victims/rights/index_en.htm

Farrall, S. (2002). *Rethinking what works with offenders.* Cullompton: Willan.

Farrall, S., Hunter, B., Sharpe, G., & Calverley A. (2014). *Criminal career in transition. The social context of desistance from crime.* Oxford: Oxford University Press.

Feeley, M., & Simon, J. (1992). The new penology: Notes on the emerging strategy of corrections and its implications. *Criminology, 30*, 449–474.

Fitzgibbon, W. (2011). *Probation and social work on trial: Violent offender and child abusers.* Basingstoke: Palgrave Macmillan.

Gibbs, A. (1999). The forgotten voice: Probation service users and partnerships. *Howard Journal of Criminal Justice, 38*(3), 283–299. Blackwell.

Hammerschick, W., & Neuman, A. (2008). Bericht der Begleitforschung zum Modellversuch 'Elektronische Aufsicht/uberwachter Hausarrest im Rahmen des § 126 StVG' [Report of the accompanying research for the pilot project 'Electronic Monitoring based on § 126 StVG']. In F. McNeill & K. Beyens (Eds.), *Offender supervision in Europe*, 2013. Wien/Graz: Palgrave Macmillan.

Hammerschick, W., Pelikan, C., & Piligram, A. (1994). Von der Fallzuweisung zum Abschluß des Außergerichtlichen Tatausgleichs- die praktischen Ergebnisse des Modellversuchs [From case assignment to the conclusion of out-of-court offence compensation proceedings: The practical results of the pilot project]. In F. McNeill & K. Beyens (Eds.), *Offender supervision in Europe*, 2013. Wien/Graz: Palgrave Macmillan.

Harris, R. (1995). 'Studying probation: A comparative approach' and 'Reflections on comparative probation'. In F. Hamai, R. Vile, M. Hough, R. Harris, & U. Zveckic (Eds.), *Probation around the world.* London: Routledge.

Hayes, H. (2005). Assessing re-offending in restorative justice conferences. *Australian and New Zealand Journal of Criminology, 38*(1), 77–101.

Hayes, D. (2015, August). The impact of supervision on the pains of community penalties in England and Wales: An exploratory study. *European Journal of Probation, 7*, 85–102. doi:10.1177/2066220315593099

Hedderman, C., Gunby, C., & Shelton, N. (2011). What women want: The importance of qualitative approaches in evaluating work with women offenders. *Criminology and Criminal Justice, 11*(1), 3–19.

Hucklesby, A. (1994). The use and abuse of bail conditions. *Howard Journal of Criminal Justice, 33*, 258–270.

Hucklesby, A. (2002). Bail in criminal cases. In M. McConville & G. Wilson (Eds.), *The handbook of the criminal justice process* (pp. 115–136). Oxford: Oxford University Press.

Hucklesby, A. (2009). Understanding offenders' compliance: A case study of electronically monitored curfew orders. *Journal of Law and Society, 36*(2), 248–271. doi:10.1111/j.1467-6478.2009.00465.x

Huisman, E., & Aanen, G. (2006). *Uit de Bak, Exodus- dak, Eigen Dak!?* [Out of prison, Exodus- roof, own roof?]. Bachelor's thesis, Exodus Utrecht, the Netherlands.

Jorgensen, T. T. (2011). *Afsoning I hjemmet: En effektevaluering of fodlaenkeordningen* [Doing prison time at home: An evaluation of the effect of electronic monitoring]. Copenhagen: Ministry of Justice.

Latimer, J., Dowden, C., & Muise, D. (2005). The effectiveness of restorative justice practices: A meta-analysis. *Prison Journal, 85*(2), 127–144.

Lemonne, A., Van Camp, T., Vanfraechem, I., & Vanneste, C. (2007). *Onderzoek met betrekking tot de evaluatie van de voorzieningen ten behoove van slachtoffers van inbreuken* [Evaluation research of the services for victims of crimes]. Eindrapport. Brussels: NICC.

Mair, G., & Mills, H. (2009). *The community order and the suspended sentence order three years on: The views and experiences of probation officers and offenders.* London: Centre for Crime and Justice Studies.

Malloch, M., & McIvor, G. (2011). Women and community sentences. *Criminology and Criminal Justice, 11*(4), 325–344.

Maruna, S. (2010). Mixed methods research: Why not go both ways? In A. Piquero & D. Weisburd (Eds.), *Handbook of quantitative criminology* (pp. 123–140). New York: Springer.

May, D., & Wood, P. (2010). *Ranking correctional punishments: Views from offenders, practitioners and the public.* Carolina Academic Press.

McCold, P., & Wachtel, B. (1998). *Restorative policing experiment: The Bethlehem Pennsylvania police family group conferencing project.* Pipersville, PA: Community Service Foundation.

McIvor, G. (1992). *Sentenced to Serve: The operation and impact of community service by offenders.* Aldershot: Avenbury.

McNeill, F. (2014, June 19). *Probation: Myths, realities and challenges.* Presentation delivered at Council of Europe Conference of Directors of Prisons and Probation Services, Helsinki. Retrieved from www.offendersupervision.eu

Moerings, M., Van Wingerden, S. G. C., & Vijfhuize, P. J. (2006). *Exodus, Op de Goede Weg? Onderzoekschool Maatschappelijke Veiligheid.* Hoofddorp: Boom Juridische Uitgevers.

MORI. (2004). *MORI Youth Survey 2004.* Retrieved from http://yjbpublications.justice.gov.uk/en-gb/scripts/prodView.asp?idProduct=187&eP=

Padfield, N. (2012). Recalling conditionally released prisoners in England and Wales. *European Journal of Probation, 4*(1), 34–45.

Padfield, N. (2013). *Understanding recall 2011* (Paper no. 2). Retrieved from http://papers.ssrn.com/sol3/papers.cfm?abstract_id=2201039

Payne, B. K., & Gainey, R. R. (1998). A qualitative assessment of the pains experienced on electronic monitoring. *International Journal of Offender Therapy and Comparative Criminology, 42*(2), 149–163.

Petersilia, J., & Turner, S. (1993). Intensive probation and parole. In M. Tonry (Ed.), *Crime and Justice: An Annual Review of Research* (Vol. 19, pp. 281–335). Chicago, IL: University of Chicago Press.

Rex, S. (1999). Desistance from offending: Experiences of probation. *Howard Journal of Criminal Justice, 36*(4), 366–383.

Robinson, G., & Shapland, J. (2008). Reducing recidivism. A task for restorative justice? *British Journal of Criminology, 48*, 337–358.

Sherman, L., Strang, H., & Woods, D. (2000). *Recidivism patterns in the Canberra Reintegrative Shaming Experiments.* Canberra: Australian National University, Centre for Restorative Justice, Research School of Social Sciences.

Stassart, E., Peters, T., & Parmentier, S. (2000). *Elektronisch toezicht. Een belevingsonderzoek bij de eerste groep van deelnemers.* Eindrapport (unpublished). Brussels: Ministerie van Justitie - K.U.Leuven.

Sykes, G. M. (1968). Points of no return: Some situational aspects of violence. *Prison Journal, 48*(2), 14–16. doi:10.1177/003288556804800206.

United Nation Declaration on Basic Principles of Justice for Victims of Crime and Abuse of Power. (1985). Retrieved from http://www.un.org/documents/ga/res/40/a40r034.htm

Van de Bunt, H. G., Holvast, N. L., & Plaisier, J. (2011). *Toezicht op Zedendelinquenten door de Politie in Samenwerking met de Reclassering.* Apeldoorn: Politie en Wetenschap and Erasmus Universiteit en Impact R&D.

Van den Dorpel, H., Kamp, E., & Van der Laan, P. (2010). *Amsterdamse Werkgestraften aan het Woord. Eerste Indrukken van een Onderzoek naar de Werkstraf in Amsterdam.* Amsterdam: Nederlands Studiecentrum Criminaliteit en Rechtshandhaving.

Van Ness, D., & Strong, K. (2002). *Restoring justice.* Cincinnati, OH: Anderson.

Vander Beken, T., & Vanhaelemeesch, D. (2012). Electronic monitoring: Convicts' experiences in Belgium. In M. Cools, B. De Ruyver, M. Easton, L. Pauwels, P. Ponsaers, G. Vande Walle, et al. (Eds.), *Social conflicts, citizens and policing.* Antwerpen: Maklu.

Vanstone, M. (2008). The international origins and initial development of probation: An early example of policy transfer. *British Journal of Criminology, 47*(3), 390–404.

Walker, N. (1991). *Why punish?* Oxford: Oxford University Press.

Weaver, B. (2010). *Multi-Agency Protection Arrangements (MAPPA) in Scotland: What do the numbers tell us?* SCCJR Briefing Paper, No. 01/2010.

Electronic Monitoring and Probation Practice

Mike Nellis

Introduction

Probation services have, perhaps understandably, had a largely ambivalent relationship to electronic monitoring (EM) technology, and while recent years have seen, around the world, a rapprochement between the two—sometimes convivial, sometimes uneasy, based on a despondent (or merely pragmatic) sense that, no matter what, EM is not going away—it would be unwise to assume that no cause for concern remains about the likely trajectory and impact of this surveillance technology (Nellis et al. 2012). English chief probation officer Whitfield (1997, 2001) and the sequence of CEP EM conferences that began in 1998 made a concerted bid to promote an integrated vision of EM, embedding it within probation programmes to support rehabilitative ends, and have undoubtedly influenced EM's development for the better in Europe (Nellis 2014a). The Council of Europe's (2014) subsequent Recommendation (instigated by the CEP) set out a human rights

M. Nellis (✉)
Law School, University of Strathclyde, Strathclyde, UK

© The Editor(s) (if applicable) and The Author(s) 2016
F. McNeill et al. (eds.), *Probation*,
DOI 10.1057/978-1-137-51982-5_11

217

framework for implementing EM—recognising that it had appeal to prison services and police forces as well as probation services—and was premised on the idea that without dynamic regulation there could obviously be bad and unduly extensive uses of EM, possibly fuelled by commercial interests. The overall political, economic and cultural context in which EM has gained prominence and momentum as a penal measure could undoubtedly make it a 'disruptive technology', and perhaps even a 'transformational technology' in respect of contemporary probation services—more so, perhaps, than one which can easily and permanently be subordinated to existing probation ideals and practices.

This chapter will explore the nature of the debate that has taken place about EM and probation, describe and appraise the available evidence, and consider the prospects for their future relationship. Firstly, however, it is important, in the first instance, to attempt a conceptual clarification of what EM actually entails as a penal intervention. It can of course be represented in discursively different ways, reflecting underlying political and professional attitudes towards it, and in different times and places it has been given both utopian and dystopian inflections, often by people who have failed to conceptualise its precise nature, misunderstood its conditions of emergence in successive waves of innovation in communication technology, and failed to distinguish between its possible and plausible trajectories as a penal measure in a pervasively digitised world.

Describing and Defining 'Electronic Monitoring'

Although initially only associated with curfews and house arrest, 'electronic monitoring' is a term which nowadays must be used in the plural, because it encompasses a range of distinct-but-related surveillance technologies. This includes the original, and still most widespread, short-range radio frequency (RF) systems, which require a signalling device (colloquially, a 'tag') to be fitted to the ankle or wrist of a defendant or offender, and for them to remain in close proximity to a transceiver in their home, which relays data about their presence or absence to a monitoring centre, either by a landline or, increasingly, the cellular telephone system. This enables curfew enforcement. Voice verification systems (still rare) use the uniqueness of a person's voice to identify them during a phone call, by matching it with a biometric voiceprint already stored, at the point of sentence, in the monitoring centre's computer, and tallying this with the location from which the phone call is made. This enables the pinpointing of a person at a single location (its commonest use), but it could in principle be used to confirm presence at a sequence of locations—home, job centre, community service placement etc.—in effect becoming a form of 'tracking'. The preferred, and increasingly popular, means of tracking an offender's movements relies on geo-location satellites (in practice, the American Global Positioning System (GPS), although Europe, Russia and China have satellite systems of their own). The precision and accuracy of satellite tracking systems, which require ankle-worn devices that both pick up GPS signals and transmit location data to monitoring centres, is invariably augmented by—and could not operate efficiently without—cellular telephone systems, and can be supported by night-time curfew requirements which require the defendant/offender to go home and charge the battery.

All the above interventions are forms of remote-location monitoring, expressions of an increasingly 'telematic society' in which the conduct and coordination of activity in many spheres—transportation, education, security, healthcare, global finance, even entertainment—is undertaken at a distance, but in 'real time' (Bogard 1996). Immediacy of communication and influence, mediated by digital technology, is a defining characteristic of contemporary society, from which no existing institutional arrangements are immune. 'The new' does not necessarily erase 'the old', but the extension of near-instantaneous access to data and people in remote spaces means that it can displace—or augment—merely local, face-to-face encounters. The digitised structures and cultures in which people live and work are reconfigured, enabling hybrid combinations of the virtual and the material through which commercial, civic and everyday relationships and transactions can be built and sustained in novel ways.

EM is telematic. In a criminal justice/penal context, these technologies enable judicial and executive authorities to restrict, regulate and enforce a suspect or offender's spatial and temporal activity (their locations, movements and schedules), at a distance, in real time if desired, potentially in a very finely calibrated way (down to the minute or second), for periods of variable duration. Contemporary monitoring technologies focus on pinpointing offenders at fixed locations, following (and analysing) the trails of offenders 'on the move' or alerting authorities when the perimeters of designated exclusion zones are about to be crossed—separately or in combination. These technological capabilities enable the enforcement of judicial or executive requirements either to be present at a certain place at a certain time (inclusion), or to be absent from it (exclusion); by showing whether an offender was at or near a particular crime scene the tracking technologies can incriminate or exonerate them (Nellis 2009a, 2010).

All monitoring technologies can be used on a stand-alone basis or in conjunction with other supervisory (social work, probation or policing) techniques, and a wide range of surveillant/supervisory regimes can be built around them, of varying intensities and onerousness. There is nothing inherent in any of the technologies that dictates precisely how they should be used; that is for policymakers and practitioners to decide, according to the penal purpose they wish to achieve. Nonetheless, monitoring technology can itself stimulate new imaginative possibilities, on a scale hitherto unfeasible, if policymakers choose to pursue them. All forms of EM impose *control* on an offender—monitors are in a position of influence over monitorees, can check, in real time or retrospectively, whether a legally imposed spatial or temporal requirement has been complied with, and can initiate a response to any perceived violation. EM control can be imposed for its own sake, for no reason beyond itself (say, at the pre-trial stage), or it can be embedded in (sentencing or post-release) programmes which are intended to be rehabilitative or punitive, or both.

EM technologies are never perfect, in the sense of being an always foolproof means of identifying an offender's location; quite apart from their own design limitations and occasional technical flaws, they remain heir to the vulnerabilities of the larger technological systems in which they are nested. But they do not have to be perfect to be useful: so long as their imperfections and potential failings are understood and allowed for in the interpretation of the location data they generate, they can still facilitate and support surveillance and/or supervision. Criticising the reliability of EM technology, which some probation services were prone to do in the early days, was always a weak way of resisting it, not least because they invariably underestimated its ever-increasing reliability (and misunderstood the sources of this, in commercially driven innovation in the wider world of everyday digital connectivity), as well as laying probation itself wide open to comparable questions about the assumed reliability of its own traditional methods.

Onerous as EM-based regimes sometimes can be, they cannot be incapacitative in the same way as cells and locks, or bolts and bars, and it is unhelpful to think of them, even metaphorically, as 'virtual prisons', as Roberts (2004) has done. EM undoubtedly introduces an element of 'virtuality' into offender supervision, at least for the monitoring centre staff, who can undertake remote mass surveillance across a whole country or region from a single site, and make tentative judgments about an individual offender's behaviour and motivation on the basis of onscreen geo-location data. They may have no personal, face-to face-knowledge of the offenders in question: at best they may speak to them by phone if curfews are not kept or if family problems arise. None of this replicates the confining aspects of imprisonment, although from the offender's perspective it may echo the panoptic gaze of a closed penal institution, the sense of being watched or, more precisely, of having one's whereabouts known by unseen authorities, for remote location monitoring is not in itself, a visual, ocular form of surveillance, although it can potentially be linked to that (Nellis 2006).

EM entails a restriction of liberty, but not full deprivation of it. The requirements it can be used to enforce—to be in, or to avoid, certain places at certain times, to succumb (in the case of GPS tracking) to incessant oversight—can be prohibitive, but never fully inhibitive. In that sense EM has always had more of a practical affinity with probation supervision than with imprisonment, and those probation services which have embraced it have understood this: offenders have a choice about whether to comply, and can, by dint of their agency, resist compliance if they are so inclined, just as they can with any community sanction or measure. A certain personal discipline is required to abide by a curfew, or to resist the temptation of criminal activity when one is wearing a tag, because there is no physical restraint on either. As such, some champions of EM claim that it can 'responsibilise' its subjects, at least for the duration of the monitoring period, and possibly beyond it. In reality, compliance may be as much to do with the increased likelihood of violation detection that monitoring entails, and the threat of more severe punishment if breach is proven. Either way, EM exemplifies one instance of what Crawford (2003) has elsewhere called an emerging mode of 'contractual governance' over offenders, and indeed citizens more generally, which he dubs 'regulated self-regulation', because it requires active cooperation from participants with the socio-technical system in which they have been 'enrolled'. With EM, arguably more so than with other community penalties, compliance requires some understanding of how the sanction works, technologically; in agreeing to regularly charge the short-life battery in GPS tracking devices offenders actively collaborate with their own monitoring. Nonetheless, not only can crime be committed while a tag is being worn, but plastic ankle straps can easily be cut through (although slower-to-remove straps containing steel bands are available), devices smashed, signals blocked with tinfoil or jammers, and transceivers tampered with. All these violations will be detected at the monitoring centre, but cumulatively these apparent weaknesses have empowered critics to claim that EM is wholly inadequate as form of control or punishment, certainly compared with imprisonment, and that at best it can only be suitable for low-risk offenders.

Contemporary EM manufacturers readily concede that EM is 'participant-dependant' (see the advertisement for Satellite Tracking of People (STOP), an American GPS tracking provider, in *Journal of Offender Monitoring* 19:2), typically seeing it as a design weakness, a technological limitation to be overcome, an impediment to more complete control, which leaves an offender with too much leeway to break the rules. STOP, in fact, marketed its one-piece tracking unit as 'the least participant dependent device available today' (idem) without apparently realising that from an 'offender management' perspective the leeway creates an opportunity for an offender to act responsibly, and to respond positively to the element of trust being shown to him (or her) by the monitoring authorities. Leaving aside the question of whether EM actually does 'responsibilise' offenders, it certainly makes them (rather literally) 'accountable', creating precise, retrieveable, time-stamped digital records of presence or absence, or of routes and movements, against which, or for which, they can be held to account.

Nowadays, not all 'electronic monitoring' is remote-*location* monitoring. The American, nineteen-sixties, precursors of what we now call EM, developed experimentally under the rubric of 'psychotechnology' (Schwitzgebel 1969; Schwitzbebel and Schwitzbebel 1971), and while they were deployed in tracking movement, they were more focussed on *remote behaviour modification.* Notwithstanding its somewhat medicalised understanding of offender motivation, the precursor visions of EM anticipated its use as a means of monitoring and rewarding good behaviour (for avoiding bad neighbourhoods, attending school or work, arriving at agreed destinations on time etc.), and formallly aligned it with rehabiliation rather than punishment. Outside the growing fields of 'telecare' and 'telehealth' which (among other things) remotely monitor the 'lifesigns' (heartbeat, respiration rate etc.) of elderly and ill people who remain in the community rather than hospital or residential care, remote alcohol monitoring was the first form of remote physiological surveillance to be developed for offenders. The first version of this added breathaliser technology to a transceiver in a curfewed offender's home, prohibited the use of alcohol for the duration of the monitoring period and randomly checked compliance, variously using photographs, voice verification and even facial recognition software to remotely confirm the identity of the person blowing into the breathalyser (as opposed to a sober surrogate). More recently, greater interest has been shown in transdermal alcohol monitoring, in which an ankle worn-device senses alcohol given off by the skin (rather than the breath), and uploads the data at regular intervals, via the internet, to a monitoring centre. Remote alcohol monitoring has been more widely used in the US than Europe, although recently pilot schemes using the transdermal technology have been established in England and the Netherlands. In England, remote alcohol monitoring has been discursively packaged by government- –as indeed EM in England always has—as a punitive measure, but to the extent that it is in practice being used to help offenders manage an alcohol problem that has led them into criminal activity, it borders on the 'coercive rehabilitation' that Robinson has identified as characteristic of late modern penalty. Remote alcohol monitoring also brings out, even more so than location-monitoring technologies, that EM is a form of 'informated touch', (Bogard 1996) the gathering and processing of data from sensors embedded in or attached to physical objects, in this case a human body. Ankle-worn tags are just such sensors, and while it is the offender's conscious mind (reflexive reasoning) over which influence is being sought, it is the corporeal presence or absence of the offender's tagged (touched) body from designated places at specified times, or the constant mapping of its mobility in physical space, mediated by digital technology, which makes the entire infrastructure of electronic monitoring possible.

Finally, it is important to conceptualise EM as something more than just an individualised, targeted surveillance technique applied to selected penal subjects, although it is emphatically that. It is also an architecture of control, an 'automated socio-technical system' which is capable—in a way that other supervision practices are not—of undertaking the mass surveillance of potentially large numbers of suspects and offenders simultaneously (Lianos and Douglas 2000; Jones 2006). Detailed rules and regulations can be imposed on offenders and enforced with a precision and speed that merely human systems could never emulate, certainly not as efficiently, and perhaps not as impartially. People are still needed to programme and tend the computers, to read the screens and make decisions about how alerts and violations are to be responded to, but many aspects of the process, for example, phone calls to offenders, are or can be automated, creating superficial efficiencies but potentially—from a probation standpoint—depersonalizing the supervision process. With EM, there are always ethical choices to be made as to how automated one wants monitoring to be (and many systems eschew automated, recorded voices, preferring live verbal exchanges between monitoring staff and offenders and their families) (Nellis 2013a). Furthermore, once one monitoring centre is created in a country, it is technically as easy (staff numbers and data overload notwithstanding) to monitor tens of offenders as it is to monitor thousands. Once an EM system is established, with a software platform that is easy to upgrade, it is relatively easy to increase the scale of its use, and this latent potential can be seen as one of its dangers.

It is not however that arguments – slippery slope & thin end of the wedge are intellectual positions should be unduly indulged; there is nothing inevitable about the expansion and future domination of EM, although there are always tendencies, contexts and conjunctures (which it is important to identify, and if possible modify) which favour some outcomes over others. Technological innovation only creates possibilities: it is, as the critics of technological determinism have long told us, commerce and politics which create and shape actualities.

EM and Probation: Evolving Relationships and Issues

As can be seen from the above, a great deal can and has been said about the forms, aspirations and potential of EM without probation being in the same frame; as often as not EM has been theorised and researched without reference to its significance for probation. Past probation practice has entailed an incidental degree of spatial and temporal regulation (residence at agreed locations, punctual appointments), and has imposed onerous requirements on offenders, but nothing resembling the reach and immediacy of EM has been within its purview. EM emerged outside probation, not from within it, and there is no immediate or obvious affinity between the two modalities of supervision. Nevertheless, ever since EM's practical inception in the USA in the early 1980s, and the beginnings of its adoption in Europe (essentially from the mid to late 1990s, although England and Wales had run a pilot in 1989–90), probation services have felt compelled to appraise its potential and consider their own future in relation to it. This is simply because the governments who have shown interest in it, largely in a modernising (and sometimes anti-welfare) spirit, have perceived it as a new, ostensibly cost-effective means of supervising offenders in the community, an area of penal practice in which probation has traditionally had a near monopoly. Crucially, finance-conscious governments, more so in Europe, but eventually in the US as well, have expressed hopes that EM—usually in conjunction with intensive probation—would constitute a more reliable, consistent and credible 'alternative to prison', or form of 'early release', thus enabling more significant reductions in the use and cost of imprisonment than forms of probation or parole supervision had hitherto enabled or achieved on their own.

Explaining the evolving interface between probation and EM is a complex story, not easily told in a short compass, partly because there is no consensus on what the sociological parameters of the story actually are. Is 'explaining the interface' to be understood narrowly as a simple technical debate about better and worse ways of doing supervision and reducing the use of prison, based on the steady accumulation of empirical evidence? Much debate in the academic sub-field of 'probation studies' has been of this kind. Much of the early academic literature on EM itself was similarly technical and utilitarian—albeit alongside a 'literature of resistance', especially in British probation circles, which declared EM to be unethical in principle, anathema to all probation stood for, regardless of what evidence may say about it. Or does—or should—'explaining the interface' between probation and EM—entail a larger set of questions about ways of mediating the impact of digital information and communication technology on established social institutions in general, and probation services in particular, a perspective which will inevitably challenge the more simplistic (empirical, technical) probation understandings of how it can be accommodated or resisted. Even the sociology of punishment has shown only limited interest in the impact of digital technology on the management of offenders (Jones 2000, Franko Aas 2004; Brown 2006; Bogard 2010); 'probation studies' has largely brushed it away.

For the time being, however, let us stick with a narrowly probation perspective on EM, and summarise the issues that have arisen. There has been, as in most penal matters, a marked element of national variation in the way EM has been used—but also, arguably, elements of cross-national convergence in policymakers' thinking about the meaning of EM (as a technology) and the purposes to which it can be put, even if the legal and policy frameworks in which it is given practical expression still differ (Nellis 2014a; 2014b). There seems to be a difference in attitude towards older, traditional probation services, and newly created ones in Eastern Europe and the Baltic states; the latter, being established after the advent of EM, and in fully digitised societies, have been more receptive to its use as a tool of supervision than older services for whom EM seemed initially to be an innovation too far. In Estonia, for example, one of Europe's most 'wired' societies, probation officers themselves have discretion, within the framework of a court order, to decide when to fit and remove an RF ankle bracelet, at whatever point in the sentence they consider it useful and necessary. Older, traditional, probation services have been sceptical of the compatibility of EM technology—so manifestly a form of impersonal surveillance and control—with their own humanistic, often social work-derived 'probation values', which typically and traditionally emphasised care and support, and merely legal-administrative forms of control (notably the threat of breach for non-compliance).

The sense of incompatibility has been heightened when governments have discursively and strategically presented EM as inherently and uniquely punitive, and—as in England and Wales—set it up as a formal rival to probation supervision. Handing its administration to the private sector rather than the probation service—a distinct feature of all British models of EM (England and Wales, Scotland and Northern Ireland), although less common elsewhere—further reinforced the sense that EM was 'somebody else's business', not probation's—and anxiety about commercial lobbying for the expansion of EM (perhaps at the expense of other community-based measures, which rarely have commercial champions) has long been a background feature of debate on its likely impact on probation services (Paterson 2007, 2012).

Despite technocratic claims to the contrary, the ideal or optimum relationship between EM and probation was never likely to be settled by empirical evaluations of effectiveness alone, helpful as these can be. Overriding Ideological and ethical considerations have always framed debate about probation and EM, and to greater or lesser degree these have been immune to arguments derived from evidence. In the broader context of ever heightening awareness of the impact automation (and robots) might have on skilled human labour, fears that EM would supplant the personal and relational aspects of supervision and reduce officer-offender encounters to a digital transaction have never been entirely fanciful: 'in the age of the smart machine, (Zuboff 1988) neoliberal imperatives will dispense with certain occupations. These fears have recently (re)surfaced in respect of plans to introduce 'kiosk-based reporting' in some of England's newly privatised probation services (Raho 2014). Perhaps paradoxically, the cost-driven use of GPS tracking to supplant the labour intensive 'intrusive policing' of persistent and prolific offenders released from prison in England has been experienced by offenders as replacing a dismal and intimidating form of human interaction with a more convivial technological one. This, in turn, has given them confidence to access serves from probation officers that they would otherwise have seen no purpose in (interview with tracked offender at Hertfordshire Police headquarters, 15th August 2014).

In the era when the pursuit of effective probation practice was dominated by cognitive behavioural psychology EM seemed inherently incapable of effecting the longer term change in attitudes and behaviour in which probation placed such store. It is quite true that EM in itself intends no more than an immediate, 'real-time', deterrent effect on behaviour—it invites the offender to consider whether his action will be detected in the here and now if he (or she) violates the conditions imposed on them—and does not seek to influence what they become in the long term. Dismissing the utility of EM to probation on these grounds alone seems unwise, if, for example, EM can be shown to be useful in other ways, such as improving compliance with therapeutic and supportive elements of a cognitive change programme. Early evidence from Canada, albeit based on a very small sample, did suggest this (Bonta et al. 2000). The use of EM house arrest as part of an intensive, cognitive behaviourally-based supervision programme seemed to help offenders to complete a cognitive change programme, and thereby gain full benefit from it (unlike the unmonitored, who had lower rates of completion).

In the later, and arguably still current, era of 'desistance-based practice'—a reaffirmation of humanistic, relational, personalised approaches to offender supervision—EM has seemed similarly marginal, even alien, to its central ambitions, an intervention that should always, ideally be done without. This, despite Hucklesby's (2008, 2009) English research showing rather precisely how even short, stand-alone EM-curfews can contribute to desistance—the experience can stimulate thinking about giving up crime, expose offenders to the good influence of supportive family and friends—which would be attenuated or lost in a prison sentence—and breaking the bad habit of association with criminal peers. The great merit of Hucklesby's research is that it shows what the specific effects of stand-alone RF EM are in the context of 12-hour-per-day maximum curfews over short periods of time, 'uncluttered' by other interventions. It isolated the effects—or some effects—that Marklund and Holmberg (2009) admit they were unable to disentangle from their evaluation of a more integrated, deliberately synergised, multi-component supervision programme in Sweden. The great danger of Hucklesby's research is that it will be read by others, irrespective of her intentions, as a justification of stand-alone EM, producing good enough effects in itself without the addition of rehabilitative measures. While there is common sense in the view that offenders may need help and support to complete an EM-order, there is danger too in the idea of 'assisted compliance', if by that social work (as opposed to texted reminders of rules and appointments) is relegated to supporting the *more important measure* of EM. In the main, EM should support probation interventions, not the other way round (see Martinovic 2010a for a partial counterview). A case can arguably be made for the short-term, stand-alone use of EM as a low-tariff measure, the equivalent of a fine, but in such cases the regime imposed should not be so onerous that additional support is required for offenders and families to bear it.

Understanding the EM Evidence Base

Like all contemporary penal measures, the efficiency and effectiveness of EM has been evaluated, with greater or lesser degrees of independence and sophistication, in almost all countries which have adopted it. Periodically, evaluations are collated and reviewed, and an attempt made to draw some cumulative, state-of-the-art message from them, which might be useful for policymakers, nationally and internationally (Schmidt 1998; Martinovic 2010b; Renzema 2012). This enterprise has not gone well. Mark Renzema, the doyen of EM evaluators in the USA, has pointed out that EM research, even when methodologically sound, is only as good as the purposes to which EM is put, and if those purposes have been ill-thought-out and/or misconceived, and if even well-conceptualised programmes have been badly implemented, evaluations will not say much that is useful (Renzema and Mayo-Wilson 2005). In his view, much early EM research was not methodologically sound, and he regretted that the expansion of EM in the USA proceeded without an adequate evidence base. In England, Mair (2006), a pioneering Home Office evaluator of EM, made a different, more telling point: although the government commissioned sound research on all its EM pilots, which showed modestly positive results in terms of reduced reconvictions, the policy commitment to EM was always greater than the results warranted, suggesting that the expansion of EM had other—ideological and fiscal—drivers apart from, and perhaps despite, the evidence of its effectiveness.

In any case, the diverse technologies which now constitute EM, combined with the even more diverse programmes and contexts in which it can be embedded, together with the variety of penal cultures which exist internationally, mean that defining and measuring its effectiveness (its impact on reducing reoffending, or reducing the use of custody, to use but two possible criteria) is far more complex than, say, probation or community service, which are far less versatile. It is significant that the Campbell Collaboration, which collates evaluations from around the world and publicises meta-analyses of the effectiveness of particular penal interventions, has yet to produce one on EM—Taylor and Ariel (2012) are the second attempt to do so—and not only because there are still too few studies using the random controlled trial method that the Consortium favours. It is fair to say in respect of EM that no study in any one country could ever be more than *suggestive* of how EM might be used in another country, because, as the 'policy transfer' literature avers more generally, the social, legal and practical nuances that create the precise effects can never be replicated cross-nationally. Nevertheless, there is much evaluative research now that is indeed suggestive of how EM might be used well.

Not all EM research has been undertaken with probation interests in mind, sometimes by design, sometimes for reasons of academic neutrality. Not all criminologists (who are not the only academics to have researched EM) are wedded to the survival or evolution of the probation service, and by researching EM neutrally, as if its relationship to existing probation practices were a matter of indifference, may inadvertently contribute to the view that probation can be sidelined or dispensed with, if EM seems to get better results. Like the CEP's strongly normative approach to EM, this chapter is premised on the view that EM will only be used wisely and well if it is shaped and constrained by the liberal humanistic traditions which underpin good practice in probation. The corollary of this is that probation services must be open-minded enough to engage with the varied potential of EM, to experiment with it, to champion its better uses and challenge its worse ones, lest—left to its own devices, and opened up to endless commercial innovation—EM becomes a dangerous technology and surveillance becomes the overriding norm in offender supervision.

For this reason, the appraisal of evidence offered here will be drawn from a recent international review of EM (Graham and McIvor 2015) specifically commissioned by the Scottish Government to inform its thinking about the future of criminal justice social work (as 'probation' is called in Scotland) and 'community justice' more broadly. Scotland had adopted an essentially English model of stand-alone RF EM, delivered by the private sector, in 1998, but now (quite unlike England and Wales) wants to develop a more integrated use of EM and social work, and to see it contribute more systematically to a reduced prison population (Nellis 2015) and is looking to other countries for relevant lessons. Graham and McIvor (2015) offer a selective rather than a comprehensive review of the literature, but touch on all the main research from the past fifteen years, highlighting both implementation processes and outcomes, for both RF and GPS EM, as well as what has been useful and difficult for probation services. The advice they offer to the Scottish government is doubtless already familiar to many European and indeed some American probation services, but it has the merit of spelling out lessons from EM research from the standpoint of academics supportive of, rather than hostile or indifferent to, the broader social work context in which offender supervision should ideally occur.

Graham and McIvor highlight clear evidence that RF EM can, broadly speaking, reduce reoffending, but there are always qualifiers. In a small US study of paroled violent offenders, Finn and Muirhead-Steves (2002) concluded that compared with a control group, EM reduced time delays in return to prison, at least in the short term, within one year. By three years there was no difference between the groups and, playing down the short-term results, give no significant endorsement to EM as a tool for paroles. The study begs many questions about what the parolees' experience actually consisted of, but tentatively signalled one finding that has been replicated elsewhere, that EM has an effect for the duration of the monitoring period but not necessarily afterwards, and that even in the monitoring period (depending how long it is) the impact may decline over time (Bonta et al. 2000; Sugg et al. 2001; Renzema 2012).

In a large, much cited and influential statistical study of 'community control' programmes in Florida between 1998 and 2002—which undoubtedly portrayed EM (both RF and GPS) as too useful for probation services to turn down—Padgett et al. (2006) claimed much higher levels of compliance with requirements, fewer technical violations and fewer new offenders for violent, property and drug-related offenders on EM compared with those not on EM. None of the sample were formally on probation but some of them were receiving some forms of court-ordered supportive, rehabilitative input, and the study tends not to accommodate this, or explain its significance to the findings, if any. Bales et al.'s (2010) follow-up study in Florida, augmenting statistical analysis with some offender accounts of experience on EM, showed similarly impressive results in terms of increased compliance and reduced reoffending—GPS more so than RF—even though offenders had largely negative views of monitoring's impact on their lives in the community. Because the positive effects were to be found only over the duration of the monitoring period, and not sustained afterwards, Padgett et al. (2006) made a clear recommendation that monitoring periods be extended for longer, playing into then current US debates about the lifelong monitoring of released sex offenders, and begging the (very plausible) question of whether positive effects would or could be sustained over longer monitoring periods. Bales et al.'s (2010) view that GPS had advantages over RF similarly played into ongoing US debates that tracking was an practice inherently superior to house arrest (Doffing 2009), and that RF should therefore be 'upgraded' to new-generation GPS, but this begs the question of whether simple, short-term curfews and house arrest are perfectly suitable for some offenders some of the time, and whether a better approach to EM would use both RF and GPS.

GPS tracking has seemingly proved its worth in the context of high-risk, paroled sex offenders in California. Geis et al. (2012) compared two large samples of such offenders between 2006 and 2009, over one year of supervision: both received treatment and supervision, but one also had

GPS imposed on them. Each group was compared on rearrests, reconvictions, returns to prison and compliance with parole regulations, and on each criteria those on GPS scored better, not always massively, but sufficient to give credence the additional intervention. Most significantly, offenders without GPS tracking were three times more likely to commit a sex-related violation than those with it. The researchers noted that the use of GPS increased and changed the balance of the parole officers' workload—large amounts of incoming data and frequent alerts, some false alarms had to be processed—but the staff were overwhelmingly in favour of the technology. Among the policy recommendations in the research was a reduced caseload (down to 20) for officers managing tracked high-risk offenders, and the use of an independent monitoring centre to filter the datastreams so that parole officers only received important information. Button et al. (2009) had been more sceptical of GPS-based supervision of sex offenders, not because of any inherent technological limitations, but because the assumptions underpinning sex offender legislation in the USA were often misconceived, privileging punishment when a more determined rehabilitative approach may have better served both offender and public interests. Certainly, it cannot have been sensible, as happed in Florida, that monitored sex offenders were subject to such draconian residence restrictions, banning them from living near schools, playgrounds and parks, that many of them finished up homeless, a community of rough sleepers under a bridge in Miami, using a portable generator to charge their GPS device batteries (Nellis 2012). Miracle Park—a rural village for some of Florida's rejected sex offenders, some on GPS—was one Christian pastor's solution to this enforced abjection (Allen 2009).

The use of EM to protect victims of domestic violence from whom perpetrators (suspected or convicted) have been ordered to stay away has grown steadily in the US and Europe. Exclusion zones may be placed around the victim's home, and in addition, victims may be given small portable receivers which would register the proximity of the tracked perpetrator wherever in the community they were—an approach dubbed 'bilateral EM'. Erez et al.'s (2012) large scale, multi-site evaluation of this in the USA concluded that GPS in particular was an effective means of ensuring compliance with court-ordered requirements, and that victims, although not without anxiety, sometimes caused by false alerts, were largely satisfied with the arrangement. The use of RF EM in this context—keeping perpetrators from victims by imposing house arrest on them—was less effective (Erez and Ibarra 2007). As with GPS tracking in a sex offender context, the technology was never conceived as a stand-alone measure, and probation services, and sometimes police forces, are almost always involved.

This outcome-focussed research produced, from three of the jurisdictions studied, some spin-off analyses which may from a probation perspective be the most important kind of research about EM, because it shows how the use of the technology is—and by implication can be—shaped by the prevailing culture of the probation service which uses it. Ibarra (2005) pioneered the study of 'surveillance as casework'. Ibarra et al. (2014) show how some services operate GPS very punitively, mystify defendants and offenders about the exact degree of electronic oversight they are subject to, and are ever alert for violations which inexorably trigger revocation and imprisonment. Other services take a more caring, collaborative approach to the surveillance of perpetrators, explaining the technology thoroughly, supporting and motivating them to comply and responding more flexibly to violations, depending on circumstance: the emphasis is more on completion of the monitoring period than catching the offender out at the earliest moment. This demonstration of variation in professional culture, among practitioners using EM in a domestic violence context, are probably relevant to all uses of EM, in the USA and elsewhere; they provide empirical confirmation that there is no technologically determined use of EM, even in ostensibly similar projects, and no single narrative in which it has to be packaged. It is hard to know, in the USA, which is more common. Kilgore (2012a, b), an American academic and former prisoner who himself experienced GPS monitoring while on parole, argues that probation and parole cultures are predominantly punitive, and that EM is simply aligned unreflectively with that, indifferent to the excessive collateral suffering imposed on offenders and their families, and contrasting this with his perception of more rehabilitatively inclined approaches in Europe.

Offender perspective research has become important in EM, but while it suffers from the same problem of generalisability as EM projects themselves—offenders respond to specific, tangible and nuanced experiences of EM in particular contexts, and to the people involved in its administration, not to a reified, abstract technology—certain common and consistent themes have emerged (Nellis 2009b). Payne and Gainey (1998; Gainey and Payne 2000), key US researchers in this field, established that EM house arrest (in this instance, a particularly onerous variant) entailed socio-psychological 'pains' distinct from those of imprisonment, and that it is far from the lenient and undemanding sentence that is sometimes portrayed in the media. Crucially, and to a greater extent than other community sanctions, EM affects not only the tagged individual but also other household members, emotionally and practically, and their response to the stresses entailed can have a bearing on whether monitoring periods are completed. Outside the home the stigma of a visible, wearable ankle bracelet can be intimidating to offenders: the difficulties of finding or maintaining employment while wearing one is exacerbated for some, particularly when the media portray tagged offenders in disparaging terms. Overall, the core message of offender perspective research on EM is that while most offenders do find them onerous, they are largely preferred to imprisonment (not least because family ties are maintained) (Staples 2005; Martinovic 2007; Vanhaelemeesch and Vander Beker 2012; Vanhaelemeesch et al. 2013). Compliance with EM sanctions is more likely if offenders perceive them as legitimate responses to lawbreaking, and part of the challenge for professionals involved in monitoring is to identify the forms of EM and the conditions of its use, alongside other supportive measures, which most help offenders to reform and desist.

Graham and McIvor (2015) conclude from their overview of evaluative literature on EM that a sufficiently strong case can be made for its further use in Scotland, and that a more integrated approach, embedding EM in other forms of supervision and support, is to be preferred to stand-alone interventions. GPS has a place, but not at the expense of RF EM. Practice elsewhere in Europe and the USA is sufficiently effective, in particular ways and contexts, to be suggestive of approaches that might be tried in Scotland in modified, even improved form. Much of what they recommend has already been undertaken by other countries' probation services, and their considered reflection on the evidence at this, arguably mature, point in EM's history, is as much a legitimation of what has happened elsewhere—a recognition that it has been right for probation to experiment with EM—as it is a spur to criminal justice social work to take greater belated ownership of EM in Scotland.

Conclusions

EM technologies have undoubtedly posed awkward and uncomfortable questions for probation services—some of which have been adequately addressed, at least for now—but may yet pose more momentous ones. The early intuition that EM was potentially a dangerous, threatening technology was not misplaced, but nor too was the intuition that it could not be wished away and had to be reckoned with, and that probation values and practices had an important role to play in ensuring that it was tamed, and its dangers minimised. Although they were unversed in the academic and policy literature on 'the social shaping of technology', Whitfield (1997, 2001) and the CEP were entirely correct in believing, however inchoately at the turn of the 21st century, that European probation services had an obligation to mould and constrain the development of EM in ways that were consistent with probation ideals, not least to ensure the political survival of probation services themselves, but also to stall the drift towards more surveillant, less humanistic forms of control.

The embedding of EM in the probation services of Sweden and the Netherlands, and the employment of social workers to administer it from within an administrative base in the Belgian prison service, gave early encouragement to the idea that RF EM could be incorporated into rehabilitative measures as a useful form of control—even if, largely for reasons of political legitimacy, it was publicly characterised as 'punishment'. From the start, it was always in England and Wales that dystopian fears about the future trajectory and impact of EM were most easily grounded. A Conservative, nascently neoliberal, government piloted RF EM as a standalone sanction and handed delivery of service to contracted commercial organisations, rather than the probation service, whose social work ethos it never ceased to castigate, and whose continued existence it refused to assure (Nellis 1991, 2003; Mair and Nellis 2013). A succession of neoliberal governments continued to expand EM and to denigrate probation as a public sector service, culminating in its almost complete privatisation in early 2015, by a Conservative-led coalition government. Parallel to this, and under the influence of an influential right-wing think tank, this government had hatched plans for a massive expansion of commercially delivered EM—an all-GPS based system, albeit based on a multi-tag which would combine both 'presence' and 'movement monitoring'—which would be implemented in mid 2015 (Nellis 2014b). While it is important to note that this grand plan, initially billed by government as something which would make them a world leader in the scale and sophistication of EM use, has so far failed to come to fruition, it is equally important to register that serious politicians actually entertained this vision, considered it feasible and desirable, and that several interlocked businesses, large and small, signed up to deliver it. It neatly illustrates the continuing 'techno-utopian' appeal of EM within the neoliberal imagination (see also Yeh 2010, 2014), for an equivalent US vision of 'mass monitoring', absurd and alarming in equal measure) and supplies the reason why public sector probation services still have something to fear from EM, unless they actively and continually try to shape it themselves (Lilly and Nellis 2012; Nellis 2013b).

In England, Dick Whitfield's insight that the probation service would be publicly and politically discredited if it did not make some accommodation with emerging EM technologies, based on best practice in Europe, and particularly Sweden, was never widely shared by his probation colleagues, and least of all by the probation officer's union, the National Association of Probation Officers (NAPO). The latter made a fatal, foolish mistake by taking a hostile government's narrowly punitive vision of EM, and its delivery by the private sector, at face value, and pitting themselves against both. A better strategy would have been to argue that there were other, better visions of how EM might be used, more commensurate with probation ideals, and to wrest control of the narrative from government and demand that EM was given to the probation service. Granted that this would have been easier said than done with the series of successive governments that proved quite so hostile to the survival of a public sector probation service, it should nevertheless have been tried—even a neoliberal, market-oriented think tank concluded that a local public sector base for EM (shared between police and probation) would have been viable, and indeed preferable to central government contracting with large service-providing corporations (Geohegan 2012).

What NAPO failed to realise (while other countries' probation services did, however reluctantly), was that there are certain forms of modernisation—organisational adaptations to wider changes in contemporary society, including technological ones—which cannot be fully resisted without rendering oneself obsolete, and that EM was one of them. The modern, post-eighties forms of EM originated in, and were an expression of, the broader information and communication technology revolution that permeates, and indeed constitutes, late modern societies, customised for use in a penal context. Their relatively low cost, compared with prison, guaranteed that Western governments would at least show interest in them: how policy on EM then played out in particular countries depended on the interests, the understanding of what was at stake and the strategic influence of particular players in the 'penal field' in each jurisdiction.

That will remain the case, but the boundaries of the traditional 'penal field' have been breached by EM and the commercial and technological momentum that drives governments to refine and perfect it are by no means played out. The broader information and communication infrastructure cannot be resisted, least all by probation services, but the forms of EM, the regimes it can be used to create and the scale of its use are amenable to shaping, if probation services are willing to engage with the process, claim EM for themselves and contest the narratives of others. The way to achieve best practice in EM—to ensure that it does not become the widespread and oppressive technology that some have pitched for—is to preserve and advance the best of probation as a humanistic endeavour. Past achievements, however well consolidated, do not guarantee future success.

References

Allen, G. (2009, December 4). Pastor offers sex offenders a 'miracle': A new start. *National Public Radio*. Retrieved from http://www.npr.org/templates/story/story.php?storyId=121089157

Bales, W., Mann, K., Blomberg, T., Gaes, G., Barrick, K., Dhungana, K., et al. (2010). *A qualitative and quantitative assessment of electronic monitoring*. Report for the National Institute of Justice. Miami: Florida State University.

Bogard, W. (1996). *The simulation of surveillance: Hypercontrol in telematic societies.* Cambridge: Cambridge University Press.

Bogard, W. (2010). Deleuze and machines: A politics of technology? In M. Poster & D. Savat (Eds.), *Deleuze and new technology.* Edinburgh: Edinburgh University Press.

Bonta, J., Rooney, J., & Wallace-Capreta, S. (2000). Can electronic monitoring make a difference? An evaluation of three Canadian programmes. *Crime and Delinquency, 46*(1), 6–75.

Brown, S. (2006). The criminology of hybrids: Rethinking crime and law and technosocial networks. *Theoretical Criminology, 10*(2), 223–244.

Button, D., DeMichele, M., & Payne, B. (2009). Using electronic monitoring to supervise sex offenders: Legislative patterns and implications for community corrections. *Criminal Justice Policy Review, 20*(4), 414–436.

Council of Europe. (2014). *Recommendation CM/Rec(2014)4 of the Committee of Ministers to member States on electronic monitoring.* Adopted by the Committee of Ministers on 19th February 2014. Strasbourg: Council of Europe.

Crawford, A. (2003). Contractual governance of deviant behaviour. *Journal of Law and Society, 30*(4), 479–505.

Doffing, D. (2009). Is there a future for RF in a GPS world? *Journal of Offender Monitoring, 22*(1), 12–15.

Erez, E., & Ibarra, P. R. (2007). Electronic monitoring and victim-re-entry in domestic violence cases. *British Journal of Criminology, 47*(2), 100–120.

Erez, E., Ibarra, P., Bales, W., & Gur, O. (2012). *GPS monitoring technology and domestic violence: An evaluation study.* Washington, DC: National Institute of Justice.

Finn, M. A., & Muirhead-Steves, S. (2002). The effectiveness of electronic monitoring with violent male parolees. *Justice Quarterly, 19*(2), 294–312.

Franko Aas, K. (2004). From narrative to database: Technological change and penal culture. *Punishment and Society, 6*(4), 379–393.

Gainey, R. R., & Payne, B. K. (2000). Understanding the experience of house arrest with electronic monitoring: An analysis of quantitative and qualitative data. *International Journal of Offender Therapy and Comparative Criminology, 44*(1), 84–96.

Geis, S. V., Gainey, R., Cohen, M. I., Healy, E., Duplantier, D., Yeide, M., et al. (2012). *Monitoring high risk offenders with GPS technology: An evaluation of the California Supervision Programme.* Final Report. Washington, DC: National Institute of Justice.

Geohegan, R. (2012). *Future of corrections: Exploring the use of electronic monitoring.* London: Policy Exchange.

Graham, H., & McIvor, G. (2015). *Scottish and international review of the use of electronic monitoring. Part 1—Purposes, uses and impact of electronic monitoring: Part 2—Comparing electronic monitoring technologies.* Edinburgh: Scottish Government.

Hucklesby, A. (2008). Vehicles of desistance? The impact of electronically monitored curfew orders. *Criminology and Criminal Justice, 8,* 51–71.

Hucklesby, A. (2009). Understanding offender's compliance: A case study of electronically monitored curfew orders. *Journal of Law and Society, 36*(2), 48–71.

Ibarra, P. (2005). Red flags and trigger control: The role of human supervision in an electronic monitoring program. *Sociology of Crime, Law and Deviance, 6,* 31–48.

Ibarra, P., Gur, O., & Erez, E. (2014). Surveillance as casework: Supervising domestic violence defendants with GPS technology. *Crime, Law and Social Change, 62,* 417–444.

Jones, R. (2000). Digital rule: Punishment, control and technology. *Punishment and Society, 2*(1), 5–22.

Jones, R. (2006). 'Architecture', criminal justice and control. In S. Armstrong & L. McAra (Eds.), *Perspectives on punishment: The contours of control.* Oxford: Oxford University Press.

Kilgore, J. (2012a). Would you like an ankle bracelet with that? *Dissent, Winter,* 66–71.

Kilgore, J. (2012b). Progress or more of the same? Electronic monitoring and parole in the age of mass incarceration. *Critical Criminology, 20*(4), 123–139.

Lianos, M., & Douglas, M. (2000). Dangerisation and the end of deviance: The institutional environment. In D. Garland & R. Sparks (Eds.), *Criminology and social theory.* Oxford: Clarendon.

Lilly, J. R., & Nelllis, M. (2012). The limits of technoutopianism: Electronic monitoring in the United States of America. In M. Nellis, K. Beyens, & D. Kaminski (Eds.), *Electronically monitored punishment: International and critical perspectives.* London: Routledge.

Mair, G. (2006). Electronic monitoring in England and Wales: Evidence-based or not? *Criminology and Criminal Justice, 5*(3), 257–277.

Mair, G., & Nellis, M. (2013). Parallel tracks: Probation and electronic monitoring in England, Wales and Scotland. In M. Nellis, K. Beyens, & D. Kaminski (Eds.), *Electronically monitored punishment: International and critical perspectives* (pp. 63–81). London: Routledge.

Marklund, F., & Holmberg, S. (2009). Effects of early release from prison using electronic tagging in Sweden. *Journal of Experimental Criminology, 5*(1), 41–61.

Martinovic, M. (2007). Home detention: Issues, dilemmas and impacts for detainees co-residing family members. *Current Issues in Criminal Justice,* *19*(1), 90–105.

Martinovic, M. (2010a). Increasing compliance on home detention-based sanctions through utilization of an intensive intervention support programme. *Current Issues in Criminal Justice, 21*(3), 413–435.

Martinovic, M. (2010b). *The complexity of punitiveness of electronically monitored sanctions: The western words analysis.* Saarbrücken: Lambert Academic Publishing.

Nellis, M. (1991). The electronic monitoring of offenders in England and Wales: Recent developments and future prospects. *British Journal of Criminology, 31*(2), 165–185.

Nellis, M. (2003). Electronic monitoring and the future of the probation service. In W. H. Chui & M. Nellis (Eds.), *Moving probation forward: Evidence arguments and practice.* Harlow: Longmans.

Nellis, M. (2009a). 24/7/365. Mobility, locatability and the satellite tracking of offenders. In K. Franco Aas, H. O. Gundus, & H. M. Lommell (Eds.), *Technologies of insecurity: The surveillance of everyday life.* London: Routledge.

Nellis, M. (2009b). Surveillance and confinement: Understanding offender experiences of electronically monitored curfews. *European Journal of Probation, 1*(1), 41–65.

Nellis, M. (2010). Eternal Vigilance Inc: The satellite tracking of offenders in real-time. *Journal of Technology and Human Services, 28*, 23–43.

Nellis, M. (2012). The GPS satellite tracking of sex offenders in the USA. In J. Brayford, F. Cowe, & J. Deering (Eds.), *Sex offenders: Punish, help, change or control.* London: Routledge.

Nellis, M. (2013a). Surveillance-based compliance using electronic monitoring. In P. Raynor & P. Ugwudike (Eds.), *What works in offender compliance?* Basingstoke: Palgrave Macmillan.

Nellis, M. (2013b). Techno-utopianism, science fiction and penal innovation: The case of electronically monitored control. In M. Malloch & W. Munro (Eds.), *Crime, critique and utopia.* Basingstoke: Palgrave MacMillan.

Nellis, M. (2014a). Understanding the electronic monitoring of offenders in Europe: Expansion, regulation and prospects. *Crime, Law and Social Change, 62*(4), 489–510.

Nellis, M. (2014b, August). Upgrading electronic monitoring, downgrading probation: Reconfiguring "offender management" in England and Wales. *European Journal of Probation, 6*(2), 169–191.

Nellis, M. (2015). Underusing electronic monitoring in Scotland. *Journal of Offender Monitoring, 26*(2), 10–18.

Nellis, M., Beyens, K., & Kaminski, D. (Eds.). (2012). *Electronically monitored punishment: International and critical perspectives.* London: Routledge.

Padgett, K., Bales, W., & Blomberg, T. (2006). Under surveillance: An empirical test of the effectiveness and consequences of electronic monitoring. *Criminology and Public Policy, 5*(1), 103–108.

Paterson, C. (2007). Commercial crime control and the electronic monitoring of offenders in England and Wales. *Social Justice, 34*(3–4), 98–110.

Paterson, C. (2012). Commercial crime control and the electronic monitoring of offenders: A global perspective. In M. Nellis, D. Beyens, & D. Kaminski (Eds.), *Electronically monitored punishment: International and critical perspectives.* London: Routledge.

Payne, B. K., & Gainey, R. R. (1998). A qualitative assessment of the pains experienced on electronic monitoring. *International Journal of Offender Therapy and Comparative Criminology, 42*(2), 149–163.

Raho, D. (2014). *The Curious Case of the Use of Reporting Kiosks in the UK Probation Service – Robohero or Roboflop?* Paper presented at the 6th Bi-annual Surveillance and Society conference, Barcelona 24th-26th April 2014.

Renzema, M. (2012). Evaluative research on electronic monitoring. In M. Nellis, K. Beyens, & D. Kaminski (Eds.), *Electronically monitored punishment: International and critical perspectives.* London: Routledge.

Renzema, M., & Mayo-Wilson, E. (2005). Can electronic monitoring reduce crime for medium to high risk offenders? *Journal of Experimental Criminology, 1*(2), 215–237.

Roberts, J. V. (2004). *The virtual prison: Community custody and the evolution of imprisonment.* Cambridge: Cambridge University Press.

Schmidt, A. (1998, December). Electronic monitoring: What does the literature tell us? *Federal Probation, 62*(2), 10–19.

Schwitzgebel, R. (1969). Issues in the use of an electronic rehabilitation system with chronic recidivists. *Law and Society Review, 3*(4), 597–610.

Schwitzgebel, R.L., & Schwitzgebel, R.K. (Eds.). (1973). *Psychotechnology: electronic control of mind and behaviour.* New York: Holt, Rheinhart and Wilson.

Staples, W. G. (2005). The everyday world of house arrest: Collateral consequences for families and others. In C. Mele & T. Miller (Eds.), *Civil penalties, social consequences* (pp. 139–159). New York: Routledge.

Sugg, D., Moore, L., & Howard, P. (2001). *Electronic monitoring and offending behaviour—Reconviction results for the second year of trials of curfew orders* (Findings 141). London: Home Office.

Taylor, F., & Ariel, B. (2012). *Protocol: Electronic monitoring of offenders: A systematic review of its effects in recidivism.* Oslo: Campbell Collaboration.

Vanhaelemeesch, D., & Vander Beker, T. (2012). Electronic monitoring: Convict's experiences in Belgium. In Cools, M. (Ed.). *Social conflicts, citizens and policing.* Antwerp: Government of Security Research Paper Series (GofS), Series 6.

Vanhaelemeesch, D., Vander Beker, T., & Vandevelde, S. (2013). Punishment at home: Offenders' experiences with electronic monitoring. *European Journal of Criminology* 11(3): 273–287.

Whitfield, D. (1997). *Tackling the tag: The electronic monitoring of offenders.* Winchester: Waterside Press.

Whitfield, D. (2001). *The magic bracelet: Technology and offender supervision.* Winchester: Waterside Press.

Yeh, S. (2010). Cost-benefit analysis of reducing crime through electronic monitoring of parolees and probationers. *Journal of Criminal Justice, 38,* 1090–1096.

Yeh, S. (2014). The electronic monitoring paradigm: A proposal for transforming criminal justice in the USA. *Laws.* Retrieved from http://www.mdpi.com/2075-471X/4/1/60/pdf

Zuboff, S. (1988). *In the age of the smart machine: The future of work and power.* Oxford: Heinemann.

Explaining Probation

Fergus McNeill and Gwen Robinson

Introduction

Most of the contributions to this collection deal with questions about probation that have obvious and immediate practical importance not just for scholars and students of the subject but also for policymakers and practitioners—and even for the wider public. This chapter is a little different, though we would suggest that it is no less important. Here, our focus is on the question: '**How we can best account for probation's emergence and development as a penal institution and as a set of connected penal discourses and practices?**' In essence, we aim to set out some possible approaches to developing a sociological account of probation. This matters—and has real contemporary import—because if we fail to understand the social, cultural and political conditions which gave rise to and subsequently have shaped probation's development, and *how*

F. McNeill (✉)
University of Glasgow, Glasgow, UK

G. Robinson
University of Sheffield, Sheffield, UK

© The Editor(s) (if applicable) and The Author(s) 2016
F. McNeill et al. (eds.), *Probation*,
DOI 10.1057/978-1-137-51982-5_12

they have done so, then we will remain poorly placed to assess or affect its prospects. The evolution of policy and practice is always and everywhere profoundly affected, not just, for example, by arguments about technical effectiveness (and cost effectiveness) but also by the extent to which a given policy or practice proposal 'fits' with the zeitgeist or spirit of the times.

Recognising that these are large questions and that this is a small chapter, we will confine ourselves to briefly exploring three of the most significant contributors to the sociology of punishment—Foucault, Durkheim and Marx—and of sketching out how their ideas have informed or might inform our understandings of probation. But a note of caution is required here: To the best of our knowledge, none of these theorists spoke or wrote directly about probation and Marx himself had relatively little to say even about punishment. Perhaps more importantly (and tellingly), most of the sociologists of punishment who have used Foucault's, Durkheim's or Marx's ideas have done so to understand the emergence and development of prisons and imprisonment in modernity or late modernity. Just as probation scholarship has been negligent in failing to address the sorts of sociological questions that concern us here, so sociologists of punishment have been negligent in failing to address probation (see Robinson forthcoming). That said, and as we will see, there are some notable exceptions both among probation scholars and among sociologists of punishment, and there is increasing evidence of the belated emergence of sociologically informed analyses of probation in a number of jurisdictions and across them (see, for example, Phelps 2013; Robinson and McNeill 2015).

Rather than taking the three thinkers in chronological order, we have chosen to reverse the chronology, partly so that we start our discussion with the theorist whose work has undoubtedly been most influential among those seeking to explain and understand probation as a social and a penal institution—Michel Foucault.

Foucault, Punishment and Probation

The publication of Foucault's *Discipline and Punish* (1977) had a profound impact on criminology and sociology. It provided a powerful illustration of the continuities between systems of regulation and control in the social and penal spheres and is, as Garland (1990) maintains, primarily a work of social theory. Despite its subtitle then, 'the birth of the prison' actually constitutes for Foucault a pretext for exposing the spread of a particular mode of power—*disciplinary power*—throughout the social body.

Discipline, in Foucault's work, is a translation of the French *surveiller*, which has no direct English translation but bears the hallmarks of terms like surveillance, observation and supervision. It denotes a method of mastering or training the human body, not via the use of bodily force or restraint but rather by exerting an influence on what Foucault terms 'the soul', which in turn directs behaviour. In Foucault's account the prison constitutes a case study of discipline: it is conceived as epitomising the institution of the 'gentler forms of control' which came to replace the violent, repressive forms characteristic of the 'classical age'. At the core of disciplinary power are the principles of individualisation and constant visibility (famously characterised by Bentham's late-eighteenth-century 'Panopticon' prison design) which work in tandem to produce compliant subjects who habitually behave in the required manner. In the realm of punishment, discipline is a mode of exercising control over individuals which is less punitive than it is corrective: its primary objective is 'normalization'—that is, a readjustment of the individual towards the 'norm' of what Foucault terms 'docility-utility' (1977, p. 137), but which today we might call 'compliant behaviour'.

Foucault's concept and characterisation of 'discipline' has proven to be useful for probation scholars, both in analysing the origins of probation as a mode of regulation, and in making sense of more recent developments. For example, Garland's (1985) *Punishment and Welfare* draws heavily on Foucault's notion of disciplinary penality in analysing the birth of the modern penal complex in Britain. Both Garland's study (in Britain) and Simon's (1993) study of the development of parole in California locate the formal–legal origins of probation in the context of the social, political and cultural shifts which coalesced around the turn of the twentieth century to inaugurate a specifically *modern* penality: one that brought the welfare and/or reform of the individual into the domain of state responsibility and, in that process, extended the reach of disciplinary power (in the Foucauldian sense). Both also describe how the modernist quest for 'normalisation' was transformed in the early decades of the twentieth century as ideas about moral reformation gave way to a more 'scientific' discourse centred on diagnosis, treatment and 'rehabilitation'.

The collapse of confidence in rehabilitation in Britain and the USA ignited intense debate among scholars working within a primarily Foucauldian framework. The early 1980s saw some British scholars predicting the demise of disciplinary power, and with it traditional probation supervision, in favour of an expansion of 'non-disciplinary' disposals which did not aim to correct or transform their subjects, such as the (then relatively new) sanction of community service (Bottoms 1980; Pease 1980). These analyses however went against the grain of other accounts which were emphasising an *extension* of discipline in the context of both formal and informal domains of social control. The so-called 'dispersal of discipline' thesis was the subject of three contributions to Garland and Young's (1983) collection *The Power to Punish* (Scull 1983; Cohen 1983; Mathieson 1983), and was further elaborated in Cohen's (1985) seminal book *Visions of Social Control*, in which the focus was the gap which Cohen perceived between, on the one hand, the rhetoric of decarceration and diversion and, on the other, the reality of the deviance-control system which he thought was emerging at that time. Cohen utilised a much-cited 'fishing net' analogy [in which 'deviants are the fish' (p. 42)] to describe the increasing extension, widening, dispersal and invisibility of the (non-carceral) social control apparatus as he observed it. It is from this source that scholars adopted the concepts of 'new widening' and 'mesh thinning' that have become staples in analyses of community sanctions and measures—and sentencing trends more generally—over the last 30 years. The idea that the proliferation of forms of social control beyond the prison should be seen as an inherently positive development was heavily criticised by Cohen, who was quick to point out that more and different community-based sanctions and measures did not necessarily imply *less* (or less-intensive) control; nor did they inevitably lead to a reduction in the use of imprisonment.

The fate of disciplinary power in the wake of the collapse of the 'rehabilitative ideal' (Allen 1981) is also the subject of the highly influential 'new penology' thesis which has been hotly contested over the last

20 years across a number of jurisdictions (Simon 1993; Feeley and Simon 1992, 1994). The new penology thesis essentially contends that late modern societies have moved on from the dominant disciplinary modes of control described by Foucault, in favour of managerial, risk-based strategies. On the basis of his research on the development of parole in California, Jonathan Simon described a decisive shift, starting in the mid 1970s, from a 'clinical' model of practice (centred on the normalization of ex-prisoners) to a 'managerial' model, characterized by significantly lowered expectations and functioning as a mechanism for securing the borders of communities by channelling their least stable members back to prison. The idea that penal (and indeed welfare) systems across a variety of jurisdictions have taken on a more 'managerial' character have become increasingly concerned with risk management is now part of criminological common sense, although whether this has been at the expense of more ambitious objectives of reform and rehabilitation continues to be the subject of debate (e.g. Hannah-Moffatt 1999; Garland 2001; Robinson 2002, 2008; Robinson and McNeill 2015). Meanwhile, Foucauldian concepts have informed some recent studies of the rise and proliferation of surveillance technologies, including the electronic monitoring of offenders which is an increasingly significant element of community sanctions and measures throughout and beyond Europe (Nellis et al. 2012).

Durkheim, Punishment and Probation

Whereas Foucault's work drew attention to changes in the ways penal power was being deployed, highlighting shifting objectives, discourses and techniques, Durkheim's influential account of penal evolution placed its emphasis on the *cultural* contexts of penal change; or more accurately on the influence on punishment of the interplay between cultures, social solidarity and the nature of the state.

Durkheim argued that social solidarity depends on the moral beliefs that unify social groups. Although solidarity's different forms reflect changes in the historical context, national setting and the division of labour in any given society, punishment of crime is always a passionate collective reaction to violations of these unifying beliefs; its rituals are important as a means of allowing us to communicate, reaffirm and reinforce them. As Garland (2013a, p. 25) puts it in his recent re-analysis of Durkheim's contribution, offending shocks 'healthy' (i.e. well-socialized) consciences into punishment as a reaction.

Two different sources of outrage—one founded in shared religious belief and one based upon respect for citizens as individuals—reflect the different forms of social solidarity that Durkheim distinguishes. *Mechanical solidarity* is characteristic of societies that are structured and dominated by the needs and interests of fairly small collectives whose unity of moral belief is religious in type. Law and sanctions here are primarily repressive rather than restitutive; their function is to express *and* to reinforce the *conscience collective* (Durkheim 1984). In contrast, the division of labour in modern societies occasions the transition to more *organic* forms of social solidarity. Although repressive law and sanctions continue to exist, the development of increased social diversity and the necessity of complex inter-group cooperation require the moral code to be based on *moral individualism*. For this reason, restitutive forms of law and sanctions develop to regulate intra- and inter-group cooperation in ways which rely less on repression and more on restoration to health of the social body (Durkheim 1958, p. 48).

Garland (2013a, p. 36) insists on a reading of Durkheim that stresses that 'the social processes of punishment, in so far as they are social, *presuppose* solidarity as well as *reinforce* it'. In other words, punishment is *both* a project of solidarity-building *and* a product of it. But like any other social institution, the form of punishment in any society may be 'normal' or 'pathological'. For Durkheim, an institution is pathological if it does not correspond with the collective conditions of social life. Often this occurs because the institution's current form still reflects an earlier period characterised by different social conditions. For Durkheim, pathological institutions represent and cause both practical and moral problems. Indeed, Sirianni (1984) argues that the conception of organic solidarity in *The Division of Labour* is as much a normative as an empirical statement, with Durkheim often collapsing the two in his discussion. Putting this another way, organic solidarity is the *goal* of modern societies; it is a 'mission of justice' (Durkheim 1984, p. 321) and not just a description of their social order. A pathological or ill-fitting penal system is therefore a failure to progress the mission of justice. Hence the importance that Durkheim accords to analysing penal evolution.

Durkheim's famous essay *Two Laws of Penal Evolution* was first published in 1899–1900. The first ('quantitative') law is that: 'The intensity of punishment is the greater the more closely societies approximate to a less developed type—and the more the central power assumes an absolute character' (Durkheim 1973, p. 285).

The lack of complexity and the strength of the shared religious beliefs characteristic of mechanical solidarity beget intense punishment and repressive laws. However, Durkheim is careful to note a second influence—the absolute power of the sovereign—and in this sense he recognizes the relationships between culture and political power.

Durkheim's second ('qualitative') law is stated thus: 'Deprivations of liberty, and of liberty alone, varying in time according to the seriousness of the crime, tend to become more and more the normal means of social control' (Durkheim 1973, p. 294).

His explanation of this development in the *form or style* of punishment relies heavily on his account of the rise of moral individualism. To the extent that offending ceased to violate religious ideals and values and came to be seen as offence of one citizen against another, forms of brutalizing punishment were less likely to be invoked. Importantly, with the rise of individualism, collective sensibilities about punishment shifted. Moral individualism requires that *both* the victim and offender be given appropriate consideration without recourse to punishment for punishment's sake.

But this qualitative evolution in punishment, and, in particular, the rise of the prison is also accounted for, in part, because of the prison's utility as a technological (or architectural) fix for a changing social problem:

[A]t the very time when the establishment of a place of detention was becoming useful in consequence of the progressive disappearance of collective responsibility, buildings were arising which could be utilized for this purpose ... In proportion as the penal law abandons the archaic forms of repression, new forms of punishment invade the free spaces which they then find before them. (Durkheim 1973, p. 298)

Consequently, a new way had to be found of (literally) holding the *individual* to account. Durkheim recognizes that this 'holding' originally developed as a place of pre-trial detention and thus as a prelude to punishment, rather than as a punishment *per se*. However, he argues that, in this case, the social function followed the new penal form; once the pains of imprisonment became apparent, its utility as a punishment became established. And as imprisonment came progressively to be associated the deprivation of liberty its punitive character relied less and less on the particular conditions or peculiar hardships of confinement. It was not merely that the deprivation of liberty displaced the mortification of the body; it was also that the penal severity of imprisonment diminished over time.

However, when he was writing, Durkheim's diagnosis of punishment at the *fin de siècle* was highly critical. He argued that institutional forms of punishment appropriate to organic solidarity had failed to emerge, meaning that punishment was failing to fulfill its cultural functions in expressing and reinforcing shared beliefs. As we have already noted, for Durkheim this was not just an empirical sociological observation; it was a normative problem. The 'mission of justice' implied in organic solidarity was failing.

Given this historical context, it might be tempting to read probation as precisely the new form of punishment that Durkheim's mission of justice required. And one might have expected probation scholars to look to Durkheim as providing ready-made the resources for a cultural account of probation's emergence. It is striking therefore that, until very recently (see McNeill and Dawson 2014) no one has done so, although Garland's (1985, 2001) work on modern and late modern penality discusses probation to a certain extent and, of course, draws to some extent on Durkheim.

Ironically, the neglect of Durkheim's ideas by probation scholars may be a result of the historical evolution of *their* subfield; that is, probation studies expanded significantly from the 1960s onwards in its scope and depth; and of course, this was the era when first Marxist and then Foucault's influences were at their heights.

Seeking to begin to remedy this neglect of Durkheim's contribution, McNeill and Dawson (2014) have recently offered a sketch of how a Durkheimian account of probation in the UK might be developed, and of how this might assist us in assessing probation's future prospects. They argue that a re-reading of Durkheim can serve to clarify how and why:

[P]robation's future development—like punishment's—may depend less on evidence of its 'effectiveness' or 'quality' and more on shifting forms of social organization; on their expression in terms of changing moral sensibilities; and on the changing dynamics of political or governmental authority … The important practical question for those interested in probation is whether, how and under which social and political conditions probation might resist or moderate these forces. To begin to answer it, we need to examine much more closely, in a range of different contexts (historical and geographical), what it is that probation has communicated (or failed to communicate) about social solidarity, to whom and for whom, and under what forms of political authority? (McNeill and Dawson 2014, p. 12)

Marxism, Punishment and Probation

The development of critical perspectives on probation owes much to the emergence in the 1970s of a series of revisionist histories of crime, punishment and social control. These revisionist histories challenged the then prevailing narrative of gradual reform towards ever more effective penal solutions to the problems that crime presented, underpinned by the inexorable progress of positivist social science. Instead, historians like Ignatieff (1983, and indeed Foucault himself) revealed the role played by penal power and its attendant technologies in the preservation of vested class interests. In essence, their challenge was that the penal system was rigged in favour of the property owners and against the dispossessed.

This kind of Marxist critique—exposing the latent functions of punishment in defence of capital—was not merely historical. Sociologists of punishment inspired by Marx were also beginning to expose the role of (then) current day penal systems in sustaining a capitalist system of economic production, based on the exploitation of wage labour (for a review of such scholarship, see Melossi 1998). As De Giorgi suggests, such analyses

contend that penal politics plays a very different role than defending society from crime: both the historical emergence of specific penal practices and their persistence in contemporary societies, are structurally linked to the dominant relations of production and to the hegemonic forms of work organization. In a society divided into classes, criminal law cannot reflect any 'general interest'. (De Giorgi 2013, p. 41)

The first serious attempt to apply Marxist ideas in understanding punishment was provided by Rusche and Kirchheimer (1939[2003]) in their seminal text *Punishment and Social Structure*. Though their arguments are more complex than the title of their seminal text suggests, their analysis centres on the relationship between social structures (and in particular economic arrangements) and penal systems and practices. The former exercise a determining influence on the latter. Thus slavery and servitude as punishments rely on and facilitate a slave economy; the development of fines requires a monetary economy; penal transportation both needs and feeds emerging colonial economies; and the emergence of the prison both requires and serves an industrial economy. More generally, fluctuations in 'demand' for punishment (and in support for certain forms of punishment) depend on the availability of material resources and in particular on the demand for labour.

However, as Cavadino et al. (2013) suggest, not all versions of Marxist analysis are equally economically deterministic in their accounts. For example, those influenced by the works of Antonio Gramsci (1891–1937) place greater emphasis on the ideological domination through which certain regimes of power manufacture 'consent'; the idea of 'hegemony' and of 'hegemonic discourses' derive from Gramsci's work which nevertheless left room for the exercise of human agency in resistance; such resistance might take the form of exposing and undermining hegemonic ideas, in our case about punishment.

Similarly, those influenced by Louis Althusser (1918–1990), while still propounding a structuralist and materialist perspective in which the economic arrangements in society are *ultimately* determining of its social order, nonetheless stress that the social 'superstructure' possesses 'relative autonomy'. In this context the dominant ideology is reproduced both through the 'institutional state apparatus' (such as education and welfare systems governing the socialisation of children) and the 'repressive state apparatus' (including the policing and penal systems, as well as the military). Whereas the institutional state apparatus applies covert forms of coercion, the repressive state apparatus is (usually) more overt in its exercise of power. That said, an Althusserian Marxist perspective allows us to recognise that penal systems serve *both* repressive and ideological functions; as well as punishing dissent, they communicate values. The links to Durkheimian ideas are obvious here.

Perhaps one step further away from a materially deterministic form of Marxism, the historian E. P. Thompson (1924–1993) propounded a 'humanistic materialism'. This approach again recognises the determining force of economic arrangements and of the material distribution of resources, but it left yet more room for agentic struggles against the social order—and specifically against the deployment of law and order by the ruling classes, even if the 'game' is rigged in their favour:

> People are not as stupid as some structuralist philosophers suppose them to be. They will not be mystified by the first man who puts on a wig … If the law is evidently partial and unjust, then it will mask nothing, legitimize nothing, contribute nothing to any class's hegemony'. (Thompson 1977, pp. 262–263)

Despite the potency and popularity of Marxist critiques of capitalist societies, they have been surprisingly rarely deployed in making sense of the evolution of probation. Again this may owe something to the popularity of Foucault's (post-structuralist) work, even if his analysis clearly bears the marks of the legacy of Marxist ideas. Indeed, it should already be apparent that Durkheim and Foucault both recognise and explore the intersections between social structures and cultures, as well as being concerned with the evolution and expression of different forms of penal power.

Marxist perspectives did however clearly influence some important revisionist accounts of the histories of probation and social work. Again, these emerging critiques were influenced as much by Foucault as by Marx; thus Donzelot's (1977) work on *The Policing of Families* charted the development of public intervention in the regulation of family affairs and in particular illuminated the totalising power of the emergent social work profession. Similarly, Mahood's (1991) *Policing Gender, Class and Family*, which includes significant discussion of the development of juvenile probation in the UK, challenged the traditional narrative of the evolution of a benign and caring welfare state by revealing how the child-saving movement served middle-class interests rather than (or more than) the interests of those whose lives it penetrated. Similarly, Garland's (1985) *Punishment and Welfare* took inspiration from both Marxist and Foucauldian perspectives (see Garland 1990, p. 132).

One or two similarly critical accounts emerged of the history of probation in England and Wales. In particular, Maurice Vanstone, by building on the work of Bill McWilliams (1983, 1985, 1986, 1987) and focussing on practice-related discourses, significantly challenged and revised the traditional story of probation's origins as an essentially altruistic endeavour, characterised by humanitarian impulses linked to religious ideals. As Vanstone (2004) notes, Young's (1976) earlier account of the history of probation stressed the role of charity in maintaining the position of the middle classes by confirming that where unfortunates failed to capitalise on the opportunities that charitable endeavours provided, they confirmed their own intractable individual degeneracy, deflecting attention from broader economic or political analyses of social problems. Among a broader range of philanthropic activities, probation emerges in this account as a class-based activity that justifies the existing social order and defends it through its mechanisms of persuasion, supervision and control.

Young's (1976) account was arguably the first and only Marxist or Marxian reading of probation's development, but Walker and Beaumont's (1981) *Probation Work: Critical Theory and Socialist Practice* was perhaps more influential in offering a fairly downbeat Marxist assessment of probation's situation and prospects at the start of 1980s, while also seeking to offer some sort of Marxist prescription for probation practice even under capitalism.

Conclusions

We wrote at the outset that our essential question was: '**How we can best account for probation's emergence and development as a penal institution and as a set of connected penal discourses and practices?**'

In writing even such a brief, introductory chapter in response to that challenging question, it quickly becomes apparent that in seeking to differentiate Foucauldian, Durkheimian and Marxist accounts of probation, it is all too easy to caricature the three perspectives. We hope that our brief summaries of some of their key ideas and analytical resources show that it is much too simple to suggest that Foucault explains punishment in terms of relationships between power and knowledge, while Durkheim lays stress on relationships between morality, culture and social organisation, whereas Marxist perspectives stress the ultimately determining influence of economic arrangements. Of course, we might have included many other social theorists, perhaps most obviously Max Weber, whose ideas have much to offer an understanding both of the professionalization of probation in the modern era, and of the impact of managerialism in late modernity.

But in reality, almost every account of the development of punishment (and of probation) is what Garland (2001) calls 'conjunctural'. Indeed, his magisterial work *The Culture of Control* is the example par excellence of an attempt to combine structural, cultural and political aspects in an explanation of penal transformations associated with late modernity. He summarises both his method and his conclusion thus:

> I have tried to show how the field of crime control and criminal justice has been affected by changes in the social organization of the societies in which it functions, by the distinctive problems of social order characteristic of that form of social organization, and by the political, cultural and criminological adaptations that have emerged in response to these distinctive problems. (Garland 2001, p. 193)

His account therefore is structural in so far as it elaborates the nature of the constraining structures that create and limit possibilities, but it insists on the interaction of structures with the choices of human actors and the contingencies to which they respond, both reflecting and giving rise to adaptations of politics and culture.

That said, in contemporary 'Punishment and Society' scholarship there are two main challenges to this sort of account that have emerged. Firstly, some suggest that Garland's analysis over-states, over-generalises and sometimes under-evidences the changes he identifies within the USA and the UK (e.g. Snacken 2010). Others have suggested that many of the social and cultural changes he relies upon to explain how penality has evolved in these two countries (very broadly those changes associated with globalisation) have also occurred in many other jurisdictions where a culture of control has *not* emerged, or not to the same extent. Thus some contemporary scholars have stressed the importance of re-examining differences in political-institutional systems (see Gottschalk 2013) and economic arrangements in order to explain differences between states subject to similar social and cultural pressures (see also Lacey 2008). These criticisms, and Garland's own work on the persistence of the death penalty in the USA (Garland 2010) has led him recently to reconsider the relationship between broader social and cultural changes and different kinds of penal states (Garland 2013b).

A second and different sort of criticism concerns the relationships between the influences *upon* penal systems and institutions and processes of transformation *within* them. Drawing on the work of French social theorist Pierre Bourdieu, Page (2013, p. 157) has suggested that major accounts of late-modern penal change 'do not investigate how contemporary crime control fields (or their sub-fields) affect agents' subjective orientation to penal practice. In other words, they do not concretely show if or how reconfigurations of crime control play out in practice'. The remedy for this neglect, he suggests, is to develop the concept of the 'penal field' to require us to take more seriously the positions, dispositions and relations of actors in that field and 'to examine how the structure and basic rules and assumptions of the penal game affect penal outcomes' (Page 2013, p. 164; see also McNeill et al. 2009).[1]

This last development, we would argue, is exceptionally important for probation scholars and practitioners. We need *both* a clearer understanding of the structural, cultural and political influences *upon* the penal field *and* a sharper grasp of dynamics *within* the field if we are to be able to engage seriously and thoughtfully with its progressive 'reform'. If we cannot make sense of why things are as they are, and of how they evolve, then we will struggle to change them for the better.

This chapter therefore is offered, in this collection, not as a contribution to debates about developing 'evidence-based practice' but rather as an injunction to pay more attention to the structural, cultural, political

---

[1] In this Page echoes Garland's development of the concept of 'penality': 'It involves discursive frameworks of authority and condemnation, ritual procedures of imposing punishment, a repertoire of penal sanctions, institutions and agencies for the enforcement of sanctions and a rhetoric of symbols, figures, and images by means of which the penal process is represented to its various audiences' (Garland 1990, p. 17).

and institutional influences upon probation—and to *how* they influence it. Whether we want to develop probation or to constrain its development, these are contexts and processes that we need to understand.

References

Allen, F. (1981). *The decline of the rehabilitative ideal: Penal policy and social purpose.* New Haven, CT: Yale University Press.

Bottoms, A. (1980). An introduction to 'The Coming Crisis'. In A. Bottoms & R. Preston (Eds.), *The coming penal crisis.* Edinburgh: Scottish Academic Press.

Cavadino, M., Dignan, J., & Mair, G. (2013). *The penal system: An introduction* (5th ed.). London: Sage.

Cohen, S. (1983). Social-control talk: Telling stories about correctional change. In D. Garland & P. Young (Eds.), *The power to punish.* Aldershot: Gower.

Cohen, S. (1985). *Visions of social control: Crime, punishment and classification.* Cambridge, UK: Polity and Blackwell.

De Giorgi, A. (2013). Punishment and political economy. In J. Simon & R. Sparks (Eds.), *The Sage handbook of punishment and society.* London and New York: Sage.

Donzelot. (1977). *La Police des Familles* [The Policing of Families]. Paris: Edition de Minuit.

Durkheim, E. (1958[1986]). The state. In E. Durkheim (Ed.), *Durkheim on politics and the state* (pp. 45–50). Stanford: Stanford University Press.

Durkheim, E. (1973). Two laws of penal evolution. *Economy and Society, 2*(3), 285–308.

Durkheim, E. (1984). *The division of labour in society.* Hampshire: Palgrave Macmillan.

Feeley, M., & Simon, J. (1992). The new penology: Notes on the emerging strategy of corrections and its implications. *Criminology, 30,* 449–474.

Feeley, M., & Simon, J. (1994). Actuarial justice: The emerging new criminal law. In D. Nelken (Ed.), *The futures of criminology.* London: Sage.

Foucault, M. (1977). *Discipline and punish: The birth of the prison* [English translation 1977]. London: Allan lane.

Garland, D. (1985). *Punishment and welfare: A history of penal strategies.* Aldershot: Ashgate.

Garland, D. (1990). *Punishment and modern society: A study in social theory.* Oxford: Clarendon.

Garland, D. (2001). *The culture of control: Crime and social order in contemporary society*. Oxford: Oxford University Press.

Garland, D. (2010). *Peculiar institution: America's death penalty in an age of abolition*. Oxford: Oxford University Press.

Garland, D. (2013a). Punishment and social solidarity. In J. Simon & R. Sparks (Eds.), *The Sage handbook of punishment and society*. London and New York: Sage.

Garland, D. (2013b). Penality and the penal state. *Criminology, 51*(3), 475–517.

Garland, D., & Young, P. (Eds.). (1983). *The power to punish: Contemporary penality and social analysis*. Aldershot: Gower.

Gottschalk, M. (2013). The carceral state and the politics of punishment. In J. Simon & R. Sparks (Eds.), *The Sage handbook of punishment and society*. London and New York: Sage.

Hannah-Moffatt, K. (1999). Moral agent or actuarial subject: Risk and Canadian women's imprisonment. *Theoretical Criminology, 3*(1), 71–94.

Ignatieff, M. (1983). State, civil society and total institutions: A critique of recent social histories of punishment. In S. Cohen & A. Scull (Eds.), *Social control and the state*. Oxford: Martin Robertson.

Lacey, N. (2008). *The prisoner's dilemma: Political economy and punishment in contemporary democracies*. Cambridge: Cambridge University Press.

McNeill, F., Burns, N., Halliday, S., Hutton, N., & Tata, C. (2009). Risk, responsibility and reconfiguration: Penal adaptation and misadaptation. *Punishment and Society, 11*(4), 419–442.

McNeill, F., & Dawson, M. (2014). Social solidarity, penal evolution and probation. *British Journal of Criminology, 54*(5), 892–907.

Mahood, L. (1991). *Policing gender, class and family in Britain, 1950-1940*. London: UCL Press.

Mathieson, T. (1983). The future of control systems: The case of Norway. In D. Garland & P. Young (Eds.), *The power to punish: Contemporary penality and social analysis*. Aldershot: Gower.

McWilliams, W. (1983). The mission to the English Police Courts 1876-1936. *Howard Journal, 22*, 129–147.

McWilliams, W. (1985). The mission transformed: Professionalisation of probation between the wars. *Howard Journal of Criminal Justice, 24*(4), 257–274.

McWilliams, W. (1986). The English probation system and the diagnostic ideal. *Howard Journal of Criminal Justice, 25*(4), 241–260.

McWilliams, W. (1987). Probation, pragmatism and policy. *Howard Journal of Criminal Justice, 26*(2), 97–121.

Melossi, D. (1998). *The sociology of punishment: Socio-structural perspectives.* Aldershot: Dartmouth.

Nellis, M., Beyens, K., & Kaminski, D. (Eds.). (2012). *Electronically monitored punishment: International and critical perspectives.* London: Routledge.

Page, J. (2013). Punishment and the penal field. In J. Simon & R. Sparks (Eds.), *The Sage handbook of punishment and society.* London and New York: Sage.

Pease, K. (1980). The future of the community treatment of offenders in Britain. In A. E. Bottoms & R. H. Preston (Eds.), *The coming penal crisis.* Edinburgh: Scottish Academic Press.

Phelps, M. (2013). The paradox of probation: Community supervision in the age of mass incarceration. *Law and Policy, 35*(1–2), 55–80.

Robinson, G. (2002). Exploring risk management in the probation service: Contemporary developments in England and Wales. *Punishment and Society, 4*(1), 5–25.

Robinson, G. (2008). Late-modern rehabilitation: The evolution of a penal strategy. *Punishment and Society, 10*(4), 429–445.

Robinson, G. (2016) 'The Cinderella complex: Punishment, society and community sanctions'. *Punishment and Society 18*(1): 95-112.

Robinson, G., & McNeill, F. (Eds.). (2015). *Community punishment: European perspectives.* London: Routledge.

Rusche, G., & Kirchheimer, O. (1939[2003]). *Punishment and social structure.* New Brunswick, NJ: Transaction.

Scull, A. (1983). Community corrections: Panacea, progress or pretence? In D. Garland & P. Young (Eds.), *The power to punish: Contemporary penality and social analysis.* Aldershot: Gower.

Simon, J. (1993). *Poor discipline: Parole and the social control of the underclass 1890–1990.* Chicago: University of Chicago Press.

Sirianni, C. (1984). Justice and the division of labour: A reconsideration of Durkheim's *A Division of Labour in Society. Sociological Review, 32*(3), 449–470.

Snacken, S. (2010). Resisting punitiveness in Europe? *Theoretical Criminology, 14*(3), 273–292.

Thompson, E.P. (1977) Whigs and Hunters: The Origin of the Black Act. Harmondsworth: Penguin.

Vanstone, M. (2004). Mission control: The origins of a humanitarian service. *Probation Journal, 51*(1), 34–47.

Walker, H., & Beaumont, W. (1981). *Probation work: Critical theory and socialist practice.* Chichester: Wiley-Blackwell.

Young, P. (1976). A sociological analysis of the early history of probation. *British Journal of Law and Society, 3,* 44–58.

Conclusion: The 12th Question

Fergus McNeill, René Butter, and Ioan Durnescu

We said in the introduction that our conclusion would summarise what can be learned from this collection, before exploring the important 12th question: what next? It makes sense therefore, to review each chapter, but perhaps a first priority is to notice again the types of questions we asked, and the types of theory and evidence to which they relate.

Our first two questions are *explanatory* in nature. They aim to summarise how we can best explain offending and how we can best explain desistance from offending. Neither of these is a question about probation—but they are questions which nevertheless speak directly to some of probation's key objectives (at least in most jurisdictions). Wherever probation is invested with a mission to control or reduce crime, these two forms of understanding will be key.

F. McNeill (✉)
University of Glasgow, Glasgow, UK

R. Butter
HU University of Applied Sciences, Utrecht, The Netherlands

I. Durnescu
Faculty of Sociology, University of Bucharest, Bucharest, Romania

© The Editor(s) (if applicable) and The Author(s) 2016   **263**
F. McNeill et al. (eds.), *Probation*,
DOI 10.1057/978-1-137-51982-5_13

By contrast, questions 3–8 are primarily *evaluative* in nature. They aim to summarise: whether and how probation affects sentencing, whether and how it affects victims, whether and how it promotes resettlement, what it achieves in and through community service, how it is seen by the general public and *inter alia* what are its costs and benefits.

Questions 9–11 return to explanation, but perhaps are more *exploratory and critical* in character. They aim respectively to explore how probation is experienced by those subject to it, how we make sense of the development of electronic monitoring (as a relatively new development in the field) and, more generally, how we can develop our understandings of the historical emergence and development of probation itself. We call these chapters exploratory and critical not to suggest that the other chapters lack these qualities, but to highlight that these chapters do not start with probation's formal purposes and test its success in pursuing them. Rather, they start with probation itself—as a lived experience, as an evolving institution and as a historical artefact—and seek to understand it from these different perspectives. We return to the importance of these different forms of questioning—explanatory, evaluative and exploratory—in our concluding remarks.

Explanation for Probation

Rob Canton opens our volume by posing the important, but almost unanswerable question: why do people commit crimes? The chapter introduces a number of the main theories of criminology in order to show that the various theoretical accounts offer more than academic insights and can be applied to enhance probation work. An important distinction discussed within the chapter is that between the 'Lombrosian project' and the 'Governmental project'. The first project aims to find the causes of crime using the methods of the natural sciences. The second project seeks for opportunities to intervene and treat those causes, thus preventing offending. Also, the important questions of how crime is defined and of how criminalization is constructed are raised. If the political choice is made to turn more acts (misbehaviours and incivilities) into crimes, then, paradoxically, there will be more crimes and more criminals.

With respect to probation practice, Canton shows that effective offending behaviour programmes are generally thought to focus on the risk of reoffending, the criminogenic needs behind the offending and to be adapted to the person in question (responsivity). But besides this 'Risks, Needs and Responsivity' approach, he also stresses the social, cultural and contextual determinants of crime. In some cases, committing crime could perhaps also be seen as a rational choice. Probation staff might often do well to look more closely at the neighbourhoods and areas in which probationers live and try to understand the problems that their clients face, and the (limited) opportunities they may have. Finally, Canton suggests that a better question than 'why do people commit crimes?' would be 'how do people stop offending?'

Our third chapter, by Lila Kazemian , addresses precisely this question. She provides an extensive overview of the available knowledge on 'desistance'; that is, the process of giving up crime. It is generally agreed that crime rates peak in late adolescence/early adulthood and gradually drop thereafter. The story behind this finding is rather complex, however, as individual predispositions, life events and other turning points and their interactions come into play here. Accordingly, the author convincingly argues that it is more fruitful to consider desistance as a gradual process rather than as an abrupt break from crime.

Many different factors may be involved, such as increasing social bonds, employment, marriage or cohabitation, military service, decreased substance use, and incarceration. While most of these factors are often positively associated with desistance, incarceration tends to have a negative effect. Also, cognitive predictors of desistance, such as shift in identity, the content of cognitions and cognitive skills are highlighted.

However, we still seem unsure with respect to the *exact* nature of the relation between these factors and desistance. For example, a recent Norwegian study found that employment is a consequence, and not a cause, of desistance. To make things even more complicated, work seems to promote desistance not through the development of increased social capital *per se*, but rather through increased associations with pro-social co-workers. Also with respect to marriage and separation we do not have conclusive knowledge yet on whether these are causes, consequences or symptoms of desistance. Accordingly, as far as future research is concerned, Kazemian pleads for an assessment of desistance that should focus not only on measures of offending, but also on mental and physical health outcomes, social bonds, integration, personality traits and behavioural variables. Finally, efforts should be undertaken to integrate desistance research and prisoner reentry research.

Evaluating Probation

George Mair's chapter focuses on the tasks of the probation service and particularly on its impact on sentencing. Presence reports (PSRs) play a key role here. The author gives an historic overview of the role of such reports with respect to providing background and contextual information for sentencers and to offering informed opinions about the likely effects of sentences on an offender. The key idea behind the PSR is that it will help 'fit' the offender to the most appropriate sentence (and *vice versa*) and that this will lead to reduced reoffending.

The chapter suggests however, that this goal is not so easy to attain, in part because it is not very clear what exactly is meant by offender/ sentence 'fit'. Also, the impact of the PSR on actual sentencing practice is rather opaque. While on the whole magistrates and judges are positive about PSRs, only a minority of them claimed that they might have passed another sentence in the absence of a report. A sense of professional ownership of their decisions by judges might play a role here. Mair extensively describes the dynamics between the probation report and sentencing and the role of pleas for community sanctions by the probation officers in this field. Finally, the impact of actual trends in probation such as (oral) 'Fast Delivery Reports', the focus on risk factors rather than contextual information and the marketisation of probation are discussed as developments that may contribute to a more punitive and less rehabilitation-oriented sentencing.

Leo van Garsse addresses the question of whether probation has any impact at all in terms of reparation of victims and communities. For a couple of decades now, the prominence of reparation and restoration among the goals of public intervention in the aftermath of crime has been obvious. Based on examples from the Belgian context, the author takes a critical philosophical stance on whether reparation is really possible. Experience shows that in Belgium at least, victims of crime often perceive the promise of being 'repaired' as an insult. Also, it is alleged that the notions of 'victim' and 'community' lack clarity. The very Anglo-Saxon concept of 'community' sounds rather vague in the context of an urbanised, bureaucratised and multi-cultural Belgian society. This makes the idea of 'the damaged community in need of reparation' as one of the crucial stakeholders in 'doing justice' far from self-evident. He also demonstrates that the relation between probation and the community is not very clear.

Finally, van Garsse concludes that probation and restorative justice aren't really joining forces. Instead, probation officers and mediators act as competing fishermen on the restricted lake of minor-cases criminal justice. He argues for an approach to probation not as a set of alternative measures to 'real punishment', but rather as a means of supporting civic participation and respecting legal protection in constructing and constantly reconstructing in practice what the notion of 'justice' means in a democratic society. Within this framework, probation-work and mediation are part of the same movement focused upon a common social-pedagogical challenge related to the promotion of human dignity in terms of civic capacity and of democracy as a shared political perspective.

Gill McIvor poses the quintessential question of what the effect of community service actually is. Unpaid work by offenders—most commonly described as community service—is available as a penal measure in many countries worldwide and has become one of the most popular community sentences among the public and the judiciary. It is applied at various points of the criminal justice process: as an alternative to prosecution, as an alternative to imprisonment for fine default, as a sentence in its own right, as a direct alternative to a sentence of imprisonment and as a condition of early release from prison.

Despite its prevalence, the penal objectives of community service have been subject to much debate and the relative emphasis placed on punishment, reparation and rehabilitation varies across jurisdictions and over time within jurisdictions. However, re-integrative community service placements seem to be more likely to encourage participants to leave 'the path of crime' than those that are primarily retributive in aim.

Accordingly, McIvor concludes that there is some evidence that rates of recidivism are lower following community service than following short sentences and that the quality of offenders' experiences of undertaking unpaid work are important in this respect. The available evidence suggests that community service within a system of proportionate punishment should aim, where possible, to require offenders to sacrifice their time while providing them with experiences and skills that enable them to pay back to society in ways that increase both their competencies and the likelihood that they are re-integrated into their communities. Efforts to increase the punitive 'bite' of community service may, therefore, be counterproductive in the longer term.

Maurice Vanstone describes probation's role as an important piece in the jigsaw when it comes to successful social integration or resettlement of people leaving prison. The question of resettlement requires both a pragmatic and a moral answer: pragmatic because punishment of the individual always has unintended negative consequences for the rest of society, and moral because punishment is haphazard and non-specific in its effect.

The chapter extensively describes the history of dealing with the deleterious effects of imprisonment in Europe, the USA and Australia both by private parties and states. He concludes that this type of work with prisoners and ex-prisoners has always been infused with the ideals of rehabilitation and has been focused on building social and human capital. Effectiveness of this work is not simply about avoiding offending but incorporates the broader concept of desistance which combines a crime-free life with positive living. Focusing on desistance-related needs should be a policy and practice focus of probation.

In this respect, resettlement work should concentrate not only on the resolution of problems and the creation of opportunities to change, but also on how people view the possibilities of change and success; and in so doing, it should support and reinforce positive thinking. Also, the reinforcement of the connections between the prisoner's family and community is essential here. This entails explicit skills to be used in high-quality probation supervision, such as communication skills, conveying optimism, empathy, being clear about roles and responsibilities, structuring skills, motivation-building and supporting self-efficacy. In short, the ability of probation workers to assist the individual in the process of motivation building has never been so important.

Faye Taxman and Stephanie Maass discuss probation's costs and benefits. They point out the elasticity of probation, which means that it can be tailored to respond to individual risks and needs as well as to the severity of the offence. Probation, unlike incarceration, which is defined by the total deprivation of liberty, can limit or constrain liberty without removing it altogether, through imposing various conditions. This flexibility yields certain benefits but also influences costs. The chapter explores probation's costs and benefits for the justice system, for the individual probationer and for the community. Ultimately, Taxman and Maass argue that the costs and benefits of probation depend on the degree to which it is proportionate to the offence, parsimonious in its restriction, reinforcing of citizenship, and capable of contributing to social justice.

The chapter by Rob Allen deals with the impact of probation on satisfying the public's desire for justice or punishment, based on examples from, among others, the Netherlands, Denmark, England and Wales. First, he stresses the importance of increasing public understanding about and confidence in the work of probation services. This has been recognised as an explicit goal of probation services in many countries in recent years. Without the general public actually knowing what, for example, community sentences really mean, it is hard for them to judge their effectiveness.

Allen examines the evidence about what the public thinks about probation and community penalties and draws out some of the possible implications for organisations and policy-makers. He shows that research over the last twenty years has consistently revealed that, in general, the public is not very well informed about matters relating to crime, but tends towards more punitive and deterrent objectives of punishment when considering serious crimes. However, surveys also show that there is also considerable support for rehabilitation.

That said, lack of knowledge about this topic, within a context of unwarranted cynicism about sentencing in general, produces headline news that is critical of probation. Allen extensively discusses drivers of public attitudes with respect to sentencing, such as crime, notions of redeemability and the influence of the media. He concludes that in terms of attitudes to sentencing, there is a need to find a way out of the 'comedy of errors'. Opinion formers with authority are crucial here to stand up for the values of probation.

Exploring Probation

Ioan Durnescu's chapter addresses the way probation supervision is experienced by offenders. This is subtly different from exploring probation's 'impact' or 'effect' since it starts not with the formal objectives of supervision but with the lived experience of the supervisee.

Supervision is defined as comprising all activities that are associated with the implementation of community sanctions and measures that have a surveillance component which is implemented in the community: probation orders, community service orders, conditional sentences, suspended sentences, deferred sentences, electronic monitoring, drug testing and so on.

He explains that it is only recently that scholars have started to investigate more carefully how supervisees live the supervision experience. Many ex-probationers acknowledge the constructive influence of probation supervision, but sometimes only after many years. People under probation supervision often report 'pains' related to deprivation of autonomy, and time, financial costs, stigmatization, forced return to the offence and life under tremendous threat. It appears that while community sanctions and measures are considered by offenders to be more constructive than prison they seem also quite demanding. He reports that research suggests that the more a probation officer is perceived by the supervisee as a helpful figure, the more positive outcomes are reported. Also the quality of the supervisee's relationships with other significant people seems to be important here. On the other hand, if the process is perceived as intrusive and lacks legitimacy, probationers seem to be dissatisfied and less engaged with the process of supervision.

Durnescu concludes that it is very important that researchers engage with these issues in order to make the impact of these punishments more transparent and to explore their legitimacy. In this respect he pleads for a more sophisticated qualitative research methodology that can do justice to the fact that supervision is not a monolithic structure or homogeneous phenomenon, but rather is very context-dependent.

Mike Nellis takes us into the fascinating, multifaceted world of electronic monitoring and probation practice. Electronic monitoring encompasses a range of distinct-but-related surveillance technologies. He thoroughly describes the various systems in a non-technical and conceptual way and also explores the debate that has taken place about EM and probation.

Contemporary monitoring technologies focus on pinpointing offenders at fixed locations, following (and analysing) the trails of offenders 'on the move' or alerting authorities when the perimeters of designated zones are about to be crossed—separately or in combination. They can be used on a standalone basis or in conjunction with other supervisory work, be it social work, probation or policing. EM emerged outside probation, not from within it, and there is no immediate or obvious affinity between the two modalities of supervision. In jurisdictions and periods where probation practice was dominated by cognitive behavioural therapy, EM seemed inherently incapable of effecting the longer-term change in attitudes and behaviour in which probation was invested. Research shows, however, that EM can reduce reoffending, but there are always qualifiers that underline the fact that there is no technologically determined use of EM. Embedding EM in other forms of supervision and support is to be preferred to stand-alone interventions. Compliance with EM sanctions is more likely if offenders perceive them as legitimate. Accordingly, the challenge for professionals involved in monitoring is to find the forms of EM and the conditions of its use which most help offenders to reform and desist.

Finally, Nellis concludes that the way to achieve best practices in EM—to ensure that it does not become an oppressive technology—is to preserve and advance the best of probation as a humanistic endeavour.

In the last substantive chapter, Fergus McNeill and Gwen Robinson take on the challenging task of explaining probation. Whereas most of the other contributions to this collection have obvious and immediate practical importance, their chapter takes a somewhat more abstract and reflective perspective. To enable the necessary bird's-eye view, they stand on the shoulders of the giants of the sociology of punishment, that is, Foucault,

Durkheim and Marx. Risking oversimplification one could argue that Foucault explains punishment in terms of relationships between power and knowledge, while Durkheim lays stress on relationships between morality, culture and social organization, whereas Marxist perspectives focus on the determining influence of economic arrangements. These structures are important aspects of the entire 'penal field', including the word of probation, because they influence the position, dispositions and relations of actors in that field and the 'penal outcomes' that are realised.

McNeill and Robinson conclude that such a broad historical and sociological perspective is very important for probation scholars and practitioners. Both of them need a clearer understanding of the structural, cultural and political influences upon the penal field and of the dynamics within the field in order to be able to engage effectively with its progressive reform.

Conclusions: What Next?

The 11 questions addressed in the chapters of this volume do not admit of simple answers. They reveal that the problem and issues which probation (formally) exists to address, the impacts of its efforts and the origins and contexts of its development are inescapably complex. How then are we to chart a way forward that might, at the very least, edge us towards a better understanding if not of what we know, then at least of the shape of our ignorance?

In a different recent collection which aims to map our knowledge and ignorance of *Offender Supervision in Europe*, McNeill and Beyens (2013) explore the question of how we 'see' (and often fail to see) offender supervision. Following Barbara Hudson's *Understanding Justice* (2003), they suggest that there are many possible ways to direct our penological imaginations. Just as criminology is a 'rendez-vous discipline' requiring many different methods of analysis, so probation is a rendez-vous practice and rendez-vous institution, situated somewhere at the interfaces between punishment and welfare (Garland 1985). Probation deserves and compels criminological, legal, philosophical and sociological scrutiny, because it raises fundamental political questions as much as urgent practical ones.

Table 1 The purposes and functions of offender supervision

Purposes or normative functions	How, when and under what conditions is offender supervision morally justified? What forms of supervision are justifiable?
Primary functions	How and on what basis are decisions about the imposition and administration of supervision to be made? What is supervision officially intended to achieve?
Ancillary functions	How and in what ways can and does offender supervision contribute to the efficient, effective and legitimate administration of justice systems, in pursuit of their primary aims?
Latent functions	Whose interests are served by offender supervision and whose interests are damaged? As a social practice, what interests and resources shape and are expressed and reinforced through offender supervision?

Source: McNeill and Beyens (2013), p. 7

McNeill and Beyens (2013) also point to Tonry's (2006) commanding and authoritative overview of the purposes and functions of sentencing. They suggest that, as well as illuminating sentencing, it provides a neat framework for analyzing sanctions. Tonry distinguishes between sentencing's purposes or normative functions (that is, its moral justifications), its primary functions (that is, what it aims to achieve, such as the proper distribution of punishment; the prevention of crime; the communication of threat, censure and of social norms), its ancillary or supporting functions (in contributing to the management of an efficient and effective justice system, and in securing legitimacy and public confidence) and its latent functions (the ways in which it reflects self-interest, ideology and partisanship, and how and what it communicates informally).[1]

McNeill and Beyens (2013) suggest that the same taxonomy of perspectives can and should be applied to probation. It can be explored in terms of its purposes or normative functions, its primary functions, its ancillary functions and its latent functions, provoking respectively legal and philosophical enquiry, criminological research and analysis, and sociological interpretation. In Table 1 we suggest just a few of the questions that this taxonomy might raise about offender supervision.

---

[1] In the Mertonian sense, the normative, primary and ancillary functions of punishment are all 'manifest' functions, in that they are all explicitly stated and understood, though perhaps to varying degrees and in different ways by different parties to the process.

Our first two chapters lie before or behind this framework, addressing wide questions about the social problems or issues that sanctions seek to address. Most of our chapters engage with probation's ancillary functions. Only our last few chapters begin to address the latent functions it serves.

No collection can do everything. But while recognising the merits of the work collected here, it is also important to note our limits. Probation scholarship stands in need of expansion—not so much (or not only) in terms of its ancillary functions, but in terms of its normative, primary and latent functions. We still need to work harder to understand what justifies probation, how exactly its restrictions and opportunities come to imposed (or should be imposed), and whose interests and resources it promotes and reinforces. All penal institutions, cultures and practices compel such analysis, because we must always punish in 'bad conscience' (Hudson 2003), aware of the harms punishment imposes, even if it might also build capacity and create opportunity. We remain convinced that, in appropriate forms, imposed in appropriate people, administered fairly, probation *can* build capacity and create opportunity, contributing to the public good and improving people's lives. But we also now know that probation hurts; it harms people's interests in that it involves court-mandated impositions on their autonomy if not their liberty. Those inevitable harms deserve to be scrutinized as much as probation's putative benefits if we are ever to arrive at a proper answer to the question of whether, when, how and in what sense 'probation works'.

References

Garland, D. (1985). *Punishment and welfare: History of penal strategies.* Aldershot: Ashgate.

Hudson, B. (2003). *Understanding justice.* Maidenhead: Open University Press.

McNeill, F., & Beyens, K. (Eds.). (2013). *Offender supervision in Europe.* Basingstoke: Palgrave Macmillan.

Tonry, M. (2006). Purposes and functions of sentencing. In M. Tonry (Ed.), *Crime and justice: A review of research* (Vol. 34). Chicago: University of Chicago Press.

Index

A

active gene-environment correlations
        (rGEs), 51
Allen, G.F., 211
Althusser, Louis, 254
Anderson, S., 46
Armstrong, S., 202
Association for the Moral
        Reformation of Prisoners,
        134
Attrill, G., 202

B

Barnes, J.C., 54
Bazemore, G., 121, 122
Beaver, K.M., 51
Becker, H., 20
Berntsen, K., 135, 142
Bersani, B.E., 41
Beyens, K., 72, 76, 272, 273

Biesta, G., 91
Bouffard, J.A., 117
Bouffard, L.A., 44
Boutwell, B.B., 41
Box, S., 17–18
Braithwaite, J., 89
Burnett, R., 25, 47
Bushway, S.D., 47
Button, D., 233

C

Cabinet Office (2008), 112
Calverley, A., 148, 212
Canton, R., 72
Carter, P., 80, 111
Cavadino, M., 254
Chief Inspector of Probation, 155–6
Christiansen, K., 135, 142
Circles of Support and Accountability
        (COSA), 171

© The Editor(s) (if applicable) and The Author(s) 2016
F. McNeill et al. (eds.), *Probation*,
DOI 10.1057/978-1-137-51982-5

Civic Justice Corps, 122
Clemmer, D., 45
Cohen, S., 248
community base, 15
community control programmes, 232
Community Payback Scheme, 112
community punishment order (CPO), 111
Community Punishment Pathfinders, 119
Community Rehabilitation Companies (CRCs), 80, 81
community service, 107–8, 191–3, 204
    criminal justice system costs impact, 114
    development, 108–10
    diversionary impact, 113–14
    effectiveness, 118–22
    penal objectives, 110–13
    recidivism, 116–18
    re-integrative potential, 118–22
    reparation, 114–16
Confederation of European Probation (CEP), 2
control theory, 24–5
costs and benefits
    community services, 191–3
    elastic sanction, 179
    jurisdictions, 180
    justice control
        community, 189–90
        implicit cost, 190–1
        pains of punishment, 191
    justice system
        breaches/violations, 187
        drug testing, 185
        elasticity, 183

electronic monitoring/GPS, 185
        formal programming, 186
        length of supervision, 184
        markers, 182
        pains of punishment, 188
        probation personnel, 188
        psychological rehabilitation, 183
        RNR framework, 182
        supervision conditions, 184–5
    principles, 181
    RNR, 180–1
Council of Europe Probation Rules, 154
Council of Europe's (2014), 217–18
Council on the Penal System (1970), 110
Craig, J., 44
Crawford, A., 222
Crewe, B., 136
crime, 11–12
    abilities, 29–30
    Chicago School, 16
    constitutional difference, 13–14
    control theory, 24–5
    and criminal justice, 160–1
    culture, 16
    desistance, 25–6
    justice interventions, 18
    labelling theory, 19–21
    motivation, 29
    opportunities, 30
    physiology, 17
    principles, 14–15
    and punishment, 165–6
    rational choice theory, 21–4
    RNR criticism, 18–19
    social factors, 15–16
    sociological perspective, 17–18

criminal justice, 29, 109, 154, 160–1
criminals, 12–13
criminology, 9–11, 28–9
Crouch, B., 202
Cullen, F.T., 43, 44
The Culture of Control (2001), 257

D

Darrow, C., 135
Davies, M., 64, 65, 199
Dawson, M., 252
Derrida, J., 91
desistance, 25–6, 36–7, 52
    cognitive transformations, 46–8
    employment, 37–9
    genetic/biological factors, 51
    identity change, role of, 48–9
    incarceration, 44–5
    marriage, 39–43
    military, 44
    peers, 43–4
    relevance, 35–6
    social and cognitive factors,
        49–51
    substance use, 45–6
deterrence, 22
DiClemente, C.C., 138
Digard, L., 203
Discharged Prisoners' Aid Society
    (DPSA), 132
Discipline and Punish (1977), 246–7
The Division of Labour (1984), 250
docility-utility, 247
Doherty, E.E., 41
Donzelot (1977), 255
Dryden, W., 141
Durkheim, E., 246
    holding the individual, 251–2

probation in UK, 252–3
qualitative law, 251
social solidarity, 249–50
sources of outrage, 250
Durnescu, I., 135, 201
Dutch research, 169
Dutch study, 117, 118

E

effectiveness, 136–44
elastic sanction, 179
electronic monitoring (EM), 203–4,
    218–25
    research, 229–35
    vs. probation, 225–9
Ellis, A., 141
Enhanced Community Punishment,
    120
Erez, E., 233
European jurisdictions, 111, 198

F

Farrall, S., 48, 137, 138, 200–1
Farrington, D.P., 40, 44
Fast Delivery Reports (FDRs),
    77–80
Fitzgibbon, W., 203
Foster, H., 4
Foucault, M., 12, 246
    collapse of confidence, 248
    disciplinary power, 246–9
Fréchette, M., 36

G

Gainey, R.R., 235
Garland, D., 10, 247, 250, 255, 257

Giordano, P.L., 37, 45–7, 49
Gladstone Report 1894, 133
Global Positioning System (GPS),
    219, 232–4
Glueck, S., 51
Good Lives Model (GLM), 25,
    121
Gottfredson, M.R., 48, 51
governmental project, 10
Gove, W., 46
Graham, H., 231, 235

H

Haines, K., 74
Haney, C., 129
Harris, R., 109
Hayes, D., 201
Hedderman, C., 206
Hirschi, T., 48, 51
Home Office's Crime Reduction
    Programme, 119
Horney, J., 39
Hough, M., 162
Hucklesby, A., 203, 204
Hudson, Barbara, 272
human agency, 46

I

Ibarra, P.R., 234
Ignatieff, M., 253
imprisonment, 130–1
Intensive Alternative to Custody
    (IAC) programme, 74
International Crime and Victim
    Survey (ICVS), 165, 166
Irwin, J., 37

J
judicial favour, 198
justice control
    community, 189–90
    implicit cost, 190–1
    pains of punishment, 191
justice system
    breaches/violations, 187
    drug testing, 185
    elasticity, 183
    electronic monitoring/GPS,
        185
    formal programming, 186
    length of supervision, 184
    markers, 182
    pains of punishment, 188
    probation personnel, 188
    psychological rehabilitation, 183
    RNR framework, 182
    supervision conditions, 184–5

K
Karp, D.R., 122
Kilgore, J., 234
Killias, M., 117–9
King, A., 166, 167
Kirchheimer, O., 254
Kirk, D., 44
Kohlberg, L., 142
Kreager, D.A., 43

L
labelling theory, 19–21
Latimer, J., 208
Laub, J.H., 36, 38–41, 44–6, 49, 50
law-abiding majority, 20

Law Enforcement Assistance
    Administration, 109
LeBel, T.P., 50
Le Blanc, M., 36, 38
length of supervision, 184
Liell, G., 202
Local Crime Community Sentence
    (LCCS) programme, 170
Loeber, R., 36, 51
Lombrosian project, 10–14
Lo, T.W., 109
Louvain Catholic University, 98
Lyngstad, T.H., 42

M

Mahood, L., 255
Mair, G., 204
Majesty's Inspectorate of Probation,
    115
Malloch, M., 206
Maloney, D., 121, 122
Maruna, S., 48, 51, 137, 138, 140,
    145, 166, 167, 202–3
Marx, 246
    capitalist system, 253, 255
    England and Wales, probation, 256
    punishment and social structure, 254
Matza, D., 23
McIvor, G., 111, 120, 206, 231, 235
McNeill, F., 46, 146, 183, 194, 252,
    272, 273
mediation, 98–9
Mills, H., 204
Minahan, A., 138
Morgan, R., 74
Morizot, J., 38
Morris, P., 135

Mouffe, C., 91
Muftić, L.R., 117
multi-modality, 15

N

National Association of Probation
    Officers (NAPO), 123,
    237–8
National Probation Directorate, 70
National Probation Service (NPS),
    80, 112
National Research Council (2014), 181
National Youth Survey (NYS), 43
need principle, 15
net-widening, 114
neutralisation, 23
New Social Defence, 94

O

offender supervision, 273

P

Padfield, N., 203
Parker, T., 130
Paternoster, R., 47
Payne, B., 235
Peeters, E., 94
Petersilia, J., 135, 137–8
Pettit, P., 89
Pincus, A., 138
Policing Gender, Class and Family
    (1991), 255
The Policing of Families (1977), 255
positivism, 10
The Power to Punish (1983), 248

pre-sentence reports (PSRs), 61–2, 70–1
  information and influence, 65–8
  objectives, 72–7
  sentencers, 69
probation, 1–6, 61–2, 158–9,
      172–4, 263–74
  Belgium of victim, 95–9
  comedy of errors, 173
  community, 81, 89–92, 155
  CRCs, 80, 81
  crime and criminal justice, 160–1
  crime and punishment, 165–6
  criminal justice system, 154
  criminal policy, 99
  developments, 154
  diagnostic ideal (1986), 63
  education, 93–4
  European Commission, 174
  FDRs, 77–80
  indicators, 69
  justice, 94–5
  knowledge, 163–4
  media influence, 167–8
  mediation, 98–9
  modernity, 153
  needs, 70
  NPS, 80
  philanthropic work, 95
  police court mission, 62
  PSRs, 65–77
  public attitudes, 165
  punishment, 169–72
  punitive public, 161–3
  redeemability, 166–7
  reparation, 87–9
  restorative justice, 86, 87
  social defence, 93
  supervision, 172
  taxpayer-funded service, 156
  UK survey, 157

  victims, 85–6, 89–92
Probation of Offenders Act 1907, 62
procedural justice, 89
Prochaska, J.O., 138
programme integrity, 15
Punishment and Welfare (1985), 247,
      255

Q

Quinsey, V., 140

R

radio frequency (RF) systems, 218,
      231–4
rational choice theory, 21–4
Rawlings, B., 143
Raynor, P., 131, 144
reparation, 87–9
resettlement, 129–30
  effectiveness, 136–44
  imprisonment, 130–2
  prisoners problems, 132, 135–6
  society, 130
  voluntary involvement, 132–3
resettlement Pathfinders study, 141
respectability package, 37
responsivity principle, 15
restorative justice, 86, 87
restorative justice process, 207
Rex, S., 200
Rhine, E., 181, 182
risk principle, 14
Risks-Needs-Responsivity (RNR)
      model, 15, 17, 25–6, 180–1
Roberts, J., 164
Roberts, J.V., 221
Robinson, G.J., 131
Rusche, G., 254

S

Sampson, R.J., 36, 38, 39, 41, 44–6, 49, 50
Satellite Tracking of People (STOP), 222
Savolainen, J., 39, 42, 43
Scheirs, V., 72, 76
secondary deviance, 20
self-reconstruction, 48
Serin, R.C., 129, 142
Shover, N., 47, 48
Simon, J., 247
Sirianni, C., 250
Skardhamar, T., 39, 42
Smith, D., 28
Snacken, S., 136, 140, 143
Streatfeild Committee, 63, 66
Strong, K., 207
strong social model, 50
strong subjective model, 50
subjective-social model, 50
supervision, 197–9, 209
    activity, 199–202
    obligations, different, 202–5
    purposes and functions, 273
    treatment, 205–6
    and victims, 206–9
Sutton, Willie, 22–3
Sykes, G.M., 136

T

Tata, C., 71, 76
Taxman, F.S., 181, 182, 191
telematic society, 219–20
Theobald, D., 40
Thompson, C.Y., 47
Thompson, E.P., 255

Tocqueville, A., 87
Tonry, M., 273
Tripodi, S.J., 38

U

Understanding Justice (2003), 272

V

Van de Bunt, H.G., 205
Van den Dorpel, H., 204
Vander Beken, T., 204
Vanhaelemeesch, D., 204
Van Ness, D., 207
van Schellen, M., 41, 42
Vanstone, M., 256
Vermont Reparative Project, 116
Visible Unpaid Work, 112
Visions of Social Control (1985), 248

W

Wandall, R.H., 76
Warr, M., 43
Weaver, B., 202
Wermink, H., 117
West, D.J., 40
Whitfield, D., 236
Wright, J.P., 43, 44

Y

Young, P., 248, 256

Z

Zamble, E., 140

CPI Antony Rowe
Eastbourne, UK
January 10, 2020